Jim Schnabel has stud He
has contributed to a number of publica ent,
the *Observer*, the *Washington Post, Science, New Scientist* and the
Economist. His first book, *Round in Circles: Physicists, Poltergeists,
Pranksters and the Secret History of the Cropwatchers*, was published
by Penguin in 1994.

JIM SCHNABEL

DARK WHITE

ALIENS, ABDUCTIONS, AND THE UFO OBSESSION

PENGUIN BOOKS

PENGUIN BOOKS

Published by the Penguin Group
Penguin Books Ltd, 27 Wrights Lane, London W8 5TZ, England
Penguin Books USA Inc., 375 Hudson Street, New York, New York 10014, USA
Penguin Books Australia Ltd, Ringwood, Victoria, Australia
Penguin Books Canada Ltd, 10 Alcorn Avenue, Toronto, Ontario, Canada M4V 3B2
Penguin Books (NZ) Ltd, 182–190 Wairau Road, Auckland 10, New Zealand

Penguin Books Ltd, Registered Offices: Harmondsworth, Middlesex, England

First published by Hamish Hamilton 1994
Published in Penguin Books 1995
1 3 5 7 9 10 8 6 4 2

Printed in England by Clays Ltd, St Ives plc

Contents

We have, however, seen and heard many men plunged in such great stupidity, sunk in such depths of folly, as to believe that there is a certain region, which they call Magonia, whence ships sail in the clouds . . . Out of the number of those whose blind folly was deep enough to allow them to believe these things possible, I saw several exhibiting in a concourse of people, four persons in bonds – three men and a woman who they said had fallen from these same ships; after keeping them for some days in captivity they had brought them before the assembled multitude . . . in our presence to be stoned. But truth prevailed.

> – Agobard, Bishop of Lyons, *Liber de Grandine et Tonitruis*, *c.* AD 800

They're strange!

Uh huh, tell me about them. My hand's on your arm. I'm with you. We're right here. Now, we're just looking back. Your eyes are very clear. What do they look like?

They're white. They look white. But a *dark* white – there's too much light.

> – Linda N, under hypnosis, recounting an alien abduction experience for researcher Budd Hopkins, 1989

Dr X

Wherever ufologists gather and reminisce about the great close-encounters of days gone by, the story of Dr X is likely to be told.

Dr X was and is a well-known and respected biological scientist who in the late 1960s lived with his wife and infant son in a house on a hillside looking out over a river valley in the south of France. On the condition that his real name not be used, he allowed his experience, and its remarkable sequelae, to be investigated and published by the French ufologist Aimé Michel.

In the early morning hours of 2 November 1968, Dr X awoke to the cries of his son and the noise of a passing thunderstorm. Seeing that his wife slept soundly, he threw back the covers and struggled to his feet. He was thirty-eight years old and in otherwise good health, but to stand or to walk caused him pain. There were two reasons for this: the first was that, several days previously, he had been chopping wood outside when his axe had slipped and had struck the lower part of his left leg, breaching an artery and causing an internal haemorrhage. He had fainted from the pain, and after treatment by a local physician had been confined to bed until the pain and the swollen pocket of blood in his lower leg diminished. On the afternoon of 1 November the wound had again been inspected by a local physician, who noted that it was still not healed and that the associated swelling and pain remained. Dr X's right leg gave him trouble as well, for ten years before, in the Algerian war, a mine explosion had fractured his skull and had caused severe damage to the left hemisphere of his brain, the hemisphere which controls the right side of the body. He had then suffered a coma, months of partial paralysis, and had lost much of his once formidable musical talent; his right-side muscle tone was weak and even now he could not stand on his right leg alone.

Therefore it was with some difficulty that he made his way from his bedroom across the corridor to his son's room. His son, a precocious boy who had walked at nine months and now at fourteen months wielded a substantial vocabulary, was standing in his crib and pointing to the lightning flashes visible between the closed window shutters. He was crying, 'Rho! Rho!' – his onomatopoeic word, based on the sound of a fire in the hearth, which he applied to all sources of bright light. With a refill of his bottle with water, the boy was quieted. However, Dr X now noted that a shutter somewhere on the house was loose and rattling disturbingly in the wind. Eventually he found it in an upstairs room, but noticed through the open window – the only one in the shuttered house – that the landscape outside was illuminated not merely by lightning but by a regularly pulsating light, whose source lay outside his field of view. Hobbling downstairs to the kitchen, distracted briefly by thirst which he quenched with a glass of water from the kitchen tap, he opened a pair of doors to his terrace and walked outside.

The centre of the storm had passed, and over the valley the rain had turned to drizzle. The strange pulsations of light, Dr X noted to his astonishment, were being emitted by a pair of large bright disc-shaped objects, silver above and sunset red beneath, several miles away. Each seemed to have an antenna sprouting vertically from its rounded apex, and an antenna sprouting horizontally from its side. Each cast a cylindrical shaft of intense white light on the ground beneath it. Approximately every second, a glow would begin at the top of each vertical antenna, as if drawn from the storm-charged atmosphere, and would travel rapidly downwards to consume the entire object, spreading in a luminescent pulse to merge through space with its twin object at the same moment that it discharged through its light-shaft to the ground, illuminating the valley for miles around. Eventually, as Dr X stood mesmerized by the spectacle, the two craft coalesced into one, the light pulsations ceased, and the united object began to move obliquely towards him up the valley, its underside alive with rotating dark bands, their widths and spacings seeming to violate the laws of perspective.

After a minute or two the craft loomed within several hundred yards of Dr X; then it seemed to notice him, and its searchbeam suddenly rotated until it bathed him and his house in an unearthly light. He threw up his hands to shield his eyes, but after a few moments he heard a bang, and the beam and the craft vanished into a whitish, fleecy shape which collapsed into evanescent vapour, ejecting skyward a luminescent streamer that exploded in a pinprick of light, its report absurdly like that of a firework.

Dr X stood on his terrace in shock for a few moments, then walked inside, sat down, diligently sketched what he had witnessed, and noted in detail the sequence of events. He went upstairs, woke his wife, and began to relate to her what he had just seen, presenting to her his notes and his sketches. In drowsy wonderment she listened, examining the sketches and his notes, and watched as her husband paced back and forth animatedly –

'Your leg!' she cried.

Dr X looked down at his left leg, suddenly realizing that it no longer felt swollen, no longer was painful. He pulled up his pyjama leg and saw that the leg was normal, the wound having somehow healed into a scar since his physician had checked it the previous day.

Dr X and his wife discussed all of this in confusion and awe, and after a time went back to bed. His wife found it difficult to sleep, but within minutes Dr X had fallen into a deep slumber – from which he began to speak distinctly, something his wife could not remember him ever having done before in his sleep. She listened briefly, and then, once it had become clear that he was discussing the luminous objects he had seen, began to take notes. Among other things, he said: 'Contact will be re-established by falling down the stairs on 2 November.'

The following morning, Dr X's wife awoke at 10 a.m. Dr X did not awaken until 2 p.m., but when he did, he felt very well. However, he had forgotten everything that had transpired the night before, and looked with alarm at the notes and sketches his wife claimed were his own.

His wife kept hidden her notes of his sleep-talk, and later that afternoon, while descending the living-room stairs, Dr X tripped – he remarked later that it was as if something had hooked his leg –

and tumbled downstairs, in the process bumping his head and suddenly recovering his memory of the events of the night before.

Dr X experienced mounting shock and distress at these and other strange events, and on the night of 13–14 November had an oddly vivid dream which involved the luminous objects and a large triangular shape. On the evening of 17 November he noticed an itching and pricking sensation on his abdomen. By midday on the 18th a triangular red rash had formed around his navel. He consulted a dermatologist, who was baffled and expressed the desire to write up the case for the Academy of Sciences – although Dr X, who had a reputation to lose, talked him out of it, wishing to avoid any publicity at all. The ufologist Aimé Michel, who happened to know Dr X socially and by now had also been consulted, suggested that the rash might be psychosomatic, a kind of pseudo-stigmatum deriving from his previous vivid dream. However, the day after Michel had made that suggestion, Dr X telephoned him to report that he had just noticed a similar rash around the navel of his infant son.

Aimé Michel soon discovered that objects similar to those seen by Dr X had been reported on 1 and 2 November in Spain, and were reported on 7 December in Morocco and on 9 December in Peru – where according to the Reuters wire the violet rays of a flying saucer had healed a customs official in Lima of his severe myopia and rheumatism.

As for Dr X, specialists confirmed not only that his leg had healed completely, but that the neurological after-effects of his war-wound had disappeared. There were, however, a number of after-effects of his close-encounter. He suffered months of depression, weight loss, and intermittent appearances of the bizarre triangular rash. Later, his worldview began to shift, as if his consciousness and his empathy with other living beings were expanding uncontrollably within him, striving to encompass everything, all life, the universe. It seemed absurd, and yet he could not help himself. In time, he would report further miraculous healings, as well as poltergeist infestations, strange fugue-like journeys that seemed to cover impossible distances, and the sensed presences of extra-terrestrial entities in and around his house . . .

Remembering Lemuria

The voices of the Fauns have often been heard and Deities have appeared in forms so visible that they have compelled everyone, who is not senseless or hardened in impiety, to confess the presence of the Gods.

– Cicero, *Of the Nature of the Gods*

About seventy-two years before Dr X's close-encounter, on the evening of Friday 25 September 1896, a man named Henry T. Clarke, of 139 Bradley Street, New Haven, Connecticut, kissed his young wife goodbye and headed for the town's railway station, where he was employed by the baggage-transfer firm of Peck & Bishop, and usually oversaw the office on Friday nights.

Henry Clarke's next memory, according to the statement he later gave to police, was of awakening after a restless sleep, alone and in a strange bed, with a brown suit in his wardrobe whereas he had left for work wearing a black one. Unable to find his wife, Clarke ventured downstairs from his room and discovered from the desk clerk that he was in a lodging-house on Third Street in the city of San Francisco, under the name 'A. Walker'. The date was Sunday 15 November, eight weeks having passed since his last recollection of consciousness.

Clarke immediately realized that he must have suffered from an extended version of the amnesic episodes which had occasionally plagued him back in New Haven. These would leave him wandering, on a workday afternoon, around the outskirts of the town, not knowing how he had spent the previous several hours. Similar phenomena, more than a decade before, had ended his career as an undergraduate at Yale, where he had been diagnosed with 'congestion of the brain'.

Clarke was a devout Christian, and coming to his senses in San Francisco he sought out a church, and a clergyman who could help him. He found William Shaw, assistant rector of St Luke's Episcopal church, who accompanied him to the nearest police station – where he was advised that he was wanted for the theft of more than $800 in cash and cheques from his former employers, Peck & Bishop, in New Haven.

'CLAIMS TO HAVE LOST HIS MEMORY,' read the headlines in the San Francisco papers. 'HIS MIND HAS BEEN A BLANK FOR WEEKS.' 'LEAVES HIS HOME IN NEW HAVEN AND CROSSES THE CONTINENT IN A TRANCE.' And Henry Clarke was returned forthwith by train to New Haven. It was never clear why he had travelled, consciously or unconsciously, so far west. Perhaps it had been the frontier allure of California, the chance of a fresh start. Perhaps in his happy entrancement he had planned, on the strength of his purloined $800, to go even beyond the confines of the continent, to travel onwards by ship, to Hawaii, Tahiti, Tonga, and Fiji – to bury his cares in humid Polynesia. Or perhaps, like the strange compulsives who would some day journey to Devil's Tower in a Steven Spielberg film, against all odds and obstacles, he had merely felt the unconscious call to attend one of the greatest wonders of his age . . .

This wonder manifested itself on the rainy evening of Henry Clarke's departure, Tuesday 17 November, in Sacramento, just north-east of San Francisco, where hundreds of people saw a strange light moving slowly, beneath the clouds and at an angle to the wind, about 1,000 feet over the city. The witnesses included the daughter of the mayor, and an assistant to the California secretary of state – who climbed to the observation deck at the top of the capitol dome to obtain a better view. Most observers reported only an intense white light, moving up and down and side to side, and apparently attached to a dark, egg-shaped mass. But some witnesses perceived more interesting features. F. E. Briggs, a streetcar motorman, heard bits of song gusting down from the object. A ranch foreman and his colleagues, several miles east of the city, also heard singing. Two barkeepers, Emil Wenzel and J. H. Vogel, and a mechanic named Charles Boyles, claimed to have heard ordinary voices coming from the object, albeit indistinct ones. M. F. Shelley, a streetcar motorman, heard someone shouting orders. Daniel Curl, a horse trainer, heard someone say 'Go up higher!' R. L. Lowry, another streetcar motorman, asserted that the object had descended low enough for him to see that the dark mass was actually a cigar-shaped dirigible, suspending a gondola on whose two sides spun wheels like a steamboat's side-wheels. The contraption, he said, was powered by two men pedalling a system of gears within the gondola. He had heard one of the airmen saying to the other, 'Throw her up higher or you will strike that steeple,' and then: 'We will get to San Francisco at half past twelve.'

'STRANGE TALE OF A FLYING MACHINE,' read the headlines in San Francisco. 'CLAIM THEY SAW A FLYING AIRSHIP.'

Arguments raged over whether the 'airship' had been anything more than an odd light, perhaps a prankster's fire-balloon, but on the afternoon of Friday the 20th a man named D. H. Ridson, working in an orchard near Tulare in the San Joaquin Valley, reported having seen a flying object that looked like 'an immense sheet spread out into the air'. Then, at dusk in Oakland on the 21st, hundreds again saw an erratically moving aerial object which appeared to have a dark, oblong, egg-shaped body, with wings and two bright lights fore and aft – the latter a searchlight which swept the ground. On the night of the 22nd, lights were seen again in the skies over Oakland and Sacramento, and now also over Folsom, San José, and San Francisco. Thousands of witnesses, aided by telescopes and binoculars, saw the same dark oblong object moving against the wind and occasionally shining an intense searchlight beam down at the earth. And once again the craft's motion was irregular: it rose and fell, jerking from side to side, almost like a boat bouncing in the waves, or like the body of a bird whose wings were flapping, or like a leaf pendulating softly as it fell through the air. The witnesses now included the servants of the San Francisco mayor, the Sacramento deputy sheriff, and the Sacramento District Attorney, one Frank Ryan, Esq. – who declared the apparition to be a manifestation of the biblically promised 'signs and wonders', indicating 'the advent of the millennium'.

On the night of the 24th, the lights were reported above Tacoma,

Washington, at 11 p.m. and in San José a half-hour later. The following night the lights appeared simultaneously above Oakland and Los Angeles.

The great airship visitation had begun, and before it ended, in the spring of 1897, somewhere in the American midwest, tens of thousands of witnesses, from fishermen to former Senators, would report mysterious lights, or dark masses drifting aloft, or distinct, dirigible-shaped craft. It was the first big UFO wave in modern history.

The arguments raged about what this phenomenon really represented, but most newspapers seemed to assume, this being the Age of Invention, that somehow, somewhere, some aeronautically inclined Thomas Edison type had designed and built a craft capable, unlike all other earthly machines, of sustained powered flight – and that this craft was fast enough to appear over several cities in a single night. Indeed, a San Francisco attorney named Collins soon claimed to be representing the reclusive, wealthy inventor who had built the airship. Not to be outdone, a former California attorney-general, a man named Hart, claimed that the inventor was *his* client, who had built the airship to drop dynamite on Spanish-held Havana. A Nebraska farmer seemed to confirm this, reporting that the airship, a propeller-powered dirigible, had landed in one of his fields, the pilots informing him that they were headed for Havana with a full load of TNT. Other witnesses told of seeing prisoners on board the craft, held at gunpoint by the crew. One report said that a fugitive criminal was the pilot. Another said that the ship was powered by an anti-gravity system, and that it had been headed for Cuba, but for some reason was now bound for Armenia, to help the oppressed peoples there. Yet another report said that the ship had been built by the British, to harass and to spy upon the United States. Still another said the ship had been built in California, and was flying to the patent office in Washington. Several witnesses claimed to have been taken aboard the ship, one for a lavish Jules Verne-style dinner party and a 100-m.p.h. cruise over Chicago. A midwestern farmer claimed he had been momentarily abducted when an airship anchor caught his trousers and yanked him aloft. A number of people reported that 'airmail' letters had been dropped into their gardens. A newspaper sketch was published in April

1897, purportedly reproducing a photograph of a double-dirigible, propeller-driven airship several hundred feet over Peoria, Illinois.

The hoax hypothesis had some evidence in its favour, too. A correspondent for the *San Francisco Examiner* reported witnessing a group of young men – employees of the rival *San Francisco Call*, he insinuated – releasing a balloon with a candle attached from the Market Street area of the city on the night of 4 November. A few months later, in Nebraska, a man was also reportedly seen flying a kite with a light attached. Not far away, in Omaha, the fire-balloon antics of two men named Roy Arnold and Jack Rogers prompted the *New York Sun* to declare, in April 1897: 'AIRSHIP WAS A BALLOON SENT UP BY TWO PRACTICAL JOKERS OF OMAHA TO FOOL THE PEOPLE.'

In Illinois, the *Peoria Transcript* released three gas-filled balloons with candles attached and sparked off their own wave of sightings – some not merely of lights, but of cigar-shaped craft with paddle-boat side-wheels. One witness, when told that the cigar-shaped craft had been merely the *Transcript*'s balloons, stuck with his story and alleged that the hoax report had itself been a hoax.

But perhaps most remarkable, among the mystery airship reports, were the stories of encounters with extraterrestrials. The *St Louis Post-Dispatch* reported the account of a man named Hopkins, who claimed to have come upon a small dirigible-shaped spaceship with four legs and three propellers.

Near the vessel was the most beautiful being I ever beheld. She was rather under medium size, but of the most exquisite form and features such as would put to shame the forms as sculptured by the ancient Greeks. She was dressed in nature's garb and her golden hair, waving and glowing, hung to her waist, unconfined excepting by a band of glistening jewels that bound it back from her forehead.

Accompanying the otherworldly beauty was a bearded male of the species, 'of noble proportion and majestic countenance'. He sat beneath the ship, fanning himself in the Missouri spring heat, and in a pleasant tone of voice explained to Hopkins that he and his lovely co-pilot were from Mars.

Not all alien encounters were so congenial. According to the *Stockton Evening Mail*, a Colonel H. G. Shaw had been travelling by buggy through the California countryside when he had come upon a group of seven-foot-tall beings, pale and thin, and emitting soft warbles. They had attempted to carry him away to their ship, a 150-foot-long cigar-shaped craft with a single large rudder, but the abduction had been aborted when Shaw proved too heavy for them. Colonel Shaw was of the opinion that the beings had come from Mars, and had been 'sent to earth for the purpose of securing one of its inhabitants'.

And then there was the story told by Joseph Joslin to the *St Louis Globe-Democrat*. According to Joslin, he had been taking a stroll through a park in the city on the afternoon of 4 April when a strange sensation had come over him, as if he were being pricked with hundreds of needles. In pain, he collapsed, and as the sensation subsided a few minutes later, he opened his eyes to see a gigantic dragon, dull red in colour, with bat wings and a large, six-eyed, horned head. Scurrying around the top of the animal were strange humanoid creatures, somewhat smaller than humans, with red skin, black heads, and no eyes. They somehow 'hypnotized' Joslin into submission, and then led him aboard, after which the dragon flapped its wings and flew aloft. Joslin was held captive on the dragon's back for three weeks, travelling over strange terrain and being tortured horribly by the little red men, whose mere touch could burn. He awoke in a St Louis hospital, having been found unconscious somewhere in the city. 'His case,' sniffed the *Globe-Democrat*, 'is diagnosed as alcoholism.'

There were animal mutilations and spaceship crashes, too. In Kansas, a prosperous and well-respected farmer, whose trustworthiness was asserted in affidavits from half a dozen prominent citizens, reported that one of his heifers had been abducted and cut to pieces by the occupants of an airship. In Texas, in the town of Aurora, it was reported that a spaceship had crashed into a windmill, and that the pilot, a Martian who unfortunately had been burned beyond recognition in the crash, had been given a decent but anonymous burial in the town cemetery.

There were even foreshadowings of the twentieth-century UFO enthusiast groups with their hilltop 'skywatching' expeditions, for 'airship parties' briefly became popular in the midwest in the spring of 1897 – although, according to local newspaper accounts, they tended to degenerate into very this-worldly activity ('kissing bees') between male and female airship enthusiasts.

The airship mystery was never conclusively solved. Instead it seems to have been forgotten, abruptly disappearing from the public eye after the middle of 1897. In this sense it was like many other isolated UFO encounters, from the 'wheels within wheels' described by Ezekiel, to the aerial objects which harassed Alexander's troops in 329 BC, to the atmospheric displays, featuring black, blue, green and red shapes – variously resembling spheres, spears, plates, tubes, crosses and hats – which reportedly frightened the residents of Nuremberg in 1561, Basel in 1566, and Tübingen in 1577.

Of course, most if not all of these pre-modern accounts probably fell, or could have been forced to fall by the authorities of the time, into the catch-all categories of divine or demonic manifestation. For example, the ninth-century historian Agobard wrote that one day in Lyons, where he was bishop, three men and a woman were reportedly seen descending from airships over the city, and because of these reports were nearly stoned by the townspeople as sorcerers. In the late Middle Ages, strange lights in the sky at night were sometimes attributed to witches who had hung lanterns from their broomsticks. And then of course there was the case of the French teenager who in 1425 encountered a strange light and strange beings who informed her that she would soon lead her countrymen against the English invaders. The beings were interpreted as angels, and the teenager became a saint – St Joan of Arc.

By the late nineteenth century, the growth of science and technology had empowered more mundane perceptions, or at any rate perceptions which fell short of the supernatural. Well before the great North American airship wave, in Chile in July 1868, numerous witnesses were reported to have seen an 'aerial construction', shaped like a bird covered with scales, making a 'metallic noise'. In 1877, in the British military training centre at Aldershot, two guards on the night watch reportedly claimed to have been stunned by 'blue fire' from a strange being who flew past them in a suit and helmet. In early 1878, a Texas farmer was said to have seen an aerial craft shaped like 'a large saucer'. In the summer of 1884 it was reported that an unknown flying machine had crashed in Holdrege County, Nebraska, scattering metal debris, melting the sandy soil, and causing severe burns and symptoms of (what we would now consider to be) radiation sickness to onlookers who approached within 200 feet. Yet none of these accounts – some of which, admittedly, like some of the 1896–7 airship accounts, were later shown to have been hoaxes – appear to have stimulated serious investigation; indeed, few had any resonance beyond the relevant local newspapers. In part, this may have been because such accounts lacked the evocative label of 'UFO' that unifies most modern reports. But even in the 1896–7 wave, with its unifying label of 'airship', the mystery does not seem to have outlasted its actual or reported manifestation in the skies.* Popular culture, to say nothing of scientific culture, was not yet ready for sustained attention to the phenomenon.

Further waves of airship sightings, involving reports of airship crashes, animal mutilations, and close-encounters with extra-terrestrial beings, occurred in the US in 1909–10, and in the US, Canada, England, Wales,† New Zealand, and South Africa in 1912–13. Reports came in only sparsely during the First World War,‡ and into the twenties and thirties. During the Second World War, Allied pilots described aerial encounters with 'foo fighters' – luminous blobs, with astonishing manoeuvrability, which often seemed to follow aircraft as they carried out their missions. It was widely assumed that these represented some German or Japanese secret weapon. But after the war, it emerged that Japanese and German pilots had also encountered the luminous blobs, and had assumed them to be Allied secret weapons.

In 1946, newspapers carried reports from Sweden of mysterious

---

* The airship mystery was only rediscovered by ufologists in the mid 1960s.

† The Welsh case reportedly involved a dirigible-shaped craft, with wheels at the bottom of the gondola and a propeller at the tail, whose crew members wore fur coats and caps.

‡ Many ufologists claim that the reported appearances of the Virgin Mary at Fatima in 1917 were in fact UFO sightings; Jacques Vallée has drawn attention to the falling-leaf motion of the lightform seen by 70,000 witnesses at Fatima in October of that year.

'ghost rockets'. Believing that the rockets were a Soviet secret weapon, the US sent a number of investigators, including the decorated pilot General James B. Doolittle, to liaise with the Swedes on the matter. Alas, no Soviet rocket debris could be found.

Then in 1947, on Tuesday 24 June, a private pilot named Kenneth Arnold, flying through the Cascade Mountains of the Pacific northwest in search of a downed Marine transport plane, saw a formation of nine bright objects in the distance. The objects seemed to reflect the sun like mirrors, rising and sinking in an odd wavelike motion as they skimmed over the mountains at . . . well, Arnold made a few calculations, and according to these it seemed that the objects were travelling at more than 1,000 miles per hour. At the next airfield, where he stopped to refuel, he told the ground crew about his sighting. At his next refuelling stop he was mobbed by reporters. Among other things, he mentioned to them that the objects had seemed to skip through the air as a spinning saucer might skip across the surface of a pond. One of the reporters therefore decided to call the objects 'flying saucers' – and the history of modern ufology began.

Of course, the idea of a flying saucer, or a disc-shaped spaceship, had surfaced previously not only in old UFO-type accounts, but also in science fiction. Flash Gordon, in the film *Flash Gordon's Trip to Mars* in the late 1920s, had made the journey in a shiny, metallic, discoidal craft, and although the rocket-shaped motif had then seemed more popular, the science fiction magazines had long been churning out occasional stories involving disc-shaped ships. None of this meant that the disc-shaped objects didn't actually exist; the enormous wave of 1947 sightings, by such people as airline pilots and military personnel whose testimony on other matters would have been accepted implicitly, made clear that such objects almost certainly *did* exist. However, it could not be denied that these objects' existence enjoyed an odd synchronicity with certain subcultures of the time. In fact, for one magazine, the Arnold sighting was less the indication of a new phenomenon than a confirmation of what they had been saying for years: that flying discs, or spheres, or foo fighters, or ghost rockets, or whatever, existed and were piloted by non-humans.

The magazine was *Amazing Stories*, and its editor-in-chief was a man named Ray Palmer. Palmer oversaw a small empire of pulp science fiction and fantasy magazines for the Ziff-Davis publishing group, and he had a good eye for the kinds of stories his readership – young, male, and lonely – liked to read: stories about unlikely heroes conquering unknown worlds and slaying space-dragons and winning the hands of virginal and lovely space-princesses, or subduing battle-hardened but even lovelier space-queens whose impossible proportions would invariably be clad, on the lurid magazine cover, in flesh-gripping ray-gun-deflecting heavy metal. Palmer's advertisers, who ranged from the Rosicrucians to mail-order authorities on What a Gal Really Wants, represented further evidence of the poignant though vulgar mixture of sexual and cosmological longing to which such magazines appealed. Palmer was widely characterized as the cynical master of the genre, the P. T. Barnum of fantasy esoterica, but the truth was, he loved stories of strange planets and space-dragons and space-bitches with thorium brassières. He felt at home in that world, for he too was young and male and lonely, and like his average reader would have made an unlikely hero. In fact, he would have made a very unlikely hero, for he suffered from a severe growth hormone deficiency – i.e. dwarfism – and to top it all off had a hunchback.

One day towards the end of 1943, Palmer's number two at *Amazing Stories*, Howard Browne, received a letter from an individual in Barto, Pennsylvania, who signed himself 'S. Shaver'. Shaver's letter began as follows:

Am sending you this in hopes you will insert it in an issue to keep it from dying with me . . .

Shaver's gift to the world was a list of some elements of an ancient language – the mother of all earth languages in fact, for it was the lost language of Atlantis. It went like this: 'A – animal (used "an" for short). B – be – to exist (often a command, as Ban means "stay away to exist". Same as quarantine). C – con – to see . . .' Howard Browne skimmed Shaver's letter and threw it into a nearby wastebasket, muttering something about 'crackpots' loudly enough to prick up the ears of Palmer, the patron saint of crackpots

– who came in from the next room, retrieved the letter, studied its contents, experimented successfully with some of the linguistic rules Shaver had set down, and after cleaning up Shaver's wild grammar and syntax, printed the letter in the *Amazing Stories* correspondence column, under the headline: 'An Ancient Language?'

Well, there were more than a few Atlantis buffs among the readers of *Amazing Stories*, and as the queries started to come in, Palmer wrote to Shaver and asked him how he had come by his information. Shaver responded with a virtually unreadable 10,000-word typescript entitled 'A Warning to Future Man'. At first glance, it looked like a badly written fantasy story. The narrator was a man named Mutan Mion, an apparently untalented abstract artist – 'Proteus in a Convulsive Nightmare', was how a colleague had described one of his works – who had lived in Sub Atlan, miles beneath Atlantis, in the golden age before the Atlantean cataclysm when mankind's ancestors, an extraterrestrial and highly advanced race of immortals, had colonized the surface and interior of planet Earth – or Lemuria, as it had been known then.*

Fate, according to Mutan Mion, had been unkind to the Lemurians. Not only had their continents heaved about violently, but their sun – our sun – had aged to the point where it had begun sending out harmful radioactive elements, uranium and neptunium and plutonium and so on, which corrupted bodily fluids and ravaged living cells and eliminated the immortality the Lemurians had once enjoyed. Most Lemurians had moved away to other, more hospitable planets, just as their forefathers had once sought refuge on planet Earth (Lemuria). But others, like Mutan Mion, had moved in the opposite direction, towards the centre of the earth, where they had created a kind of high-tech subterranea, an underworld accessible only through caves, and had written Warnings to Future Man in hopes that some day, someone would find them and publish them.

Palmer continued to receive a steady stream of Shaver stories,

---

* The Lemurian legend usually refers to a lost continent beneath the Indian Ocean, of which Madagascar is the only remaining protrusion; but Shaver had broadened the term to encompass the Atlantean legend and the rest of the planet, too.

from which it became clear that since Mutan Mion's time the corruption of the ex-Lemurians had progressed; when they weren't foraying above the surface in high-tech flying machines, they were down below, focusing deleterious energy rays on humans up above, to control them and to torture them. As a matter of fact, they had been focusing deleterious energy rays on Shaver for a number of years. They really had it in for poor Shaver, whose full name was actually Richard Sharpe Shaver. A photograph of Shaver taken seven years later shows a strongly built man, dressed like a lumberjack in a flannel shirt and woollen cap, with a boxer's nose, boxer's teeth, and a broad, slightly sinuous grin. He had worked as an overhead crane operator and welder at a Detroit auto-body shop but then the cave people had begun beaming the deleterious rays at him, through his spot-welding gun of all things, interrupting his thoughts with strange voices and causing him to do things he didn't want to do. About this dark period of his life he (with Palmer's editorial help) later wrote:

Suffice it to say that my enforced escapade, which I was blindly urged into by the subtle energy of the telepathy machines and other incomprehensible mechanisms using rays and forces that surface man never heard of, ended with my arrest and sentence to a state prison. To this end, I, a well-intentioned human being, had been brought, by those potent rays in the hands of evil idiots in earth's hidden caverns!

The ex-Lemurians who focused deleterious energy rays on people were known as detrimental robots, or 'deros'. They were robots, according to Shaver, because they were slaves to their own ray machines, their brains having been particularly poisoned by the radioactive solar emanations. But there was a small sect who focused a different kind of ray – a 'telaug' ray – which was beneficial and promoted wholesome thoughts. The telaug-ray people were known as 'constructive robots', or 'integrative robots', or 'teros'. It was all vaguely reminiscent of the underworld that the science-fantasy novelist Abraham Merritt had described, about twenty-five years before, in 'this-is-a-true-story' novels such as *The Moon Pool*, *Conquest of the Moon Pool*, *The Snake Mother*, and

The Face in the Abyss. Shaver didn't consider himself a plagiarist, however; he insisted that Merritt's stories had been non-fiction dressed up as fiction in order to get published. Moreover, according to Shaver, Abe Merritt hadn't seen the full picture; for instance, his cave-people had been restricted to local underworlds, such as below Mexico, whereas the real ex-Lemurian underground was everywhere beneath us.

Anyway, it came about one day that among the ex-Lemurians who lived in the vicinity of the prison where Shaver was an inmate, there was a power struggle, won by the teros. The deleterious rays ceased, and the blissful telaug rays began. One night, lying in bed, Shaver was visited by a young woman, Nydia, who was one of the teros. She had white-gold hair, and very pale skin, and eyes that were somehow too large, and she was less than five feet tall, but she looked good to Shaver. She explained to him the situation with regard to the deros and the teros, and said she needed a surface-dwelling man for a mission – to help her defeat the deros and re-establish the ancient and advanced science of Atlantis and Lemuria, including the science of immortality. Thereafter it became Nydia's habit to visit Shaver at night in his cell in the state prison, and although for various complicated reasons involving the telaug rays and perceptual screens and so on they weren't able to consummate their love, she promised eventually to take him away from the prison with her, down to the fabled underworld, where they could cavort as they pleased. One night a prison guard appeared at the door to Shaver's cell, accompanied by Nydia. The guard looked as if he were in a trance. He opened the cell, and let Shaver out. Nydia led Shaver outside and through the wilderness of eastern Pennsylvania, or wherever it was, and into a cave and down and down, and as soon as she and Shaver were safe within the tero-held underworld . . .

her . . . flower-red mouth sought mine like a starving animal scenting meat . . . Nydia spent exactly one week showing me that what happened to Tannhäuser in the Hollow Hill with the goddess Venus can still happen to mortal man. She had studied the uses of the antique pleasure mechanisms under masters – some of whom I met later . . . tremendous stimulation generators poured super-powered pleasure impulses through every nerve of my body at their full capacity. If a man could die of pleasure, I am sure that I would have died then.

Nydia later brought Shaver to the underworld library, where the history of the Lemurians was recorded on a kind of telepathic microfilm. After 'reading' the microfilm, Shaver could remember things about ancient Lemuria as if he had experienced them himself. In fact, so intense was this virtual reality that until Nydia calmed him down, he refused to believe that it had only been virtual. He thought he had spent a few centuries as a succession of Lemurian scientists and warriors and artists, when actually he had been sitting in a chair for a few minutes, under the caressing eyes of Nydia.

Shaver's first report from these telepathic microfilm sessions was, of course, the 'Warning to Future Man'. Palmer, seeing 'a sure-fire circulation-getter', quickly transmuted it into a 31,000-word odyssey entitled 'I Remember Lemuria!' and ran it in the March 1945 issue. *Amazing Stories* was never quite the same again. As controversy raged over whether Shaver was insane, or a liar, or an unlikely hero, subscriptions to the magazine rose dramatically,* and from all over America, ordinary people started writing in describing *their own experiences* in the ex-Lemurian underworld. As for Shaver, his writings became enormously popular. Ray Palmer was obliged, in his editorial column, to apologize whenever an issue came out without a Shaver story. And whenever a new Shaver story did emerge, other writers, such as the young Ray Bradbury, might find their own contributions to *Amazing Stories* rejected or shoved aside for a month or two. In time, the Shaver *œuvre* – or the Shaver Mystery as it became known to aficionados – included such stories as *Thought Records of Lemuria, Cave-City of Hel, Quest of Brail,*

---

* According to Palmer's later account, when Shaver was notified that wartime rationing of paper would prevent *Amazing Stories* from printing extra copies for the Lemuria issue, the writer repeatedly threw his shoes on to the floor of his house to attract the teros' attention, then telepathically requested their intercession with the Ziff-Davis circulation director – who shortly thereafter told Palmer that he had decided, quite out of character, to steal 50,000 copies' worth of paper from another Ziff-Davis pulp, *Mammoth Detective*.

and *Mer-Witch of Ether-18*. Palmer himself would hedge a little about whether he believed the Shaver Mystery was entirely genuine, but he insisted that, in any case, the majority of it was true. He would tell stories such as the one about the night during a visit to Shaver's farm, when he himself had heard the voices of the deros discussing their recent kidnap and dismemberment of a human woman. Palmer also began to claim, in editorial asides to the readers of *Amazing Stories*, that the 'dero sycophants' – surface-dwelling fellow travellers of the detrimental robots – had begun to harass *him* in an effort to stop further publication of Shaver's revelations . . .

By mid 1946, reports were appearing regularly in the newspapers about sightings of strange lights or objects in the sky, often by soldiers on night sentry duty. Palmer and Shaver contended that these sightings, along with other such reports throughout history, were sightings of the spacecraft flown by Shaver's cave-people, or by space visitors related to the long-departed Lemurians.* In August 1946, the back cover of *Amazing Stories* depicted a squadron of flying saucers.

The following spring, Lemuriamania reached its peak, and Palmer ran an all-Shaver issue, which was still on the news-stands when the Kenneth Arnold sighting hit the papers. For Palmer and the rest of the Shaver fan club, Arnold's flying saucers were proof, if proof were needed, of just about everything Shaver had been saying. For others, of course, Shaver and Palmer were lunatics and charlatans – and yet the flying saucers were there, just the same, as merely the most tantalizing element in an ineffable alchemy of mystery, artistry and madness.

The flying saucer wave of 1947 was followed by waves in 1952, 1957, 1961, 1964–8 and 1973–4, in each of which thousands of UFO sightings and related experiences were reported from around the world. Even in the intervals, when markedly fewer reports were received, the phenomenon continued in the public consciousness,

---

* Shaver would later contend that the apparently erratic, oscillatory movements of the mysterious flying objects were actually manoeuvres designed to evade the UFO-sniping deros' deleterious rays.

and by the middle of the 1950s it had stimulated large-scale government interest, an extensive network of flying-saucer research organizations, and an explosion of books, articles, and films about the subject, from US Marine Major Donald Keyhoe's sensational story in *True* magazine, 'The Flying Saucers are Real', to Hollywood's *The Day the Earth Stood Still*, in which a flying saucer pilot and his robot sidekick come to Washington to preach world harmony and non-aggression.

And as with the airship mystery a half-century before, the flying saucer mystery included much more than naked-eye sightings of lights or objects in the sky. There were reports of ground markings left behind by the craft, or burned patches where nothing would ever grow. There were reports of animal mutilations. There were multiple-witness reports of flying saucer crashes, such as the one said to have occurred near Roswell, New Mexico, a few days after Kenneth Arnold's sighting in the Cascades. There were even photographs of flying discs, often quite elaborate, with windows, antennae, and perhaps an identifying symbol.

And then there were the alien contact, or close-encounter stories, which began in what seemed to many to be obvious charlatanry, but evolved into something a good deal less explicable. The first well-known UFO contactee of this era was a man named George Adamski, who in a 1953 book written with a British aristocrat, Desmond Leslie, claimed that he had been visited repeatedly by friendly, utopian, saucer-flying Venusians. The success of Adamski and Leslie's *Flying Saucers Have Landed* was followed in 1954 by the success of contactee Truman Bethurum's *Aboard a Flying Saucer*. Bethurum, who had been a workman laying asphalt in the California desert, claimed to have been taken aboard a saucer from the planet Clarion. He described his experiences with the saucer captain, a lovely and talented Clarionite named Aura Rhanes. 1954 also saw the publication of Daniel Fry's *White Sands Incident*, according to which the visiting aliens had stressed the need for greater understanding between the two nuclear superpowers, the US and the USSR. In 1955 the superbly named Orfeo Angelucci, a mechanic with Lockheed Aircraft in Los Angeles, came out with his own contactee story (published by Ray Palmer) according to which the aliens, who themselves had names like Orion, Lyra, and

Neptune, would meet him in various prosaic places such as the Greyhound bus terminal in downtown Los Angeles. On one occasion they spiritually transported him to their planet, and he met many more aliens, including Jesus, who told him that a glorious New Age was beginning, but it took him a while to remember that episode because the aliens had induced amnesia which lasted for some time.

There was Cecil Michael, who took a *Round Trip to Hell in a Flying Saucer*, with aliens who could materialize at will. There was Howard Menger, an unemployed sign painter who was visited by benevolent space brothers. There was Buck Nelson, who flew to Mars, Venus, and the moon, and later tried to sell the hair he had pulled from a Venusian St Bernard. And just about everyone had heard of George van Tassel, who had gone back in time with aliens who had shown him the true history of the earth; van Tassel would hold annual UFO conventions at a place called Giant Rock in the California desert, and sometimes, to get the juices flowing, he would secretly send up helium-filled balloons with flares attached.

A lot of the contactee cases never made it beyond local newspaper stories and brief write-ups in the UFO enthusiast magazines. For example, there was a case from France in which the aliens wore diving suits, and a case from somewhere in Scotland in which the aliens had high foreheads, and breathing tubes in their nostrils, and claimed to come from Mars. There was a case from Italy, where a man saw a landed saucer, and two-foot dwarves with dark blue coveralls, green faces, huge dark eyes, and red belts which emitted a suffocating, paralysing vapour. There was a case from Canada, where a nickel miner was hypnotized by flying saucer occupants and awakened, alone, several hours later. There was a case from Birmingham, in the English Midlands, where the aliens had high collars (like Flash Gordon's rival, Ming the Merciless) and communicated with humans using telepathy, and had landed to scavenge for titanium. There was a case from Peakskill, New York, where a woman was hospitalized for shock after she and her husband saw a spacecraft and a female alien; the alien had been dressed in luminous clothing with a hood and glasses, and had been holding a tube in one hand and a box in the other. There were even cases where

UFO occupants looked like animals, such as the bat-man seen near a flying saucer in Kent, in 1963.

And as had been the case with the airship mystery, some of the alien encounters had a decidedly sinister tone. This trend became especially evident in the early sixties, with reports such as the one involving a poor Brazilian diamond prospector, who had been walking along a road when dwarf-like aliens, according to witnesses, disintegrated him with an energy beam from their spaceship. Then there was the case in which an Argentinian truck-driver, forced into a ditch by a flying saucer in the road, had to fight off its occupants – three 'shiny metal robots' – with a revolver.

A few years later, in 1965, came the unnerving news of the Antonio Villas-Boas case.

The case itself was said to have occurred on the afternoon and evening of 15 October 1957. Villas-Boas, the son of a Brazilian farmer, had been ploughing one of his father's fields near the town of São Francisco de Sales when suddenly his tractor stopped and a ship with a tripod arrangement of legs dropped down beside him. According to Villas-Boas, he was taken aboard the ship by four short, grey-suited aliens. They seemed to communicate by a system of barks. The barking aliens stripped him, took blood samples, rubbed a brown liquid on his body, and then left him in a cold room with acrid smoke seeping in through a pipe in the wall, until he vomited. Then one of the aliens, a nude female, came into the room. She had high, wide cheekbones and a pointed chin. Her skin was pale and freckled. On her head she had whitish-golden hair, somewhat like Shaver's Nydia, but her armpit hair and pubic hair were bright red. She wore no perfume, but her captive nevertheless was able to detect a feminine pheromonal odour. She began to caress young Villas-Boas, who would later remember:

I caught hold of the woman, responded to her caresses with other and greater caresses ... It was a normal act, and she behaved just as any woman would, as she did yet again, after more caresses. Finally, she was tired and breathing rapidly. I was still keen, but she was now refusing, trying to escape, to avoid me, to finish with it all. When I noticed this, I cooled off, too. That was what they wanted of me – a good stallion to improve their own stock. In the final count that was all it was. I was angry, but then I resolved to pay no importance to it. For anyway, I had spent some agreeable moments. [But] some of the grunts that I heard coming from that woman's mouth at certain moments nearly spoilt everything, giving the disagreeable impression that I was with an animal.

Villas-Boas was said to have suffered, for months afterwards, from something like radiation sickness.

In 1966, the year after the Villas-Boas case came to light, a book was published describing the Hill case. Barney and Betty Hill, who in a 1975 TV movie would be portrayed by James Earl Jones and Estelle Parsons, were an interracial couple who lived in Portsmouth, New Hampshire. Barney was an assistant dispatcher at a post office in Boston, but was also a prominent member of the local NAACP and served on the New Hampshire Advisory Board of the US Civil Rights Commission. Betty was a social worker, and like her husband was active in the civil rights movement. Both were respected in their community, and their integrity seemed unimpeachable.

One night in September 1961, after a brief holiday in Canada, they were driving home in their '57 Chevrolet. Barney was at the wheel. It was a clear, crisp night, illuminated by a moon that was nearly full. Somewhere in northern New Hampshire, a hundred-odd miles from home, Betty noticed that a star beneath the moon seemed to be getting brighter. Over the following minutes it seemed to approach them, blinking red, amber, green and blue, as it descended in a spinning, swooping, falling-leaf motion. Finally, Barney stopped the car in the middle of the road, and taking a pair of binoculars with him, went towards the object. With the binoculars he saw what looked like a 'glowing pancake', except that it had portholes through which he could see figures wearing dark uniforms. Terrified, Barney returned to the car, but as he and Betty drove away, they heard a strange beeping noise coming from the car boot. Their senses seemed to fade, and then they heard the beeping noise again – just before realizing that they had travelled about thirty-five miles further down the road. They arrived home about three hours later than expected, and when they did, they noticed that the car boot now had strange circular areas where the paint appeared to have been polished. Betty put a compass on the circular marks and found that it spun wildly. Barney had a strange compulsion to examine his groin, where a few weeks later a ring of warts appeared. Both of their watches had stopped.

Betty, who followed the UFO subject with interest, reported the sighting to the Air Force, and also to what was then the best-known American UFO research organization, the National Investigations Committee on Aerial Phenomena, or NICAP. That might have been the end of it, but Betty began having strange dreams concerning the episode, and the Hills' home became plagued by poltergeists and by visits from strange men who, for example, would pretend to want to read their gas meter, despite not being employed by the local gas company. Barney soon developed a series of anxious neuroses which apparently stemmed from the incident, and eventually he felt obliged to seek psychiatric treatment. After a series of unsuccessful visits to various other specialists, he and Betty were introduced to Dr Benjamin Simon, a well-known Boston psychiatrist who often used regression hypnosis to cure anxiety. When Simon regressed Barney, and later Betty, he was astonished to learn that the period between the first series of strange beeps and the second was filled, in the Hills' subconscious memory, with an account of being taken aboard a flying saucer: Betty had been stripped, had been given a medical-type examination involving sampling of skin and hair, and had watched as a long needle was painfully inserted into and then retracted from her abdomen. Barney had apparently had a sperm sample taken, via a suction device whose outline corresponded with the circle of warts that later developed. Barney seemed to have been in a stupor during much of the abduction, but he remembered that the aliens had greyish, almost metallic skin, and reminded him vaguely of a tribe of Magellan Straits Indians he had once seen pictures of at an anthropology lecture.

Betty, for her part, recalled that the aliens had had large Jimmy Durante noses. She had been alert enough to have a lengthy discussion with what she took to be the saucer crew's leader. The leader spoke to her in accented English, joked about Barney's dentures, allowed her to look through a book with vertical, oriental-style writing in it, and also let her see a space map, depicting the star system where he and his crew had come from. Eventually Betty and Barney were led off the craft – Barney being more or less carried – and they watched as the spaceship became an orange glow and disappeared into space. Then they got into their car, experienced the second series of beeps, and remained for the most part amnesic about the experience until confronted by Dr Simon with the tapes of their regression hypnosis sessions.

Dr Simon was an experienced psychiatrist. He had heard a lot of wild stories in his day. He was confident that reports of encounters with flying saucers and their occupants were so much fantasy, probably originating, in the Hills' case, from the nightmarish dreams Betty had been having since the incident. The dream content, which Betty had previously shared with Barney, had been similar to the memories of the abduction produced by both Betty and Barney under regression hypnosis. Simon began to challenge the Hills as to whether the story really had any objective truth to it. 'Now,' he would say during the regression sessions, 'from whom did you learn about the experience? You didn't really have it, did you?'

But Barney and Betty stuck to their story, despite the fact that, in conscious conversation, neither seemed to want the experience to have been true. The Hills continued with hypnotherapy for a few years, came to accept the reality of the experience, and eventually, after inaccurate local news reports began to leak out, told their story to the journalist John Fuller, whose book, *Interrupted Journey*, was published on the crest of the 1964–8 UFO wave.

That wave included several other close-encounter cases, including that of Steven Michalak, who claimed to have happened across a landed flying saucer while walking in the Canadian woods one day in 1967; it had left him dazed, and with a strange pattern of dot-like burns on his abdomen. Herb Schirmer, a Nebraska highway patrolman, had a similarly amnesic encounter with a UFO on a rural road in December of that same year. However, relatively few cases were reported between 1968 and the autumn of 1973, when the next, extraordinarily intense wave of UFO sightings and close-encounters began.

The most sensational case from 1973 was that reported by Charles

Hickson and Calvin Parker, shipyard workers who on the evening of Thursday 11 October had been fishing from a pier on the west bank of the Pascagoula River, in the town of Pascagoula, Mississippi, between Biloxi and Gulfport on the coast of the Gulf of Mexico. Some time near dusk, according to their account, a strange blue lightform had whizzed down the river towards them and then had stopped to hover over a marshy area nearby. Parker, who was only nineteen, 'went hysterical' (in Hickson's words) and collapsed unconscious shortly after seeing the craft open and disgorge several aliens, but Hickson recalled clearly that the aliens had floated over to the pier, and had floated both himself and Parker aboard. The aliens had each been about five feet tall, with leathery, elephantine grey skin, and claw-like hands, and a slit for a mouth, and conical projections where noses and ears should have been. They didn't seem to have eyes, although Hickson remembered seeing a big disembodied eye-like shape floating above him as he lay on some kind of examination table inside the craft. Eventually Hickson and Parker were floated out again, and the spaceship and the aliens disappeared. The men fled to a nearby police station, and told their story, and despite the craziness of that story, the lurid science-fiction sound of it, just about everyone who met them was impressed by their anxiety and trauma. When Parker and Hickson were taken to nearby Keesler Air Force base for a medical examination, they were given an extraordinary, Spielbergesque reception, with a motorcade-type escort and a team of masked, gloved military doctors who tested them for residual radiation and took skin swabs in case any extraterrestrial biological molecules had rubbed off on them. The local sheriff in Pascagoula also believed the two men; when left alone in an office with hidden microphones, they had convincingly expressed their shock at what had happened to them:

HICKSON: Well, Calvin, when they brought you out – When they brought me out of that thing, *goddamn* it I like to never in hell got you straightened out.
PARKER: My damn arms, my arms. I remember they just froze up and I couldn't move. Just like I stepped on a damn rattlesnake.
HICKSON: They didn't do me that way.
PARKER: I passed out. I expect I never passed out in my whole life.

HICKSON: I never seen nothin' like that before in my life. You cain't make people believe –

PARKER: I don't want to keep sittin' here. I want to see a doctor –

HICKSON: They better wake up and start believin' . . . they better start believin'.

PARKER: You see how that damn door come right up?

HICKSON: I don't know how it opened, son. I don't know.

PARKER: It just laid up and just like that those son' bitches – just like that they come out.

HICKSON: I know. You cain't believe it. You cain't make people believe it –

PARKER: I paralysed right then. I couldn't move –

HICKSON: They won't believe it. They gonna believe it one of these days. Might be too late. I knew all along they was people from other worlds up there. I knew all along. I never thought it would happen to me.

PARKER: You know yourself I don't drink.

HICKSON: I know that, son. When I get to the house I'm gonna get me another drink, make me sleep. Look, what we sitting around for? I gotta go tell Blanche [his wife] . . . what we waiting for?

PARKER: I gotta go to the house. I'm getting sick. I gotta get out of here.

[HICKSON *leaves the room.*]

PARKER [*alone*]: It's hard to believe . . . Oh, God, it's awful . . . I know there's a God up there . . .

In 1975 came the celebrated Travis Walton case: Walton, according to the story, had been one of seven woodcutters who had seen a UFO land one night in Sitgreaves National Forest in Arizona. Walton had run towards the UFO, but had been zapped unconscious by a beam of blue light. His friends had fled, and when they returned, Walton was gone. He reappeared five days later, some miles away, incoherent and apparently frightened. He remembered only that he had briefly awakened on board the ship, and had seen big-headed, big-eyed, hairless aliens, and then later some silent beings, apparently human but with peculiarly slanted eyes.

By now, of course, the tabloid newspapers and UFO-book publishers loved this kind of thing, and Walton, Hickson, Parker, and the others all received wide coverage in newspapers, magazines, and books. They made a fair amount of money, too. And many ufologists were willing to believe them; after all, they seemed to have penetrated deeper into the UFO mystery than anyone else had done.

But some of the more orthodox-sounding ufologists, such as the academic astronomer Allen Hynek, seemed to play down such cases. To these ufologists, a science that studied an elusive, non-repeatable phenomenon, and which depended heavily on the testimony of untrained eyewitnesses whose truthfulness could almost never be known, had to proceed with extreme caution where such outlandish tales were concerned. And in any case, they argued, close-encounter and abduction tales were relatively rare. For every Barney and Betty Hill, for every Cal Parker and Charley Hickson, there were hundreds of UFO sightings with multiple, independent witnesses, perhaps also backed up by radar, or by burned or swirled vegetation where the UFO had alighted. This was the solid ground on which ufologists should build their science.

But then along came Budd Hopkins, and the ground shifted.

3

Budd

A work of art enters life very much like another human being –
complicated, loaded with overtones and meaning, mysterious,
enticing, obsessive, and beautiful. There's no way to control
how it will be used, how it will be read, and that's part of the
excitement of it.

> – Budd Hopkins, in conversation with the conceptual artist
> Douglas Huebler, *Arts Magazine*, April 1972

They had been driving carelessly and happily through the receding
remnants of a summer afternoon storm, when their station wagon
crested a slight rise and the conversation suddenly trailed off into
suspenseful silence. After a moment, Joan said nervously, 'Are you
guys looking at what I'm looking at?' 'Yeah!' responded Budd and
Ted, sitting either side of her on the broad front seat. They
couldn't take their eyes off the thing. It was there in the sky
ahead of them, and slightly to the left, framed by the windshield of
the station wagon which now tilted gently down Massachussetts
State Route 6 towards Provincetown, at the sandy, curled terminus
of Cape Cod. The object was small and apparently motionless,
with a distinctly elliptical shape, now darkly shrouded by the cool
scudding clouds, now dully metallic in the sunlight. It simply hung
there, as if to mesmerize them . . . Neither Joan nor Budd nor Ted
seemed to want to say out loud what it looked like. It might sound
crazy! Ridiculous! For they were not the sort of hard-luck people to
whom such absurd experiences seemed always to happen. Neither
did they consider themselves visionaries. Not in such a literal sense,
anyway. They were merely very respectable people, intellectual but
worldly, thriving here in the warm inner circles of Cape Cod
summer culture. They had just driven up from Budd and Joan's

beautiful beach house in Truro, which Budd's friend the architect Charles Zehnder had designed the year before. And of course Budd, Budd Hopkins, was himself an up-and-coming young artist on the Manhattan Abstract Expressionist scene, known and respected by his peers, intelligent and darkly handsome, with black mischievous eyebrows, and black hair flecked with strands of white, like paint streaks on his studio floor, and painterly hands which gripped the steering wheel of his station wagon here on Route 6, as he met the gaze of the strange object that looked for all the world like –

No one wanted to say it. It was preposterous. And yet there it was. And here they were, headed to a cocktail party in Provincetown, at the home of Hudson Walker, a formidably wealthy art collector who some day would endow the Walker Art Institute in Minneapolis, and who now, in August 1964, represented with his elegant wife, Ione, one of the fundamental nodes on the artists' and writers' and agents' and publishers' and dealers' and collectors' and patrons' circuit here on the Cape . . .

As they watched the object, Joan and Budd and Ted exchanged brief bursts of speculation, noting among other things that the object was at least a mile away and a good thousand feet up, and so could have been nearly anything. It could have been the Provincetown sightseeing plane, the one that looked like Lindbergh's *Spirit of St Louis*, the one with the old-fashioned fat piston engine that someone said had been built by the same company which had built Lindbergh's engine . . . the fat engine and the fat happy plane which was always flying tourists very very slowly over this part of the Cape . . . Except that the object which had seized their attention was not moving at all, and was definitely a dull aluminium colour, not yellow like the sightseeing plane which they had seen a hundred times but never like this.

'Maybe it's a weather balloon,' ventured Budd, or Ted, or one of them anyway, and it began to seem that the object was indeed a weather balloon, tethered to the ground. None of them had ever seen a weather balloon with an elliptical shape like that, but it was still quite a distance away and they couldn't see it very well, and anyway it had to be something conventional. It looked odd – there was no getting around that – but there had to be some kind of explanation . . .

As they neared Provincetown, the angle of the object rose higher above the car, and they all craned forward against the windscreen to keep it in view. It looked more circular now, from below. It looked more like a weather balloon. Perhaps its tether was merely too small to see from this distance. Presumably the military had it up there for some purpose, measuring something in the air or whatever they did.

But as the station wagon turned off the highway on to the road to the Walkers' house, the weather balloon suddenly lurched from its position in the sky and, moving at an unearthly speed against the wind, disappeared into the distance . . .

Elliott Budd Hopkins, Jr was born in the late spring of 1931, the second of three children of Elliott Budd, Sr, a businessman and Army reserve officer, and his wife, Eleanor. They lived in the coal and steel town of Wheeling, West Virginia, in the little industrial sliver of that rural state which juts northward between Pennsylvania and Ohio, on the east side of the Ohio River valley. In the winter of 1933, when he was two and a half, Budd caught polio, and his right leg became paralysed. The paralysis wore off after a year, but in the interval the growth of the leg had been stunted somewhat, giving Budd a noticeable limp, and removing any hope of athletic prowess. Budd turned inward slightly, learned to draw, and became so enthusiastic about his talent that when his father went off to war in Europe, Budd would send him sketches, via the microfilmed V-mail system, of every week's cover of *Time* magazine – Churchill or Patton or Humphrey Bogart or whoever. But neither Wheeling, West Virginia, nor the Army base in Memphis, Tennessee, where the family was briefly stationed during the war, was a place where children dreamed of becoming artists, and when at seventeen Budd began to search for a suitable university, his career plans were vague. His father's plans for him were not: he wanted Budd to become a businessman like himself, by way of a degree in business administration. When Budd and his father would go for university interviews, his father would ask: 'How is the business administration department here?' At Oberlin College, near Cleveland, the man behind the dean of admissions' desk responded proudly to the effect that Oberlin had one of the best business administration programmes in the middle west. In fact, Oberlin then had almost no business administration department, and the night before Budd's interview, the dean of admissions had shot himself in the head; the fellow behind the desk was actually the football coach, who had been hauled out of bed that Saturday morning – it was the Easter vacation, and most of the faculty had disappeared – to keep up appearances until a more suitable admissions interviewer could be found.

Budd settled in at Oberlin, whose mediocrity in the field of business administration aided him in his attempts to resist this career direction. But his father was footing the bill for tuition and living expenses, and their relations anyway had been strained by Budd's youthful dabbling in Left politics, and so when Budd began to develop a career interest in art, he kept the matter from his father as long as possible. In the spring of 1952, however, the Abstract Expressionist Robert Motherwell came to Oberlin to run a seminar on the history of modern art. Motherwell focused on current developments in New York painting, and soon worked up for Hopkins and the other students a great bright image of the Manhattan art world, full of bold strokes such as Jackson Pollock and Mark Rothko and Barnett Newman and Bill de Kooning and Jack Tworkov and Clyfford Sill and Franz Kline and Frank O'Hara and Philip Guston and their lofts and studios and bohemian watering holes and muses and vital energy . . . Hopkins soon declared art as his major, and as his chosen profession, and after graduating from Oberlin the following summer, he moved to New York. He enrolled at Columbia University, and attended some art history classes, and worked as a clerk in the campus bookstore, and started painting watercolours – small-scale stuff, bright and surreal and vaguely organic, somewhat after the manner of Arshile Gorky, the Armenian who had come to New York and had been one of the founders of the Abstract Expressionist movement but had died just after the war, in true bohemian style, of despair and a broken neck at the age of forty-four.

Hopkins shared a studio with the painter Harold Pessarilo for a few months, and then shared one with Alfred Scondovitch down on 15th Street. Scondovitch's studio had more space, and so Hopkins started to expand his scope somewhat and began to switch from watercolours to oils. By now, late 1954, he had quit Columbia and was becoming more fully immersed in the New York art scene. He would work on a painting for a while and then might go over to a gallery opening on 10th Street, or to the Cedar Tavern on University Place, or to the Club on 8th Street, to hang out among the other artists and drink and talk art theory and maybe watch Pollock get drunk and pick a fight with someone – although the scene wasn't complete yet, for occasionally, to pay the rent, he would have to make his way over to the Museum of Modern Art, for a part-time job behind the information desk.

Actually, working at the Modern wasn't so bad; a lot of other young artists worked there, such as Bob Ryman and Scott Burton. In any case, working at the Modern, and hanging out at the galleries on 10th Street or at the Cedar or the Club, plugged Hopkins fairly quickly into the network, which then consisted of only a few hundred artists and critics and gallery owners and so on. He met some people who introduced him to Franz Kline, and soon he was spending a good deal of time shooting the breeze over at Kline's studio. He drifted into the orbit of art dealer Elinor Poindexter. He got to know the Modern's docent, Abraham Chanin, and began to act as substitute lecturer in Chanin's absence – in the summertime, when Chanin and a lot of others in the New York art scene tended to go away somewhere such as Cape Cod.

The museum lectures led to a job as an art history teacher at Wagner College on Staten Island, which enabled Hopkins to quit his job at the Modern's information desk. In the autumn of 1955 he helped Elinor Poindexter to set up her gallery – whose exhibition in the winter of 1955–6 included some of Hopkins's drawings. By the summer of 1956, the year that Jackson Pollock died, aged forty-four, Hopkins was lecturing again at the Modern, exhibiting oils at Poindexter's gallery and at the Tanager Gallery, and had sold his first work, a small watercolour, to a Mr and Mrs Mones. He also spent a few weeks up at Cape Cod, where he met more artists and dealers and collectors and critics, including Hans Hoffman, the crusading monk of Abstract Expressionism, who preached purity, chastity, abstinence from illusory three-dimensionality, the preservation of the virgin picture plane by the unification of forms and colours on a starkly two-dimensional surface. In the fall, Hopkins held a one-man exhibition at the Poindexter Gallery, earned some favourable reviews, married a lovely nineteen-year-old named Joan Rich, and moved with her to a large studio apartment on 8th Avenue. He was twenty-five years old, the very picture of the hot young artist in New York.

Hans Hoffman's sermons notwithstanding, Hopkins's paintings still had a touch of that gaudy, Gorkyish, organic surrealism. To an irreverent layman, some of Gorky's work might have looked like jungles on fire, as viewed through a mescaline haze . . . bleeding trees and exploding toucans . . . and there was the same aura about some of Hopkins's works, a suggestion of fire and foliage, life and depth, with perhaps a sun-like circle providing a sharp focus. His work was a good deal flatter than Gorky's, dimensionally speaking, although it probably wasn't flat enough to suit Hoffman. Anyway, as the years went by, Hopkins's work became less organic, and at the same time more organized; the soft curves of the jungle began to harden into urban angles. Shapes like the circle gave way to lines and rectangles. The sense of a landscape, however surreal, began to disappear, for the most part leaving hard-edged, rectilinear, abstract . . . expressions . . . just hanging there in outer space.*

By the summer of 1964, Budd Hopkins's works had been exhibited at the Poindexter, Tanager, March, Davida, Marino, Parke-Bernet, and Zabriskie galleries in New York; at the Tirca Karlis and Martha Jackson galleries in Provincetown; at the Athena Gallery in New Haven; at the Kasha Heman Gallery in Chicago; at Art Galleries Ltd in Georgetown; at the Chrysler Museum in Provincetown, the Baltimore Museum of Art, the City Art Museum of St Louis, the Columbus (Ohio) Gallery of Fine Arts, the Contemporary Art Center in Cincinnati, the Westchester Art Society exhibit, the Pennsylvania Academy annual exhibit in Philadelphia,

---

* In his review of post-Modern art theory, *The Painted Word*, Tom Wolfe noted the Hoffmanesque loathing of the old-style realist paintings which had the pretence of three-dimensionality and, at least in an illusional sense, could be 'walked into'. Abstract Expressionist paintings, with their lack of any sense of up and down, were impervious to this mode of entry – but, as other critics noted, sometimes retained a sense of depth, and therefore were vulnerable to more advanced forms of locomotion. 'Perhaps you can't *walk* into an Abstract Expressionist painting,' joked Wolfe, 'but you can *fly* through. Right! You could take a spaceship!'

the Art Dealers Association group exhibition in New York; at the Festival of Two Worlds in Spoleto; and on the CBS television special, *Exhibit*. He had sold a painting to the Whitney Museum, and many others had gone to private collectors, including Joseph Hirshhorn, who was later to endow much of the Hirshhorn Museum. He had rented a house on West 16th Street, and had overseen the design and construction of the beach house on Cape Cod. Abstract Expressionism was no longer quite as much in the vanguard of art, of course, thanks to Jasper Johns and Roy Lichtenstein and Robert Rauschenburg and Andy Warhol and the ironic-realist attractions of Pop Art, but its momentum would carry it a good deal further, and anyway there was enough order, enough mystery, enough outer space left in Hopkins's works for his style, to some critics, to begin to seem quietly but robustly *post*-Abstract Expressionist, without succumbing to the new vogue of Pop. Besides all of that, Hopkins seemed like a decent, respectable guy. The *New York Times*'s Brian O'Doherty would soon be writing that 'He is not the sort of fellow you are going to read about in the glossy columns where kookiness and personal charades are the usual price of admission.'

Hans Hoffman and Mark Rothko were among the luminaries at Hudson and Ione Walker's house in Provincetown on that August afternoon in 1964, but their presence didn't prevent Budd and Joan and their houseguest, Ted Rothon, from mentioning the thing they had seen over Route 6. In fact, since seeing the thing zoom off suddenly, Budd and Ted and Joan had had no more than a minute or two to collect themselves before they had arrived at Hudson and Ione's front door. The shock – of having a saucer-shaped hole put in one's worldview on a lovely Cape Cod cocktail party afternoon – had still not worn off. They weren't sure that they were in a party mood any more.

However, the artist Giorgio Cavallon perked up at the mention of amazing things in the sky. From his house nearby, on the bay, he had seen unusual objects flying around on numerous occasions. He spoke about his past UFO sightings, and one or two other people entered into the conversation, for they had seen some strange things, too.

A few days later, the newspapers reported a rash of sightings of strange objects in the sky further down the Cape. Budd and Joan talked over the subject with a Columbia University history professor and his wife, who were staying nearby, and they all decided to sit out on a clear night and watch and wait. The thing over Provincetown had been so obvious; maybe all one had to do was to wait long enough and watch carefully, and one would see something. Anyway, it was a beautiful night; the sky was a pointillist glory of stars. They brought out blankets and drinks, and sat gazing heavenwards, and the stars fell one by one, in streaks of glowing stardust, and the surf purred gently at their feet, and . . . over there . . . 'It's moving!' Yes . . . But it was only an aeroplane, headed for Boston or London or somewhere mundane, and after an hour or so they gave up, unenlightened and covered with mosquito bites.

Budd and Joan continued to hear strange stories, however, about such things as lights in the woods near Wellfleet, and lights zooming across somebody's pond. Finally, Budd phoned up Otis Air Force Base, on the south end of the Cape, to report the sighting over Route 6. The officer he spoke to at Otis was cordial, and thanked him for the information, but didn't seem eager to shed light on the subject of UFOs, and Budd couldn't help wondering whether this officer, and other people in the government, knew a hell of a lot more than they were telling the public. Like many others at the time, Budd had become somewhat suspicious about the government after President Kennedy's assassination the previous autumn. The idea that Kennedy had been killed by a lone, meaningless assassin just didn't seem right. There was too much about the case that didn't fit that hypothesis. Surely the government, with all its investigative resources, could see what was so obvious to ordinary people such as himself. Similarly, if he and his wife and a friend could watch, without even trying to, as a metallic-looking object performed high-speed manoeuvres in the sky, in an area that was presumably covered by Air Force and probably also civilian radar, then the government surely had seen it, too, and many more like it. *Why weren't they telling us anything?*

Budd went out and bought a few books about UFOs, and realized that the phenomenon was not only widespread, but was also fairly resistant to prosaic explanations. The things appeared simultaneously on independent radar screens. They flew hypersonic circles around jet fighters. They left burn marks in ground vegetation. Their behaviour seemed anything but random and unintelligent. It began to seem altogether plausible that the thing he had seen above Route 6 had been an actual spacecraft, perhaps piloted by aliens on a reconnaissance mission.

But beyond buying an occasional UFO book, and reading articles about the subject in the popular press, Budd didn't pursue the matter. He was still in the launch phase of his career. He wasn't about to drop everything and become a flying saucer enthusiast, with all that implied. And in any case, although many of the sighting reports were convincing enough, the contactee and close-encounter and abduction stories that now and again surfaced in the popular press sounded utterly absurd. When a serialized excerpt from John Fuller's book on the Betty and Barney Hill case appeared in *Look* magazine in late 1966, Budd dismissed it as more UFO-nut madness – hallucinations probably, or a hoax.

Oddly enough, however, by 1966 the formerly banished curvilinear forms had begun to creep back into Hopkins's work. In that year he finished *Sun Black*, a swarm of white and grey rectanguloids, centred on a large black circle. The day he finished it, Joan walked into the studio and . . . 'Where did *that* come from?' Budd himself wasn't sure. His next few works went back to the old rectilinear forms that had dominated his style since the late fifties, but soon the large central circle began to assert itself again, dominating his style and becoming, in the words of critic April Kingsley, 'his personal image', imbuing each painting with 'hypnotic force – with a place in the painting where energy can be concentrated and from which it may be dispersed'. A painting, for Hopkins, became something like a person; it was organized, orderly; it had a physiognomy. The circle was the head, or perhaps the Cyclopean eye. In 1968, Hopkins painted *Gemini I*, the first of several paintings named after the zodiac, and like *Sun Black* it seemed to have a certain mesmerizing power, the viewer's eye being drawn down mottled streaks of white towards the centre of a large dark circle. If one simply stared at the picture, and wasn't astigmatic or a complete philistine, one would eventually get the sense – the slightly eerie sense – that the thing was staring back. The actor

Maximilian Schell, who bought the painting, told Hopkins it called to mind Stanley Kubrick's just-released film *2001: A Space Odyssey* – in which an advanced alien race plants an enigmatic black monolith on some Cenozoic savannah, to telepathically jump-start human cultural evolution; and also in which, in several ominously silent scenes, the lens of the computer HAL is shown staring out at the human astronauts and the interior of their spaceship. Hopkins went to the movie and didn't feel the connection, but he was willing to admit that the central circle had an arresting quality. The Gemini series was followed by Aquarius and Scorpio and Virgo and Libra, and Hopkins sold a fair number of them.

By the early seventies, Hopkins's interest in UFOs hadn't developed much further, but it hadn't disappeared. After thoroughly reading John Fuller's book about the Hill case, he decided it might be plausible, after all, that aliens would wish to abduct people briefly, to take tissue samples or whatever. Biologists and zoologists did that kind of thing all the time with animals here on earth. Why should a superior, alien race be different? By the time the Pascagoula case made the news in 1973, Hopkins had joined NICAP, and although his participation didn't go beyond magazine subscriptions, he would occasionally tell UFO stories at cocktail or dinner parties, and would attempt, albeit unsuccessfully, to interest people such as Kline and Rothko and Motherwell. In New York art circles he began to get the reputation as something of a saucer enthusiast. People would come to him with sighting reports they had heard about, or with their own experiences. 'Hey Budd, you'll like this one . . .'

In the summer of 1975, Hopkins couldn't help but hear about a series of a dozen or so UFO sightings along Cape Cod around Provincetown, Truro, and Wellfleet. Some of the sightings, such as one involving an object above Provincetown harbour, had had several independent witnesses, including police officers and some of Hopkins's personal friends. The UFO was variously described as a luminous globe, emitting occasional beams of light; or as a disc-shaped craft with windows.

Nothing really came of that episode, but one evening that November, when Hopkins was back in New York for the cold months, he left his house to buy some wine for dinner. He crossed

16th Street to a liquor store, picked out a bottle of Soave, and was fishing some money out of his wallet when he noticed that the old man behind the counter, George O'Barski, seemed to want to get something off his chest. O'Barski was pacing back and forth behind the register, shaking his head morosely, complaining about how one of his knees had gone arthritic, and – apropos of nothing – how 'a man can be driving home, minding his own business, and something can come down out of the sky and scare you half to death'.

Naturally, Hopkins pumped him for the whole story, which was as follows. One night, all the way back in January, O'Barski had closed up the liquor store and was driving home, heading first to an all-night diner in Fort Lee, New Jersey. Somewhere in North Hudson Park, on the New Jersey side of the river, his radio began to pick up static. He was fiddling with the dial when he noticed a bright object to his left, zooming forward past the car. Through the open window – for it was an unseasonably warm night, with a breeze blowing up from the Gulf – O'Barski heard the object making a strange droning noise. It stopped over a nearby playing field, and seemed to hover over the ground. The thing was saucer-shaped, about thirty feet across, and had windows along the side. O'Barski by now had slowed the car to a crawl, and watched as a door in the thing slid open and emitted a ladder that stretched to the ground. About a dozen little humanoid figures, looking like children dressed in snowsuits, descended the ladder and began to take soil samples. They used what looked to O'Barski like big spoons, shovelling dirt from this New Jersey ballfield into things that looked like little plastic department-store shopping bags, the kind with handles. They moved quickly but apparently were oblivious to O'Barski, who was only about twenty yards away. They took the samples they wanted, and then ran up the ladder into their saucer. The ladder retracted and the door slid shut, and the saucer zoomed silently off towards Hackensack. O'Barski, apparently a teetotaller, drove home, took two aspirin, climbed into bed, and pulled the covers over his head. In the morning he drove through Hudson Park again, stopping at the place where he had seen the flying saucer. He walked out on to the field and found fifteen small holes, and like doubting Thomas in the Bible, didn't believe the thing had really happened until he felt the holes with his own hands.

Hopkins contacted the Texas headquarters of the Mutual UFO Network (MUFON, formerly the Midwestern UFO Network, which by the mid 1970s had superseded NICAP as the main UFO research group in the US) and MUFON directed him to their New York state director, a stage and television actor named Ted Bloecher. Bloecher contacted another New York ufologist, Gerald Stoehrer, and the three of them looked into the case. They found fifteen little bare patches in the field, where O'Barski had found the holes, and they also found a park custodian who remembered filling the holes, having assumed they had been caused by dogs. Then they tracked down the doorman who had been on duty in a nearby apartment complex on the night of O'Barski's sighting, and he remembered how he had seen a row of bright lights over the field, and how the lobby window had mysteriously cracked just as he was getting on the phone to call someone about the strange lights. He had reported it to a police lieutenant who lived in the apartment complex, and who told Hopkins that he had assumed that the doorman had been drinking. Another doorman had seen a similar light hovering over the field about six days previously.

Hopkins wrote down an account of his investigation, and within a few months got it published in the *Village Voice*, under the headline – 'SANE CITIZEN SEES UFO IN NEW JERSEY'. The rest of the press jumped all over it. UFOs in New Jersey! UFOs were normally the stuff of *National Enquirer*-type tabloids, but the *Voice* was a reasonably serious paper, and Hopkins was no obscure hoaxmonger; a lot of important people had heard of him. A little box beneath the article contained a picture of the handsome, salt-and-pepper-haired artist, and the comment that his work had been collected by the Whitney and the Guggenheim. Well, all right, he was only an artist – and some of these modern artists were a bit odd, like Warhol with his homemade sex movies, or Pollock, who had once urinated in Peggy Guggenheim's fireplace during a dinner party ... But Hopkins seemed to have covered the story with remarkable thoroughness.

The press attention was only part of it, of course. Hopkins now began to receive calls and letters from ordinary people around the

New York City area – and from around the country, when the *Voice* story was reprinted in *Cosmopolitan* of all places. People who had had some kind of UFO experience wanted to report it to someone who sounded as if he knew what he was talking about. And Hopkins was fairly easy to reach, his phone number and address being listed in the Manhattan directory.

Whether Hopkins wanted it or not, he was now becoming a full-fledged UFO researcher. He would remain an active painter, and his works would continue to sell well among collectors, but his career seemed to have reached its apogee. At any rate his bohemian days were over. In fact, had he been a true bohemian, he would probably have been dead, for in the spring of 1976 he was forty-four years old – the terminal age for Gorky and Pollock – and was weeks away from turning forty-five. He had divorced Joan in 1971, but then had married April Kingsley in 1973, and with her had had a daughter, Grace, who was now one year old. He had bought the house on 16th Street. He had put down roots, and was settling into middle age. Painting wasn't everything any more, and UFOs – well, why not?

Most of the reports that Hopkins received, like most reports that any UFO researcher received, concerned sightings of lights in the sky. But occasionally there would be an O'Barski-style close-encounter, in which a spacecraft or lightform was viewed close up. Sometimes the close-up sighting would be associated with a puzzling lapse of time that the witness couldn't account for. Even the O'Barski case seemed to involve something along those lines, for O'Barski recalled that he had left his liquor store at about 1 or 2 a.m., and hadn't arrived home until 3. It should have been no more than a half-hour drive at that time of night, even taking into account a five-minute stop at Hudson Park. What had happened to the missing time?

A few days after the *Voice* article came out, a woman telephoned Hopkins and explained that on a recent night some small alien-type creatures had appeared in her bedroom. Could he help her make sense of it all? Hopkins invited her over, and it turned out that she was an unemployed schoolteacher, with a serious weight problem, and not very well groomed and so on. Ted Bloecher was there, too, listening to the story, and the woman began to describe her experience in some detail – for example how she had been taken on board the aliens' spaceship, and how the aliens had told her about the culture of their planet, where there was a fair and equitable distribution of wealth, and they didn't allow homosexuality and various other things, and at one point in the conversation with the aliens their leader had shone some kind of flashlight at her, and she had telepathically asked what it was for, and the alien had telepathically said it was to help her cope, and –

'I've had it!' interrupted Bloecher, throwing down his pencil and notepad and standing up. 'You've gone past my limit of belief. I don't believe a thing you're saying and I'm getting out of here.' And with that he walked out.

Most subsequent investigations went more smoothly, although Bloecher and Hopkins would often disagree, sometimes vehemently, with raised voices and slammed-down telephone handsets, about the proportion of literal truth contained in such abduction accounts. In fact, Bloecher, who had catalogued the close-encounters reported by a variety of witnesses during the UFO wave of 1947, wasn't certain what to make of such accounts, although he agreed that they deserved study.

In any event, Hopkins soon theorized that episodes of 'missing time' served to mask alien abductions, just as in the Barney and Betty Hill case. He decided that the appropriate tool for removing this mask, as in the Hill case, would be regression hypnosis.

Hopkins turned to his friend Bob Naiman, a psychiatrist with a private practice in Manhattan. Naiman liked abstract art and had bought some of Hopkins's paintings, and he and his wife, an art dealer, moved around the same cocktail party circuit as Budd and April. He also specialized in the use of hypnosis, usually to help people give up addictions such as smoking and overeating. Some time around the end of 1976, Hopkins mentioned to Naiman that he had a few close-encounter cases in which regression hypnosis might bear fruit. Would Naiman be interested in helping them out? Well, Naiman wasn't exactly into UFOs, but Hopkins was a friend, and the project seemed interesting. Early in 1977, Hopkins began bringing missing-time cases to him. He would generally do it on a Saturday, outside of Naiman's regular office hours. Naiman would sit in his office chair and the missing-time subject would lie nearby on a couch; Hopkins and Bloecher would sit over in a corner, taking notes and running a tape recorder. Naiman would talk to the subject for a half-hour or so, trying to extract as much conscious recollection of the incident as possible, and trying to gain the subject's confidence; then he would use relaxation techniques to induce a hypnotic trance, putting the subject into a deep, relaxing sleep . . . and then leading her back down the memory trail to the episode of interest. Naiman, with his distinctively deep, avuncular voice, would ask all the questions, but as the encounter proceeded – usually towards an abduction, just as Hopkins had suspected – the two UFO researchers would scribble their own questions and hand them to the psychiatrist. *What colour are those eyes? What size is that table? How long is that needle?*

Some of the more bizarre accounts involved more than one person, just as the Hill case had. In one of the early cases, during the big UFO wave of the autumn of 1973, seven young men and women, in three cars, driving home from a club near the Appalachian town of Kent in western Connecticut, had seen a big *Close Encounters*-style mothership emit several small lightforms. The youths had driven towards the lightforms, but had lost sight of them while on a deserted dirt road. Doubling back, they had seen a car parked beside the dirt road with a young woman behind the wheel. They decided to ask her for directions. Then suddenly a double column of about two dozen hikers with lighted hats appeared, and walked along the road past them, chanting something they couldn't quite make out . . . and the next thing they all remembered, they were sitting in their three cars and the hikers had gone, along with the fourth car, and a short while later, while they were driving around looking for the hikers to ask them if they had seen the UFOs, the police stopped one of their cars and asked them what the hell they were doing out at this time of night, 2 a.m. – when as far as they knew it shouldn't have been any later than 11 p.m. Hopkins and Bloecher drove out to Kent and interviewed the seven witnesses. 'What did these hikers look like?' they would ask, and invariably the young witness would say, 'Well, you know, they were just hikers.' And Hopkins and Bloecher would say, 'OK – how were they dressed?' And one kid would remember, 'They were dressed like hikers, in blue jeans,' while another would insist that the hikers had been wearing shorts. Then Hopkins asked, 'What did they look like when viewed from behind?' But oddly, none of the kids seemed to remember having seen the hikers from this angle.

Virtually all of the witnesses appeared to have been through some kind of harrowing experience. One of them, a twenty-one-year-old woman, went with her husband for a life insurance medical examination a few weeks after the event, and for the first time in her life, and without being able to explain why, she felt utterly terrified of going into a doctor's surgery. So her husband went in first, and had the usual cursory check, involving a blood pressure test and a blood test and saying 'Ahhhh' and submitting to palpations and probes here and there – and when he came out, he couldn't find his wife; it turned out she was in the ladies' room, locked in and mute, so thoroughly and unutterably frightened that she had lapsed into a catatonic state.

Eventually Hopkins and Bloecher were able to get the most mature witness, a young man of twenty-five, into Naiman's office in Manhattan for regression hypnosis. Naiman took the subject back to the night in question, and now he remembered a row of humanoid figures in suits and lighted helmets coming towards them, and the figures lining up around the cars, surrounding them, and shining their helmet lamps at them – and at that point the young man's eyes opened wide and he sat bolt upright on Naiman's couch, spontaneously emerging from hypnosis, and when he had collected his wits he made it clear that he wanted nothing more to do with hypnosis or UFO researchers.

Hopkins went out to Kent several times, to try to persuade more of the kids to come in for hypnosis. He had no success. For one thing, the kids' parents were against the idea. The father of one girl let it be known that if those two New Yorkers with their talk about hypnosis and aliens came around again he'd give 'em two barrels of birdshot with his twelve-gauge. The man's wife, however, quietly took Hopkins aside and said, 'You think my daughter was taken into that ship, don't you?'

'Ma'am, I'm afraid so,' said Hopkins.

'I think so, too,' confided the woman. 'But I just want you to know, Julie's doing well in school right now, and she's got good friends. She's got a normal life. Let's just let sleeping dogs lie.'

Another case could have come right out of the old *Twilight Zone* show. It involved a New Jersey public school teacher, Jed Burgess, who one night in 1961, while a young Army officer, had been driving from New Jersey to a new posting at Fort Jackson, South Carolina. He had travelled a fair distance down into North Carolina when he realized that he was running low on petrol, and that it was too late to find a service station open. He decided to find a motel in the next town and finish the drive in the morning. But before he reached the next town, he came upon a man standing in the highway, signalling him to detour down a narrow dirt road. Burgess complied, then realized that the man had addressed him by his name – or at least by his rank; he wasn't quite sure – despite the fact that he, Burgess, was wearing civilian clothes. Burgess was puzzling over this when his car engine stalled, and the headlights and radio went out. The car kept moving, however, forward and upwards . . . Burgess started to say the Lord's Prayer, and the next thing he knew, it was a bright sunny morning and he was in a motel room – in Fort Jackson, South Carolina. His car was out in the parking lot, undamaged, and its fuel gauge read the same as it had back in North Carolina. Hypnosis indicated that his detour had included an abduction and medical examination inside a spaceship, at the hands of small grey aliens.

By the end of 1977, Bob Naiman was doing three or four regression hypnosis sessions every Saturday. Each session took over an hour, and could be exhausting; the hypnotist had to be on guard almost constantly. If an uncovered memory were obviously stressful, he would have to decide quickly whether to bring the patient out of the hypnotized state, or whether to keep him going with emotional-distancing techniques ('This is all in the past. It's not really happening. It's just like you're watching a movie'). On one occasion, in the early days, a subject claimed that his arms had become paralysed, and even when Naiman brought him out of the trance, the young man remained paralysed for several minutes. Even with the distancing techniques there could be problems. Naiman didn't want them to work *too* well. He wanted the subject to stay in a trance, to recall events clearly. Without focused, close-up recall, the patient might begin to 'confabulate' – which is to say, in psychiatric parlance, he might begin to make things up, according to how he consciously or subconsciously *believed* that events should proceed.

Nevertheless, Naiman kept it up for months, accepting no more than an occasional honorarium in the form of a small painting from Hopkins. He wasn't necessarily convinced that these abduction accounts were all literally true, but he felt that there must be something here – certainly something worth looking into. The abduction events, their sequence, the abductors – they were all described so *similarly* by people who themselves were manifestly different, and who couldn't have known one another. He talked it over with one or two other psychiatrist friends, and they agreed that it didn't sound like anything in the textbooks.

Hopkins by this time had more or less immersed himself in the abduction phenomenon. He could think and talk of almost nothing else. One summer in the late seventies, on a short-hop flight from Boston to join April on the Cape, he ran into his ex-wife Joan, who had remarried and was headed out to join her own spouse. Budd still saw Joan every now and then – she occasionally visited the studio, to see his latest work, or dropped by the gallery where his pictures were sold – but lately she had noticed a change taking place in him. He seemed to be almost obsessed with his ufological research. She was to a certain extent sympathetic, since he had shared with her some of the evidence for the reality of the phenomenon, but she didn't like to dwell on the subject. It depressed and disturbed her, as it might anyone, and anyway, even if aliens were kidnapping people right and left, it didn't seem that there was much one could do about it. On the flight out to Provincetown airport, Budd began to tell her about some of his latest cases, going into some of the spookier details, and how it was all real and something had to be done about it, and finally Joan had to ask him to change the subject. She understood what he was saying, and she respected his work, but it was just too . . . much.

In his studios in Manhattan and on the Cape, Budd began to focus his work on four basic designs. He called them Guardians, Temples, Altars, and Ixions. The Guardians were constructed from smooth, three-inch-thick pieces of wood cut into odd shapes, painted with wedges and arcs at the top and vertical bars jutting down out of them; they seemed to Joan to be descendants of that curvilinear oddity, *Sun Black*, which had so surprised her a decade before. Actually, to Budd the Guardians had consciously been inspired by ancient Near Eastern bas-reliefs, those flatland processions which so often led endlessly around the faces of temples and other important buildings. Another inspiration had come from Piero della Francesca's fancy-perspectived paintings of religious figures, especially his winged *St Michael*, the eternal Guardian, triumphantly grasping the severed head of a snake.

The Temples, at least in terms of their prosaic parts, were large square conglomerations of painted wood, intended to be hung on the wall. The Altars, meant for the floor, were pieces of dark unpainted wood, a few horizontal and a few vertical. The Ixions were similar to the Guardians, except that, for example, their heads tended to be completely rather than incompletely circular. The name for them had been inspired after Budd had finished his first Temple, and had dedicated it, in an artistic rather than a frankly spiritual way, to the Greek goddess Hera, wife of Zeus, the ruler of the gods. Budd had taken out a paperback guide to Greek mythology and had read about Hera, and had taken a particular interest in a story about a fellow named Ixion, an ambitious mortal who had once attempted to seduce Hera. Hera had promptly informed Zeus, who had fashioned a fake Hera from cloud-stuff and had placed it in Ixion's bed; Ixion had taken the evanescent bait – and for his impudence had been tied by Zeus to a fiery wheel and flung eternally across the heavens . . .*

Early in 1978, Hopkins was introduced by Ted Bloecher to one of Bloecher's fellow actors, Michael Bershad, whose story was particularly interesting. He had no conscious recollection of ever having seen a UFO, but for years, and for no apparent reason, he had felt a certain dread whenever he travelled along a particular stretch of highway near his house. Hopkins and Bloecher decided to bring him in to Naiman. By this time Naiman, to reduce his workload, was beginning to pass some of the incoming abductees to other psychiatrists and psychologists who were trained in hypnosis – for example, the distinguished author and academic

---

* Later classical writers suggest that Ixion's wheel of misfortune spun not in the heavens but in the underworld.

Robert Jay Lifton, a professor of psychiatry and psychology at the City University of New York. Lifton was a neighbour of Naiman's, and had also collected some of Hopkins's paintings. Like Naiman, he was somewhat sceptical about whether the abduction accounts were literally true, but at the same time he wasn't sure quite what to make of them.

However, Lifton always seemed to be travelling somewhere or writing books, and wasn't able to absorb more than a trickle of cases, and when Mike Bershad came along, he was sent to George Fisher, a colleague of Naiman's whom Naiman himself had trained in hypnotic techniques. Fisher and Bershad and Hopkins and Bloecher gathered one Saturday morning in Fisher's office, and the investigation began. Bershad was asked to remember what he could consciously. He told them that a few years ago he had lived in a suburb of Baltimore, Maryland, and would often drive out US Route 40 to the town of Frederick to visit his girlfriend. He had been seeing this girl for about a year, driving out every day or so, and coming back at all hours, and one night in the autumn of 1973 ... well, he couldn't remember very much, perhaps he had seen a light in the sky, and perhaps not, and perhaps he had pulled the car over, but anyway he had had the feeling of being watched, and he had wished that the car would go faster, and he had arrived home a little later than he had expected, with the weird sense that something had happened to him out there on Route 40.

Fisher put him into a trance, and the following scenario emerged: Bershad had been driving along that night when he had put down the window to get some fresh air. Then his eyes had begun to stare at the dashboard, and somehow the car had been pulled off on to the shoulder, and he had found himself outside the car looking at a fence. From behind the fence emerged some figures dressed in black. Then somehow a big brass-like clamp was placed over his left shoulder, and he was unable to move except in the direction the clamp took him. He was approached by one of the figures, who wore a black turtleneck-type suit and underneath had chalky, putty-like skin. Somewhere above them there was a bright light. 'It's day,' said Bershad, 'but it's night.' By the time Fisher brought him out of the trance, Bershad seemed to be experiencing severe stress.

Fisher soon gave up hypnosis, after having difficulty in bringing another abductee out of a trance. He could just imagine the malpractice lawsuits if that kind of thing continued to happen. The fact that the abduction stories bore similarities to each other might be of some psychiatric interest, but he didn't want to be the one to pursue it.

Bershad didn't undergo another hypnosis session until late in 1978, this time on the couch of Aphrodite Clamar. Clamar was a therapist who used hypnosis on some of her patients. Naiman had met her at a party and had told her about the UFO abductions he and his colleagues had been investigating. The abduction accounts were now regularly including scenes of genital or gynaecological examination, and one of the female abductees had requested a female hypnotist, to lessen her embarrassment. Clamar had agreed to help out on an occasional basis. As it turned out, however, the female abductee never arrived for her hypnosis session, and so the first case Clamar handled was Bershad's.

Clamar brought Bershad back to the night in 1973 on Route 40, and Bershad was able to enlarge upon the story somewhat. While driving, he had seen two lights in the sky, reflected on the windscreen. They disappeared into a wooded area by the side of the road, where he pulled over and got out of the car. He felt a sense of dread, that he shouldn't be there, but then a telepathic voice explained to him that everything would be all right. Three aliens stood in front of him, with putty-white faces and large black glistening eyes. Their heads were oversized, shaped like inverted teardrops. Their feet, or their boots, were shaped like almonds. They seemed to have bad knees; they had trouble walking. One of them dug a hole in the dirt next to the car.

That was all that Bershad could remember, until early 1980, in another hypnosis session with Clamar, when he remembered the clamp again, and that it had been connected to a saucer-shaped craft: he had been led up a ramp into the craft, and the clamp had let him go, and there had been a quiet humming inside the ship, and he had walked around for a while and eventually had found himself on a table in a round, white room, wearing some kind of a diaper, and a big metallic bulb on the end of a stalk had come down from the ceiling and – Christ, the thing looked like one of those things one saw in a dentist's surgery, or like a ray gun out of some horror sci-fi movie. But something about the room, with its curved edges, made it soothing, hypnotic even . . . The table seemed almost to have grown out of the floor . . . And now the big metallic bulb, with all kinds of appendages and attachments sticking out of it, was coming down, and one of the attachments was digging into his back. It hurt like hell, and every so often – *What the* – ? His leg twitched. It was as if he were one of those frogs stretched out on a slab in high school biology class, and some pimple-faced students were playing with his nervous system. Then the aliens pressed a little cylinder, a little tube-like thing, into his stomach, prodding him with it. And then a stirrup-like arrangement grabbed his thighs and lifted his legs up, spreading them slightly, and the putty-faces came over and prodded him some more and –

Hopkins knew a Brooklyn neurologist, Paul Cooper, who was interested in abstract art, and who might also be willing to help out with Hopkins's UFO research. He spoke to Cooper and arranged for him to meet with Bershad. Cooper listened to Bershad's story for a couple of hours, and came away disturbed by the whole thing. The business of the leg twitch – it was exactly what would happen if one stuck a probe in the base of the spinal column and stimulated the femoral nerve. And it was not something that just anyone would know . . .

By 1980, Budd Hopkins had listened to the stories of several dozen UFO close-encounter witnesses. A remarkably high proportion of them – well over half – turned out also to have experienced missing time during their close-encounters. Of the missing time subjects who agreed to undergo hypnosis, almost all turned out to have been abducted. To Hopkins, it began to seem that the abduction phenomenon, contrary to the popular belief among ufologists, was anything but rare. It began to seem, in fact, that if one could remember having seen a UFO at close range, one was more than likely to have been taken inside it.

Moreover, the Bershad case suggested that abductees might not even have the memory of a UFO close-encounter. All that Bershad had had to go on, apparently, was his vague unease about a certain stretch of highway, the sense that *something* had happened to him somewhere out there. And yet ... under hypnosis, a frightening abduction scenario had emerged, complete with putty-faced aliens, round white rooms, examination tables, and painful and degrading medical-type procedures. Hopkins had only come across Bershad because Bershad had known Ted Bloecher. How many other people were out there with only a vague sense that something traumatic had happened to them, that somehow a few hours of their lives had disappeared? It began to seem possible that the UFO abduction phenomenon was not only widespread, but was also largely *invisible*.

There were some other interesting aspects of the abduction phenomenon that had begun to surface. For example, the Virginia Horton case: after NBC had run a piece about abductions on its *Nightly News* show late in 1979, featuring Hopkins and Clamar and Mike Bershad, Horton had telephoned Dr Clamar with her story. She was a corporate lawyer, living on the east coast, with a husband and a family and an ordinary life. She had always been fascinated by the possibility of space travel, but strictly human space travel – NASA and the astronauts, that kind of thing – and had never been very interested in strange phenomena such as UFOs. A friend of hers, who also knew Clamar, had seen the NBC show and had told her about it, and now Virginia remembered that some strange things had happened to her as a child. Once in the summer of 1950, when she was six, she had been at her grandfather's farm in Manitoba, and had gone into a barn to gather eggs from the chickens – and the next thing she knew she was out in the yard again, with an itch on the back of her calf. She pulled up the leg of her jeans, and saw that she was bleeding from a neat surgical-type wound. Her jeans were undamaged, and she couldn't think of any reason for the wound, or remember how she had got back into the yard. After her friend told her about the abduction story on NBC, Virginia called her mother to ask if she remembered the incident. She didn't, but she did remember a time when the family had been on a picnic somewhere in France. Virginia, then sixteen, and her brother had been exploring a nearby forest but had become separated. Her brother had been looking for her for at least half an hour but couldn't find her and when she finally reappeared, her dress mysteriously spattered with blood, she claimed that she had been with her brother until just before she had emerged from the woods; otherwise, all she could remember was that in the woods she had met a beautiful deer.

Under hypnosis it turned out that when she was six in Manitoba she had been taken into a bright room in a spacecraft by grey aliens who had explained that they were from far away, among the stars, and that they only wanted to take a piece of her home, and that it would be best for her not to remember anything afterwards. At one point a big box-like thing, attached to a retractable arm, similar to the thing that Bershad had seen, came down from the ceiling and emitted a tubelike instrument which rubbed the back of her leg at the place where she later found the incision. And when she had been in the woods in France, and had seen the deer – well, the deer turned out to have been a peculiarly *grey* sort of deer, with peculiarly large black eyes, and inside the spaceship her old friends (for it was the same group) showed her star maps and told her they were from another galaxy and spoke about the importance of biological diversity and the preservation of species, such as the human species . . . and she talked them into giving her a short ride a few hundred miles up, and at one point they laid her down gently on a table and inserted a needle-like instrument into her left nostril, giving her a slight nosebleed which explained the blood on her dress.

The idea of aliens sticking things into abductees' nostrils wasn't too new; quite a number of the abduction cases which had been investigated and publicized by other UFO researchers in the seventies had turned out to include this kind of thing. Sometimes the witness remembered seeing something on the end of the needle that wasn't there when the needle came out again, as if some kind of neurological monitor had been implanted in the forebrain. The Horton case merely confirmed that the nasal-implant motif was a common one. But the case also suggested some new and interesting things about the abduction phenomenon. First, there was the matter of the scar on her leg. This kind of thing didn't appear too often in the literature, but it seemed to be happening to a great many of the abductees whom Hopkins looked at. An 'unexplained' scar not only indicated what the aliens might be up to; it also provided researchers with a general marker, often connected to a sense of missing time, which suggested that a given individual had previously been abducted.

Another new feature of abduction phenomenology was suggested by the fact that Virginia's deer in the woods in France had clearly been a 'screen memory', put there by the aliens or by Virginia's own frightened perception. The screen memory concept suggested that many other cases might also be masked by such prosaic recollections.

Finally, the fact that Virginia had been abducted at least twice suggested that abductions in general might not be isolated, once-in-a-lifetime events for the abductee. Each abduction might represent part of an ongoing, lifelong research programme, involving for example tissue and cell sampling, the ultimate purpose of which only the aliens knew.

In the dozens of other missing-time cases he studied during the late 1970s, Hopkins also found that abductions didn't have to take place in the woods, or on a lonely stretch of road. They could just as easily be initiated when the abductee was inside a house. Howard Rich, a friend of Hopkins's, had been watching the old horror show *The Night Stalker* one night in 1979 at his mother's house at the edge of the New Jersey Pine Barrens. Suddenly there had been a blue light in the room and Rich had grabbed a gun and had gone outside, and then for some reason had dropped the gun, and when he had come back inside, only a few minutes later he thought, another programme was on the TV, and he felt like hell, as if something had happened to him out there. Under hypnosis at Aphrodite Clamar's, it emerged that Howard had been taken into a spaceship and had experienced the usual routine.

Philip Osborne had had an even more frightening experience. A New York journalist who found himself oddly drawn to UFO stories, Osborne contacted Hopkins after the NBC programme and recalled to him that on several occasions in the past few decades he had awakened in his bed at night with a sense of terror and paralysis. Under hypnosis it turned out that one night, while a university student in Pittsburgh, he had sensed something else's presence, a face at the window perhaps; he had got out of bed and dressed himself and walked up to a deserted mansion at the top of a hill, where he had somehow entered a flying saucer and then had lain on an examination table above which two glowing spheres hovered. He saw pinkish, translucent-skinned humanoids with metallic eyes, but also an all-metal robotic creature which somehow was reminiscent of the Tin Woodman in *The Wizard of Oz*. Anyway, the important thing was that the aliens had taken him from his own bedroom, controlling his mind to make him come to them.

By the middle of 1980, when these patterns had emerged for Hopkins, the abduction phenomenon was being taken seriously by an increasing number of UFO researchers, many of whom had written or were writing books about their findings. Ralph and Judy Blum's *Beyond Earth: Man's Contact with UFOs* had been published by Bantam in 1974. Coral and Jim Lorenzen, founders of the Aerial Phenomena Research Organization, had compiled *Encounters with UFO Occupants* and *Abducted!*, which were published by Berkley Books in 1976 and 1977. Ray Fowler had written *The Andreasson Affair*, about the abduction experiences of a Massachusetts housewife named Betty Andreasson, and Prentice-Hall had published it in 1979. Shortly thereafter Prentice-Hall had also published *The Tujunga Canyon Contacts*, by parapsychologist Scott Rogo and ufologist Ann Druffel, about a series of bedroom visitations and abductions which had been suffered by a group of young women in southern California from the 1950s to the 1970s. Even abductee Travis Walton had a book out – *The Walton Experience* – which Berkley had published in 1978. But to Hopkins, none of the authors of these books had taken his own systematic view of the phenomenon. None clearly articulated the patterns which Hopkins believed had become common in abduction accounts. None showed that the sense of 'missing time' might be the only strong indication that an abduction had occurred. None argued, as Hopkins felt he could, that this and other aspects of the phenomenon indicated the presence of an invisible epidemic. *The Invisible Epidemic*, in fact, was the working title for Hopkins's own book, which he had been writing since 1979.

Ted Bloecher had been against the book, arguing that several more years of study, at least, were required for an accurate analysis of the abduction phenomenon. But to Hopkins, Bloecher's opposition to the book, and his apparent love-hate passion about the subject as a whole, indicated that a deeper motivation was at work. Hopkins began to suspect that Bloecher himself had been abducted, somewhere in his childhood; Bloecher's subconscious denial of this, Hopkins believed, was reflected in his touchiness about the phenomenon.

Hopkins didn't think there was much more he could do about it, however, and anyway he wasn't going to sit on his thesis any longer; he went ahead with the book and sought a publisher.

His search didn't take long. One day in 1980 he was in the office of Ira Wender, a collector who had just bought one of his smaller works, a study for a much larger multicoloured triptych, *Mahler's Castle*. Wender wanted Hopkins's aesthetic advice on where and how to hang the thing in his office. While they were in the office, Hopkins asked Wender whether his wife Phyllis, a literary agent, would be interested in looking at his book on UFOs. She might be, said Wender, so Hopkins called her up and she sounded interested, and it turned out that in a few days she was going to have lunch with Richard Marek, the eponymous head of a small imprint at Putnam's. Hopkins dropped off a few chapters at Phyllis Wender's office, and she read them and liked them and passed them to Marek at lunch, who phoned up a few days later, a week or so having passed since Hopkins's initial inquiry, and said he wanted to publish it. Marek prevailed upon Hopkins, however, to jettison his original title, *The Invisible Epidemic*, which somehow sounded too medical, like some kind of new Andromeda Strain. Hopkins thought about it for a while and eventually came up with an alternative, *Missing Time*. Marek liked it, and the book was published, with a short afterword by Aphrodite Clamar, who discussed her hypnotic techniques, the apparent clinical normality of the abductees she had hypnotized, and her frustrating inability to establish, despite the apparent outlandishness of the abduction stories, that they were fantasy rather than reality.

4

Unto the Daughters of Men

There were giants in the earth in those days; and also after that, when the sons of God came in unto the daughters of men, and they bare children to them, the same became mighty men which were of old, men of renown.

– Genesis 6:4

Missing Time was published in the summer of 1981. It didn't make a great impact on the mass market, selling only about 10,000 copies in hardcover, but it made the UFO research community sit up and take notice. Around the time of publication, at an annual MUFON convention held in Cambridge, Massachusetts, Budd Hopkins gave a lecture in which he outlined several of the accounts he and Bloecher had investigated. He put them into categories which were like Close Encounter categories,* except that the categories varied not with the intensity of the event, but with the degree of conscious recall. A Type 1 case involved at least partial memory of the abduction episode; Charley Hickson and Travis Walton, who hadn't needed hypnosis to remember being abducted, were Type 1 abductees. A Type 2 case involved a conscious memory of a UFO, and perhaps of its occupants, and also a sense of missing time, but nothing about an abduction; the Kent, Connecticut case, and

---

* A Close Encounter of the First Kind, or CE1, is just a close-up sighting of a UFO. A CE2 is one which includes other pronounced effects on the immediate environment, such as vehicle ignition interference or a burn mark on the ground. A CE3 is a sighting of spaceship occupants. A CE4 involves being taken inside the ship. A CE5 – named recently although based on an old concept – would be an encounter initiated by humans on the ground, for example by shining lights into the sky, or by making telepathic requests for the aliens to land.

perhaps even the O'Barski case, were Type 2. A Type 3 case – a typical one being a bedroom visitation – involved a conscious memory of a UFO and/or its occupants but without a sense of time lapse. A Type 4 case involved only a sense of missing time, and a Type 5 case involved not even that; a Type 5 abductee had only a vague sense of buried trauma, perhaps associated with a certain geographical location, or with a scar on his or her body. Hopkins suggested that the Type 1 and Type 2 cases, the really sensational ones, were like the tip of an iceberg, the vast bulk of which – that is, the Type 3, 4, and 5 cases – lay below the surface of ufological consciousness. This phenomenon in all its manifestations could be so large, suggested Hopkins, that abductions might be as common as UFO sightings. Indeed, he added provocatively, they might even be more common.

Hopkins gave the same lecture at a few other UFO conferences around the country that summer. Some conference-goers enthusiastically supported his conclusions; after all, those conclusions seemed to make sense of a lot of strange data that ufologists had been puzzling over for years: often there would be a report of a UFO close-encounter, and one witness would remember a strange bright light that had burned her eyes, and another witness would remember seeing aliens standing above her on an operating table, and another would remember nothing at all, and the case would be thrown out. But if the aliens were landing and were trying to blank out witnesses' minds, and if different people had different susceptibilities to the blanking-out process, then such reportorial discrepancies made perfect sense.

Even so, many ufologists scoffed, and after Hopkins delivered a lecture at a meeting in Chicago, one of the scoffers was David Jacobs. Jacobs had been regarded as one of America's leading authorities on the subject of UFOs ever since the publication of his 1975 book, *The UFO Controversy in America*. The book had sprung from his PhD thesis, the first American doctoral dissertation to attempt an exhaustive account of the history of UFOs in popular culture. Jacobs had been interested in UFOs ever since his teen years, and somehow had managed to pursue this unorthodox interest, investigating cases and giving papers at UFO conferences and so on, while also pursuing a successful academic career at

Temple University. One of the reasons he had managed to do this was that his views on the UFO subject were relatively moderate. He did not believe, for example, that George Adamski and Truman Bethurum and George Fry and Orfeo Angelucci and the other prominent contactees who had flown to Venus or wherever and back were anything but charlatans or lunatics. He did not believe that the Barney and Betty Hill story was anything more than a shared fantasy. He had similar reservations about the cases Budd Hopkins had investigated.

One day in the spring of 1982, Jacobs received a telephone call from Tracy Tormé, a Hollywood scriptwriter and son of the singer Mel Tormé. Tracy was a bona fide UFO enthusiast, and in years past had even investigated some of his own cases; on this occasion he was headed east and wanted to speak to Jacobs about the government's conspiracy to suppress the truth about the phenomenon. Jacobs and Tormé met in New York City, at an apartment owned by Universal Studios, and then went for a walk in Central Park and talked about whether there was a government conspiracy and cover-up and so on. At one point Tormé mentioned that Jacobs should meet Budd Hopkins, the artist and abduction researcher. Well, all right, why not? thought Jacobs, and eventually they found their way down to the house on West 16th Street. Hopkins was there with a few abductees, and Jacobs started talking to them about their experiences, and as the conversations went on it became clear to Jacobs that these people weren't quite as deluded as he had imagined they might be. They were anxious and disturbed about what had happened to them, there was no doubt about that; but otherwise they seemed completely sincere and ordinary. The most impressive thing about them, as far as Jacobs was concerned, was that they weren't taking a position on the subject, other than to argue that something traumatic had happened to them. They weren't trying to convince him that they had been taken to Saturn or Alpha Centauri and had been told the secrets of the universe. They weren't trying to push the usual contactee business about how the peoples of the world must come together in peace and brotherhood or else. They were merely frightened.

As Jacobs was leaving, he happened to mention that he and his wife would be staying in Cape Cod for a few weeks over the summer. Where in Cape Cod? asked Hopkins. A little town called Wellfleet, said Jacobs. As it happened, Hopkins had lost the Truro house when he and Joan had been divorced, but then had built another one – in Wellfleet. So Jacobs visited Hopkins in Wellfleet over the summer, and the two became close friends. To Jacobs, Hopkins was an unusually thoughtful and intelligent individual who was also seriously interested in UFOs. He didn't see that combination too often in a person. What was more, he and Hopkins had pretty much the same view of the UFO phenomenon – i.e. that it represented some kind of visitation of the earth, for some unknown reason, by alien beings of advanced intelligence who flew around in spaceships. They politely disagreed about the abduction phenomenon, but as time went on, and Hopkins told Jacobs more about his research, Jacobs began to wonder whether Hopkins might be on to something after all.

In late 1983, Hopkins received a letter which had been sent to him care of his publishers from an Indiana woman named Debbie Tomey. Tomey had read *Missing Time* and was responding to Hopkins's general invitation, printed at the end of the book, to share abduction experiences with the author. She was thirty something with two children, aged three and four, but had been divorced for a few years and lived at her parents' house, which was a nice house with a garage and a pool surrounded by tall maple trees in an Indianapolis suburb called Copley Woods. She enclosed some photographs of an apparently burned patch of grass in her yard, and in a several-page letter recounted a strange experience she'd had which related to the burned patch. One night that summer, she wrote, she had been about to go out to a friend's house when she had noticed that there was a light on in the pool house outside, and the pool house door was open, despite the fact that she distinctly remembered having shut it a few hours before. She wondered whether a burglar might be prowling about, so before going to her friend's house, she drove down the driveway to where she could see the pool house – but now the pool house light was off and the door was closed. She drove over to her friend's house, and when she got there she phoned her mother to tell her that the pool house door was closed and the light was off. But her mother by now was in a state, having seen a bright spotlight on the bird feeder near the pool house. Debbie came back and walked around the place with her father's .22, but found nothing very interesting or unusual except her dog Penny who was hiding under the back of one of the other family cars and had to be coaxed out. The next morning the patch of browned grass was there, and nothing would grow on it and the birds wouldn't go near the patch or the bird feeder and even the dog avoided the place. The patch was about eight feet in diameter, with a straight avenue emerging from it and terminating about fifty feet away in a sharply defined arc.

Tomey noted that her sister had had an odd experience with a UFO when she had been a teenager, and that she and her mother had identical scars in the same places on their legs. Actually, Debbie had two such scars, one that had been there as long as she could remember, and one that had appeared when she was about thirteen. But she didn't have any idea how she had come by either of them.

Hopkins began to travel out to Indiana to conduct interviews, and sometimes would bus Debbie Tomey to New York for hypnosis sessions, and after a few months a disturbing new facet to the abduction phenomenon had begun to appear. Actually, it had been there all along; it was just that Hopkins had tended to downplay it, suspecting that it might just be fantasy, and in general not being comfortable in talking or writing about it. But in the Copley Woods case, it was so prominent that he could no longer ignore it: when the aliens would abduct Debbie or another female member of her family, as it seemed that they often did, they would bring her into their spaceship and would take off her clothes and lay her down on a table and put her legs into a stirrup-like contraption, as in a gynaecologist's room, and would insert various instruments into her, vaginally or by a laparoscope-type needle device through her navel as they had used with Betty Hill, and sometimes this would be quite pleasant and sometimes it would be extremely painful. Sometimes it was as if they were planting something inside her, and other times it was as if they were taking something away from her. In one of the hypnosis sessions, Debbie remembered being on the table, and a few months pregnant, with her legs spread and a terrible pressure within her loins, and she began to scream: 'It's not fair! It's mine! It's mine!' And it became clear to Hopkins that the aliens, which in Debbie's case tended to appear as the usual grey ones, were impregnating her with alien chromosomes and then after a few months were harvesting the hybrid grey-human foetuses for incubation elsewhere. As the investigation wore on, Hopkins uncovered an episode in which the aliens apparently presented the little grown-up hybrid to Debbie. The girl-grey was a few feet tall, with a slim body and ivory skin and a big head and high cheekbones and no eyelashes or brows, and unnervingly sparse blonde hair, the colour of cotton, which in certain places didn't quite cover her scalp. Despite the girl's sickly unearthliness, Debbie couldn't help feeling a pang of maternal affection for her.

Perhaps the oddest thing about this hybrid breeding programme was that as soon as Hopkins recognized it, it began to show up prominently in other abduction accounts. Women would write in saying that something strange had happened to them, leaving an unexplained scar or a sense of missing time, and after Hopkins had interviewed them or had hypnotized them – for he had learned the technique from Bob Naiman and Aphrodite Clamar, and was doing it on his own now – it would become clear that somewhere in their pasts they had had pregnancies which had simply disappeared, without a miscarriage or anything. Often the pregnancy itself would be mysterious. In one case, a woman told Hopkins she had become pregnant at thirteen, after a vivid dream in which she had seemed to have intercourse with a large-headed, large-eyed being. She had sworn to her parents that she had never slept with a man before; they hadn't believed her; but when she had gone to see a gynaecologist about getting an abortion, the gynaecologist had noted with some puzzlement that her hymen was still intact.

A similar motif would appear in men's accounts: a young man would be naked on the table and his legs would be spread somehow and then something would be placed over his penis and perhaps also a kind of helmet would be placed on his head and he would feel very strange and disoriented, as if a profound neurological manipulation were under way; then suddenly he would ejaculate and his sperm would be sucked out and after that he would be set back down in his bedroom or wherever he had been, with a vague sense of having been traumatized – although sometimes there was only the evanescent and not entirely unpleasant screen memory of intercourse with a lovely female alien. It had happened in the Michael Bershad case, although Hopkins hadn't mentioned it in *Missing Time*; but now he was hearing it from virtually every male abductee who came to him.

By this time, David Jacobs would often come to New York to sit in on Hopkins's hypnotic regression sessions with abductees. The sessions were impressive, but there were a few things about the accounts that kept him wondering about the literal reality of it all. First of all, in a typical account the abductee would be in bed, and then would see a light outside or would sense a strange presence in the room, and then suddenly she would be inside the spaceship, with no recollection, even under hypnosis, of how she had been transported there; and just as often she wouldn't remember how the aliens had put her back into bed. Moreover, if one looked at the history of abduction accounts, one couldn't help but notice the weird variety of aliens and experiences reported. Charley Hickson had seen aliens with lobster claws and elephant skin and conical noses, while Philip Osborne had seen aliens with pink translucent skin, and a shiny robot helper. Jacobs had a good deal of respect for Hopkins's work, but even so there were times when he would feel a certain frustration, listening to one of Hopkins's abductees talk about jumping suddenly from bed to spaceship, or hearing her describe some fantastic alien anatomy. *He* wanted to be the one to ask the questions, not the fellow sitting in the corner taking notes.

Jacobs began to study Hopkins's hypnotic induction technique, and began to read books about hypnosis. In the summer of 1986 he went to a hypnotists' conference in Philadelphia, where various mesmeric techniques were discussed. Finally, in August of that year, he decided he was ready, and asked Hopkins to send him any abductees he knew from the Philadelphia area. Hopkins, who was happy to lighten his own load of abductees, sent him Melissa Bucknell, a twenty-seven-year-old who worked in real estate management. Melissa came over to Jacobs's house in the suburbs one day, and they talked briefly about what period of time they were going to try to illuminate with the regression, and then the time came for

Jacobs to put her into the trance. Jacobs, who had never put anyone into a trance before, was fairly nervous. Of course he knew, as anyone who knew anything about hypnosis did, that hypnotic trance induction depended primarily on the willingness of the subject to be inducted, and not on any magic words or intonations the hypnotist might use. Nevertheless, the subject's willingness in turn depended on the confidence she had in the hypnotist. He had to sound as if he knew what he was doing, as if he had done this kind of thing before, many times, and knew all the ropes. Also he had to sound trustworthy. Any hint of Bela Lugosi or Norman Bates, anything false or sinister or perverted in his tone, and the abductee was likely to freeze up entirely. Actually, that part of it Jacobs could handle. He didn't look or sound sinister at all. He was a rumpled, cherubic, middle-aged university professor (with his curly, prematurely grey hair, and his bushy eyebrows, he looked as Einstein might have looked had Einstein's wife been an exceptionally good cook) with a wife and kids and a nice Victorian house in the suburbs, as normal and conventional as you could ask for within ufology; and to top it off he was used to dealing with young people.

But to sound as if he knew the ropes – that was a problem. He just knew that if he tried to memorize an induction sequence . . . *your body is becoming more and more relaxed . . . a warm feeling is spreading up from your toes . . .* he would forget something or say the wrong thing and the thought would shoot through the abductee's mind that this guy Jacobs was a novice, a virgin, and she would make excuses and leave, and maybe would tell all the other abductees that Jacobs was someone to steer clear of.

So Jacobs tried an old actor's trick: he put together a fairly standard induction sequence, and set it down on an index card, and when Melissa Bucknell lay down on his couch, he sat a little way behind her, so she couldn't see him without effort, and for good measure he told her to close her eyes, and then he held the index card up and read out the induction sequence. He sounded a little wooden, reading the sequence from the card, but Melissa had been through hypnosis before with Hopkins, and she seemed to slip into a trance without any trouble at all.

Jacobs brought her back to the afternoon in 1966 when she had been six years old, playing out in a field with friends, and suddenly a flying saucer had appeared and she had found herself inside it. Her clothes had been removed, she had been placed on a table, and she had undergone a gynaecological-type examination, in which something apparently had been planted near her left ovary. Then she remembered going down a hallway and meeting a group of small grey aliens, one of whom she was directed to touch on the head, making her feel a sudden emotional flood of love and warmth. After that she went into a room and there was a meeting of some other aliens, and they turned to her and explained that she would grow up to be a good and strong and intelligent woman. And then she was floated back down to the field again.

Jacobs was relieved. Despite being embarrassed at the gynaecological details, he felt that the session had gone reasonably well. He said goodbye to Melissa, and then sat back to listen to the recording he had made of the session, to analyse how well he had – *Uh oh* . . . After he had listened to the tapes for a few seconds, it became clear that Melissa had been speaking so quietly that her voice had barely registered. There was no way that someone listening to the tape could hear what she was saying. He had nothing to show for his trouble, other than his own unaided memory of her abduction account.

Well, fortunately Melissa was amenable to further regression sessions, and every month or so from then on she would come back to Jacobs for more. After two or three of them, Jacobs decided to bring her back to the day covered in the first session, when she had been six years old and playing in the field. By this time his confidence had grown, and he was able to go through the induction sequence without the index card. He put Melissa into a trance, and led her back to the day in question . . . a sunny summer day, playing in the field with her schoolgirl friends . . . and as before the flying saucer came along and took her up into the ship and the aliens removed her clothes and placed her on a table and reached inside her with their chilly instruments and planted something near her left ovary, and then they floated her back down to the field again, where her friends were, and –

Jacobs gently asked her what had happened to the part about walking down the hall and touching the alien's head and feeling the warmth and love and then walking into the flying saucer conference room and being assured that she, Melissa, would grow up to be a lovely and good and strong woman. What about all of that?

Oh, *that*, said Melissa. Well . . . I guess I just sort of imagined that. I don't think it really happened . . .

Jacobs was horrified. He had *believed* the business about the flood of love and warmth and the conference room and the promise that Melissa would grow up to be a strong and lovely woman. Not that the aliens would have meant any of it – they liked to say all kinds of things to placate abductees; sometimes it seemed as if they would say whatever the abductee wanted to hear. No, the point was that the business of the alien's head and the flood of love and the conference room had seemed to make sense in the overall context of alien behaviour, and had helped to fill the narrative gap between the gynaecological procedures and Melissa's return to the field. But it had only been imagined! Confabulated!

Jacobs resolved that from then on he would make his primary goal the development of a technique that would be immune, or as immune as possible, to confabulation and imagination and screen memories and anything that wasn't absolutely accurate. He didn't have any formal training as an electrical engineer or a physicist, but even he could see that he was dealing with what the engineers and the physicists called a signal-to-noise problem. What the aliens had really done was the signal, and what the abductee only imagined they had done was the noise. With the right investigative technique – the right signal-processing algorithm – he should be able to go down into the idiosyncratic, culture-fed noise of imagination, however confusing it seemed, and pull out the true and pure signal.

What he began to do was this: whenever he heard something that was new or strange in an abduction account – something the aliens had said or an instrument they had used or some creature the abductee had seen inside the spaceship or some symbol or diagram on a spaceship bulkhead – he would note it down, but then lay it aside, treating it as confabulation or screen memory, until he heard the same thing later from the same abductee – or better yet, until he heard the same thing from *another* abductee. Budd Hopkins had already done some interesting work in this area, noting down symbols one abductee claimed to have seen inside a spaceship, and comparing them with symbols other abductees had seen. Hopkins by now had pages and pages of remarkably similar symbols which had been seen by abductees who had never met, and who lived in different areas of the country.

The same kind of thing began to happen to Jacobs, and as the months went by, and he gathered around himself a widening circle of abductees, he felt that he was beginning to learn a lot more about signal and noise. Confabulations and screen memories, he noticed, seemed to occur most often at the beginning of the abduction sequence, when the abductee had just seen the flying saucer or the aliens and was maximally frightened. At this point, which was also the point at which conscious recall ceased and missing time began, hypnotic recollections of the aliens could go all over the place, from bat-men to robots to Venusian love-goddesses. And recollections of what the aliens had done in those initial moments would also go all over the place, or would simply be skipped over, which explained why this part so often was missing from the narrative. Later on, as the aliens worked their grey magic and the abductee began to settle down, her memory would settle down, too, and the aliens would be seen more clearly as four-foot-tall putty-faces, with big glistening black eyes and crania shaped like inverted teardrops, and there would be the table and the speculum and the laparoscope and the usual instruments of torture. In one case, one of Jacobs's abductees remembered at the outset of her abduction confronting a human-looking being with shoulder-length hair. Although only four feet tall, he seemed good-looking. Guessing that this was a screen memory, Jacobs waited until later in the account and then double-checked. When the alien was walking past the abductee for some reason, Jacobs asked the abductee, 'Can you see his back?'

'Yes.'

'Can you see any hair?'

'Um. No.'

'Can you see his ears?'

'No . . . Um, I don't think he looks human, actually.'

Sometimes an abductee's memories would become clearer and less confabulated at all points in the abduction sequence, the more regression sessions she had had. Often Jacobs would wait until the second or third regression with a given abductee to ask what the aliens had looked like. For most abduction researchers, '*What do they look like?*' was the first question to ask, as soon as the abductee had been regressed to the episode of interest; but for Jacobs, it had begun to seem like a naïve invitation to confabulation and confusion.

Jacobs would usually ask his first questions on the telephone, after an apparent abductee had called him or had written to him requesting hypnosis. He would ask the woman (and about 60 per cent of those who approached him were women) whether she had any scars acquired inexplicably during childhood, or whether she could remember any episodes in which her family, say, had thought she had been lost for a few hours, when she herself hadn't noticed the time go by at all. He had a whole list of queries like this that he would go through in an easygoing, conversational manner, and usually after an hour of this sort of thing he could decide whether the woman was psychotic, or had had some kind of religious experience, or was merely making too much of an episode that was likely to have been prosaic, or in fact was likely to have experienced an abduction and was worth adding to his circle of abductees. If she fell into any of the first three categories, Jacobs would say something such as, 'Well, Jane, the situation you are describing really does fall outside of my area of expertise,' and he would then gently suggest that she take her story elsewhere, perhaps to a psychiatrist. If she seemed like a probable abductee, Jacobs would warn her that hidden memories were like the contents of Pandora's box, and when unleashed could cause her and her loved ones all kinds of anguish and trauma, and if she was happy and had a stable life with husband and kids and so on, then she probably would be better off without hypnosis and without inquiring further into the subject. If she was experiencing trauma and anguish now, however, and it looked as if hypnosis might help her to bring the source of the trauma to the surface, and then to integrate it into her life and worldview somehow, and if she had listened to Jacobs's warnings and still wanted the hypnosis, and if she lived within a few hours' driving distance, then Jacobs would send her a pamphlet that he and Hopkins had worked up, which gave the same sorts of warnings, and he would invite her to call him back in a week to see whether she wanted to proceed. If she did, and then showed up for the hypnotic regression, Jacobs would treat it as a dry run, knowing that the abductee would be nervous about lying down on a strange man's couch and maybe letting slip her most intimate and embarrassing secrets; he would wait for a further session before he began seriously to gather data. Sometimes the relationship would end with the first session; the material that emerged would be so frightening, so wrenching, that the abductee would regret having come to Jacobs in the first place. But more often the relationship would not end with the first session, and the abductee would return for hypnosis until every abduction event in her life had been uncovered.

Sometimes an abductee would undergo a dozen or so sessions, covering everything from her childhood to the present, but then would begin to have more abductions, sometimes several times a week, sometimes only hours before a scheduled session, and so she would keep having to come back. Had Jacobs considered himself merely a ufologist, he might have considered turning some of these multiple abductees away; the material was piling up, and he would never be able to analyse it all. But he was becoming a therapist more than anything else. He wanted to use the material to further the aims of ufology, and of mankind in general, but in virtually everything he did he governed himself by the goals of the therapist. The primary object of his regression sessions was not to understand what the aliens had planned for planet Earth, or even to establish the reality of the abduction phenomenon; it was to enable the abductee to integrate her abduction experiences into her life – i.e. to be healed. Typically, the abductee would come to him with all kinds of anxieties and neuroses concerning inexplicable events that had happened to her at various points in her life. She would be unable to sleep with the lights off. She would be unable to make love to her husband. She would have strange obsessions about locks and closets and windows and whether her children were safe. By bringing the abduction events to the surface, by making them somehow explicable, Jacobs – like Hopkins and the others – hoped he could help his abductees to live normal lives again, or at least as normal as possible under the circumstances.

In a weirdly analogous fashion, Jacobs through his abduction investigations was healing his own fractured view of the UFO phenomenon. When he had been a young student, poring with fascination through UFO magazines, he had imagined that the phenomenon might have to do with a race, or perhaps several races, of beings of advanced intelligence who were coming to earth in spaceships. But somehow his understanding had never progressed; it had been impossible for him to figure out precisely *why* the aliens were here. Close-encounter cases, as recalled consciously by their witnesses, never seemed to have any consistent pattern, and some could be utterly bizarre, such as the Dr X case. To Jacobs, the utter incomprehensibility of the Dr X case, when it had surfaced back in the late sixties, had forced him to admit to himself that after all his meticulous historical research, he really didn't know anything about UFOs. But now, in the light of the abduction phenomenon, the Dr X case – and many other cases like it – had begun to make a frightening kind of sense.

With his own abduction research, and his use of a more rigorous methodology, Jacobs was becoming a powerful advocate for the idea that abduction accounts were more or less literally true. But Eddie Bullard's work would soon become just as persuasive, even though he had never hypnotized an abductee in his life.

Eddie Bullard, more formally known as Thomas E. Bullard, was a lanky, friendly folklorist in his late thirties. He had been hooked on UFOs ever since 1957, when as a third-grader in the little town of Haw River, North Carolina, he had heard about a wave of sightings of egg-shaped craft in the south-western part of the country. His mood at the time had been celebratory: the Russians, who a few months earlier had lofted Sputnik, clearly were now invading from space, and World War Three would start and he wouldn't have to go to school.

Alas, the UFO wave passed without international incident, but Bullard became increasingly absorbed in the culture of ufology; he would watch just about any movie with an it-came-from-outer-space theme, and would read any of the available UFO magazines. He attended the University of North Carolina, taking a degree in English Literature, and then decided to go on to do a PhD in folklore. Studying folklore was something like studying literature;

both had to do with the verbal aspects of culture. But folklore concentrated more on unwritten, unofficial tales. Bullard was especially interested in modern folklore, the 'urban legends' that persisted in public consciousness despite the official, orthodox doctrines of science and Presbyterianism and *Time* magazine. Bullard knew just which urban legends he wanted to write about, and after arriving at the University of Indiana, where the department specialized in modern folklore, he began a PhD thesis comparing the ufological lore, not unfavourably, to that of ghosts and goblins and heavenly portents and so on.

He finished in 1982, and set about finding a job. Unfortunately, with only three or four folklore departments in the country, and given his own slightly *outré* choice of expertise, there wasn't much hope of finding real academic employment, so he stayed on at the university as an assistant librarian, and settled down to life at a cramped desk in the bookstacks, where the work was somewhat depressing but at least afforded him time for research into the field that he loved.

Not long afterwards, Bullard heard that the Fund for UFO Research, a non-profit organization which channelled money from philanthropic UFO enthusiasts, wanted to commission a catalogue and comparative study of alien abduction accounts. Bullard applied for the job, was accepted, and quickly immersed himself in the esoteric lore of abductions, cataloguing every account he could find in the better-known UFO books and journals, from Antonio Villas-Boas's to Debbie Tomey's. With his expertise as a folklorist, Bullard expected he would pretty quickly be able to establish whether abduction stories had a coherence implying a common origin, or whether, taken together, they were incoherent and idiosyncratic, their contents and sequences changing from abductee to abductee according to his or her urges and imagination and esoteric knowledge.

After four years and an analysis of 270 abduction accounts, Bullard did find a certain amount of garish variation. There was a case from Peru in which the aliens had been one-legged and mummy-like, with oblong patches of jelly for eyes. There was a case from Texas in which the aliens had worn medieval-type armour. There was a case from Argentina in which a woman and a man and their car had been taken into a sulphur-smelling UFO and examined genitally by aliens with rat-like faces and duck-like feet. There was a case from Illinois in which a man had seen a whirlwind and then had been attacked by eighteen-inch-tall screeching frog-like beings. There was a case from Georgia in which a sixty-three-year-old man, out for a walk with his dog one morning, had been paralysed and then undressed by aliens in a cow pasture, while inside the aliens' spaceship another human captive had been screaming: 'I am Jimmy Hoffa!'

Nevertheless . . . on the whole the accounts had a consistency – in their general themes, and especially in their sequences – which suggested that they were not entirely idiosyncratic. The aliens tended to be four or five feet tall, with large and ugly putty-coloured heads and big black eyes, and after establishing a kind of mental control over the abductee they typically would take off her clothes and would lie her down on a table and perform medical experiments, with special attention to her reproductive organs, and with perhaps a forebrain or ovarian implant for good measure, and then they would dress her again and would warn her not to remember any of this, except for whatever message they wanted her to bring the world, and then they would bring her back down to her bed or her car or the woods, leaving her in a state of dishevelment and shock.

Bullard set up an entire motif-index for abduction stories, and found that even apparently minor and superfluous motifs appeared again and again; for instance, dozens of abductees had reported that the aliens didn't like to be looked at directly. They would often force the abductee, telepathically, to avert her gaze, or even to close her eyes. Bullard also noted what had frustrated Jacobs – the abductees' frequent inability to remember how they had entered the alien craft – and termed it 'doorway amnesia'. Bullard found further similarities in the symbols seen, the instruments used, the aliens' clothing, the way they walked, the way their lidless eyes glistened, their odour, their emotionless and clinical manner, the hazy brightness of their spaceship interiors, and so on.

In a further analysis, Bullard separated the accounts by richness of content and by reliability – the latter determined by the general reputation of the case investigator and the source publication, and by the credibility of the abductee as judged by the case investigator. Bullard found that the high-content, high-reliability cases were more consistent than the high-content, low-reliability cases, suggesting that the more one weeded out hoaxes and delusions, the closer one got to the typical, archetypal story of the speculum-wielding greys.

Through his work, Bullard developed a new respect for investigators like Budd Hopkins and David Jacobs, who believed in the essential literal truth of the accounts. Bullard himself, despite living with this material for four years, wasn't yet ready to concede that aliens really were coming to earth and abducting people. Frankly, he didn't know what the hell was going on. But he was willing to argue that *something* was going on, something very strange.

5

Whitley

It is a clear crisp evening in the early autumn of 1985. The horror
novelist Whitley Strieber, his wife Anne and their son Andrew, and
their friends Alex and Sarah, are in the Strieber jeep, driving
upstate from Manhattan. They are going to spend a carefree few
days at the Striebers' vacation home in the woods . . .

Dusk falls. There are evergreens and hills. Some time after dark,
the jeep turns into the driveway by a large wooden house. The
motion-detectors around the house trip and the house alarm sounds
and spotlights go on everywhere. Strieber's wife clicks the keys on
the alarm console and the alarm stops. Young Andrew rushes into
the house, into his room, and . . . Something is in there. The kid
looks around, frightened. A little metal mobile is hanging from the
ceiling, like one of those Calder sculptures, and it is moving as if a
breeze is blowing. On a table there is also a flying monster mobile
that the kid has made from one of those model shop kits, and it is
moving, too. The kid screams. Whitley rushes in. The kid tells him
that . . . there is a spider in the room, as in fact there is, on one of
the tables. They throw the spider around and everyone laughs
about it. Whitley jokes, 'You know, I'm glad this is not my room.'

'It might not have been a spider I saw,' says Andrew, sounding
worried. But no one hears him. They have all gone to bed.

Later, when everyone is asleep, and a full moon stares down at
the Strieber cabin, the Calder mobile in Andrew's room starts to
swing again. The motion-detectors start to burble and blink a bit, as
if they sense something. Whitley and everyone else in the house
remain fast asleep. After a while, the motion-detectors increase their
activity, until they seem to go haywire, blinking and beeping like the
console of a spaceship. The spotlights go on outside. Whitley gets
up and goes out of the bedroom to look down at the living-room. A

fire is burning hazily in the grate but nothing seems amiss. The spotlights go off. Whitley goes back into the room and sits in a chair, looking at the door. 'Is that someone there?' he wonders aloud. The door opens a few inches and Whitley has a glimpse of a big and glistening and slanted black eye, belonging to a distinctly non-human face. The door closes and Whitley puts his head in his hands. He thinks he is hallucinating. He must be hallucinating. Then there is something like a burst of lightning from above, and the house is bathed in light – *Close Encounters* blue-white – with striated shadows flickering through it. Whitley takes it all in calmly, as if it's just the usual nightmare. His wife is still fast asleep. Downstairs, Andrew is asleep, but the kid's bedroom window seems to be opening of its own accord. The light is everywhere. It's as if a blue-white sun is shining outside. Alex, who is a big Romanian, jumps awake in bed downstairs. *What the – ?* That light . . . as bright as day . . . Sarah's awake now, too. So is Andrew. He's squinting at the light, and at his window which is opening by itself. Things are happening fast now. In Whitley's bedroom, one of the little black-eyed fellows has come up to his chair. He's dwarflike, and wears some kind of robe, and is holding a short, luminous wand up to Whitley's forehead. There is a deep electronic humming sound. *Unnnnnnnmmmmmmmmnnnnnn* . . . The wand locks on to Whitley's forehead; he's no longer in control of himself. They're picking his brains, like a laser reading a compact disc. Downstairs in the kid's bedroom, two alien hands with long ET-like fingers and Nosferatu nails throw open the curtains. The kid screams. Whitley knocks away the laser wand that was hooked to his forehead. The kid's legs, clad in Spiderman-suit red pyjamas, are squirming as he and the bed are slowly defenestrated. Upstairs, Whitley is wondering what the hell is going on. The compact disc goblins have gone away, now. He hears Andrew's screams, and goes downstairs to his room. Andrew cries at him: 'There was something here. It was very bad.'

Whitley grabs the kid, turns him upside down, and says, 'Whoa, shake it out, boss. It was only a nightmare.'

'They had me, dad,' protests Andrew.

'Nightmares do that, you know, sometimes,' explains Whitley.

Anne Strieber sleeps like a log, doesn't hear anything. But in the morning, Andrew protests again that what he saw and felt wasn't a dream. Whitley tries to laugh it off. He figures he had a bad dream, too. His wife isn't surprised; he'd had a big dinner the night before, and he always has nightmares after eating a lot.

But the business of the light has got under Alex's skin. Sarah remarks on it, too: 'There were a lot of lights. It was very hard to sleep.' 'I can't belief you didn't see it,' says Alex, in his accented English. 'It vas like day.'

Whitley admits that he had wondered in the night whether there might be a fire outside, but then says he thinks it must have been the floodlights, or the full moon. Alex and Sarah protest that it wasn't the moon, it wasn't the floodlights, it wasn't a dream. Whitley changes the subject but Alex continues to brood about it, in his dark middle-European manner, and after a few hours he says abruptly, 'OK, I vant to go home.' Whitley and Anne try to talk him out of it, but Alex only gets worse. 'TAKE US HOME, VITLEY!' he booms. And they all drive back to Manhattan.

Whitley Strieber was the son of a well-to-do Texas attorney. He had been born at the end of the Second World War, and had grown up in the suburbs of San Antonio, in a nice Catholic family with brothers and sisters and Mass on Sundays. He had a distinctively soft, full-lipped face (which would later grow into a remarkable resemblance of the Spanish prime minister Felipe Gonzalez), and a certain emotional fragility about which his mother later would tell an interviewer: 'I never saw a kid cry like Whitley. He'd cry at everything in sight.' But he had friends in the neighbourhood, and his pursuits were fairly ordinary for a boy in the 1950s, such as painting and drawing, and playing in the woods and fields of suburban San Antonio, and making fireworks and fertilizer bombs, and launching balloons full of natural gas with long fuses attached so that at a certain altitude, the balloons would explode like little Hindenburgs, and pieces of burning plastic would rain down gloriously. Space and the Space-Race particularly fascinated him, and he and his friends became fairly adept at building and launching model rockets. But Whitley was also interested in the other side of extraterrestrial exploration – the question of other worlds and other entities. He and his friends used to talk often about such things as little green men; in fact, as a joke once, Whitley had a friend down the street paint him green.

Strieber went to the University of Texas and then to film school in London, and in the late sixties moved to New York to work in advertising. Despite having been raised as a fairly strict Catholic, he dabbled a bit in alternative religions – Gurdjieff, Eckhart mysticism, witchcraft, and so on, increasingly so as he neared middle age. He had always wanted to be a writer, and he wrote a number of novels, but none of them seemed marketable until 1976 or 1977, when, apparently inspired by the sight of a pack of dogs in Central Park, he wrote a story about a pack of ultra-intelligent wolves that roamed Manhattan and ripped people's throats out.

The Wolfen was published in 1978 by William Morrow, and it sold well enough to be made into a TV movie a few years later. *The Hunger* followed in 1981; it was about a boyfriend–girlfriend team of vampires who went around at night chloroforming and strangling people and then, when the victims were on the point of death, lancing their carotid arteries with scalpels and sucking them dry. The vampires, like most vampires, had a certain kind of blood, a mutant strain of cells which fed upon, and therefore caused their host to crave, human blood. They had to have human blood or the vampire blood would start to consume them from within.

In 1982 came *Black Magic*, about an old Iranian magician, Hassan, and his blue-eyed psychic boy wonder whom the KGB captured after the downfall of the Shah. The boy had a terrific talent for mind control and psychokinesis and other such things, and by broadcasting the kid's psychical energy with special low-frequency electromagnetic antennae, secreted at strategic locations around the US, the KGB hoped to destroy the US nuclear arsenal and then turn the country of baseball and apple pie and spacious skies into a colossal mind-controlled slave labour camp. At the beginning of the book, as the Shah is falling and the CIA are pulling up stakes, a harassed Tehran station officer goes out to meet Hassan and the boy wonder, and the kid gives him a little demonstration, and suddenly the poor CIA man is hallucinating like mad:

Now there came a thought. It was not like other thoughts; it had form and substance. It was pictures and smells and a sharp, maddening shriek of a sound. The pictures were long, blurring tendrils. Snakes. The thought was snakes, hundreds of them, swarming in the cavities of his brain.

As the man from the CIA reeled in psychic agony, wrote Strieber, the psychic boy wonder was 'going through his subconscious like a rat in sewage'. Later in the book, the Soviets captured an American woman and probed her brain with an electrified gold needle. In retrospect, such passages made it clear that Strieber had been having his own otherworldly encounters for many years.

In 1983, Simon & Schuster published Strieber's *The Night Church*, about a diabolist sect within the Catholic Church, bent on world domination. The members of the Night Church would go around snatching children and then brainwashing them with hypnosis, making them new members of the Night Church, and sometimes sacrificial victims. They were very good at hypnosis and could brainwash just about anyone:

Jerry had the weird feeling that this was all some kind of a dream, but it felt like real life. Only it couldn't be.

The Night Church controlled what was supposed to be a philanthropic medical research institute, but was really using the institute to develop a mutant strain of bubonic plague. Members of the Night Church would be vaccinated, and then the plague bacteria would be released and the human race would be destroyed and the Night Church would reign over the ravaged earth. In one scene, a character who is trying to expose the truth about the Night Church tells a reporter friend to suspend his disbelief. But the hard-bitten reporter won't believe him, and they argue:

'You're setting yourself up for a put-down. You been takin' rides on a UFO or somethin'?'
'I wish I had. I'd be better off gettin' fucked over by little green men than by the Night Church.'

Strieber's next novel was *Wolf of Shadows*, a children's story about a wolf, written for an environmental organization known as the Sierra Club. He soon returned to the horror track, however, with *Cat Magic*, a novel about witches and black cats and fairies and fairy-abductions and shape-shifters and mind control and medical experiments and the secret of youth and lost Lemurian-type civilizations in the mountains and caves of western New Jersey and Pennsylvania. The fairies, 'small, solid beings who are very real', were 'a Paleolithic survival', having been exterminated in western Europe during the Middle Ages for their pagan beliefs, but having lived on in some parts of America.

These [fairy] men had sharp faces with pointed noses and large eyes. Perhaps they looked so different precisely because they were almost human.

In one scene, a woman named Mandy is abducted by fairies, feeling terror at first but then becoming calmer.

Never had she felt so thoroughly explored, so – somehow – examined. She had the eerie feeling that whatever had held her had also been in her mind. And was still there, looking and discovering, moving like a strange voice in her thoughts.

The fairy people, whose queen was known as the *Leannan*, had a civilization based on harmony with nature and generosity and absence of avarice, and powerful magic. Their allies the witches attempted 'to create a world where even fairy could be understood, which meant one where men no longer thought of the earth as something separate from themselves but viewed humanity as one organ in the living body of the planet . . .'

Strieber pushed the living-earth theme even harder with *Nature's End*, which was about an air-polluted, overpopulated twenty-first-century dystopia, and with *Warday and the Journey Onward*, which recounted a post-nuclear-war twenty-first-century dystopia. Both were co-written with fellow Texan James Kunetka. *Nature's End*'s dedication page read, 'This book is dedicated to the human future', while *Warday*'s dedication was more specific, but no less grand: 'This book is respectfully dedicated to October 27, 1988, the last full day of the old world.'

The this-is-a-true-story dedication by now had become a Strieber staple, but with *Warday*, the line between fiction and non-fiction had been blurred just a little bit more. The narrators were not ex-CIA men or missile-silo officers or presidential aides, or fictional characters that a writer could just make up. The narrators were Strieber and Kunetka! The biographical details they gave – the names of their wives, their kids, where they had gone to school, what they had done in their careers – were true, up to mid 1985 or so, and thereafter were pure invention, although ... there was nothing in the text itself to indicate where the shift had occurred.

Strieber apparently was working on another novel when the incident occurred at the house in upstate New York. According to Strieber's account in his book *Communion*, and in the later film version,* he did not devote much conscious thought to the incident at the time. However, it apparently churned up quite a storm in his subconscious. He began to feel a vague anxiety, a fear of New York, which among other things caused him to tell his wife that he wanted to move back to Texas. They put both the Manhattan apartment and the house upstate on the market, and closed on a house in Austin, the state capital, and found a private school nearby for Andrew, but then Whitley developed a phobia concerning the sky over their house-to-be in Austin, and he didn't want to move down to Texas after all, and Anne threatened to divorce him if he didn't pull himself together, so he pulled himself together, and they stayed in New York. Then winter came, and Christmas, and they went to the house in the woods again, and this time the blue-light business began to make sense.

On 26 December, at about eight-thirty in the evening, Strieber turned on the burglar alarm and then, as apparently had become his habit since the strange incident in October, went around checking closets and looking under beds for hidden intruders. By eleven he was asleep. In the middle of the night he awoke to a whooshing,

---

* The passage at the beginning of this chapter is from the film, the screenplay for which was penned by Strieber. In the book, 'Alex' is the Romanian émigré writer Jacques Sandulescu, and 'Sarah' is the writer Annie Gottlieb.

whirling noise, coming from the living-room downstairs. Strieber looked over at the burglar alarm panel on the wall, and noted that it had not been tripped. He started to settle back into sleep, but then he noticed that the bedroom door was moving. Around the edge of the door came a small creature, humanoid, about three and a half feet tall with large black eyes and a smooth rounded hat with a four-inch brim. The thing wore a kind of breastplate etched with concentric circles. The thing came into the room, and ... rushed headlong at Strieber ... and the next thing Strieber knew, he was in motion, naked, floating spread-eagled out of the room. Then suddenly he was next to a small depression in the woods, where somehow the earth was bare despite the eight inches of snow that lay everywhere else. He was sitting across from a small person in a grey-tan body suit. To his right stood a goblinesque figure in blue overalls, a female it seemed, who was doing something to the side of Strieber's head and at the same time was trying to explain something to him. Then Strieber was launched through the trees and into the sky; he saw the branches fly past and then the forest from above, and finally he found himself on a bench within a circular, domed chamber with a greyish-tan ceiling and a ribbed, vaulted construction like a capitol rotunda. The chamber was messy, with old clothes lying around, and the air was dry and stuffy. Four kinds of entities attended to him, ranging from a robot-type to hooded blue goblins (reminiscent, perhaps, of the Beatles' nemeses, the blue meanies) to five-foot tall greys with slit mouths and mesmerizing black eyes. Strieber felt a depersonalizing emotional rush that made him feel as if he were regressing to the level of an animal. One of the entities appeared with a box from which it removed a thin needle. Strieber, somehow becoming aware of what the entity intended to do with the needle, pleaded with it not to go through with the operation, assuring it that 'You'll ruin a beautiful mind.' One of the creatures, the woman again, asked Strieber in a midwestern-sounding accent what they could do to make him stop screaming, and Strieber said, 'You could let me smell you.' Another creature, a male one, said 'Oh, OK, I can do that,' and put his hand against Strieber's face. The hand smelled like cardboard, and also a little like cinnamon. Then the creature with the needle put the needle into Strieber's head, and there was a bang and a flash, and Strieber felt like weeping and sank back into a nest of little arms. Next they put a foot-long grey and scaly and narrowly triangular proctoscope-type thing with wire mesh on the end into Strieber's rectum and colon, from which they seemed to extract samples of tissue or whatever. Then one of the creatures took Strieber's right forefinger and made an incision; Strieber blacked out and awoke the next morning in bed with a sore rectum, and with the memory of having seen a barn owl at the window. After two days of anxiety, he sat down and wrote a short story, 'Pain', about a man who encounters an enigmatic blonde dominatrix named Janet. He is not sure whether she is an angel or a demon, but she is something supernatural. She imprisons him in a magical cabinet and tortures him sexually until he undergoes a shamanic apotheosis, a soul-deep transformation, and emerges with a new insight into the world, a new spiritual strength.

Despite this attempt at catharsis, Strieber's anxiety continued. He would act strangely, would argue with his wife, would lose his temper with his son. He wondered whether a small wave of UFO sightings that had been reported in the area had anything to do with his problems. His brother had given him a book for Christmas, *Science and the UFOs*, by Jenny Randles, a British ufologist, and Peter Warrington, a British astronomer. At the end of the book there was a description of an archetypal UFO abduction, and a brief mention of some of the work that the researcher Budd Hopkins had been doing. Strieber looked Hopkins up in the phone book, and called him.

Hopkins took the call, and listened to Strieber's story, and then invited him over. He was impressed that Strieber was a moderately well-known novelist, although he was a bit unnerved that Strieber had been known for horror novels. Anyway, Strieber came over to Hopkins's house on 16th Street, and told Hopkins some more of the story, and began to weep and to wonder aloud what was happening to him, and Hopkins listened and then started asking a few questions – could Strieber remember any similar experiences: any strange lights, any unusual phobias, any scars? Well . . . yes. Strieber could remember the strange blue light back on that night in October, and he could remember having this thing about checking closets at night for hidden intruders, and at his apartment in Manhattan and at the cabin in the woods upstate he had burglar alarms and motion-detectors and an Uzi submachine gun —

Hold on, said Hopkins. Is your cabin in a high-crime area or something? Well . . . no, said Strieber, but when he had been living back in Texas, he had been threatened by a right-wing group because of his political views, and this right-wing group had threatened to kill him, and to kidnap his son, and although he had fled Texas as a result, he also had thought it prudent to take certain measures to keep himself and his family safe.

Well, all right, said Hopkins, who now wanted to know about the October events, which he felt were connected to the December events. Hopkins suggested that Strieber might want to ask his wife and his son and Jacques and Annie what they remembered from the October incident.

Hopkins also expressed concern about Strieber's emotional health. Strieber claimed that he was feeling suicidal, and that on the previous day he had nearly jumped from his high-rise apartment. Hopkins suggested that Strieber might do better to see a psychiatrist than a ufologist. Strieber agreed, and in fact began to see two psychiatrists — Hopkins's old friend Bob Naiman, and Don Klein, the director of the New York State Psychiatric Institute. Both would use regression hypnosis on Strieber, but the idea seemed to be that Naiman would concentrate on therapy, and Klein — whom Hopkins had been cultivating for some time as a possible convert to abduction research — would concentrate on unveiling Strieber's experiences. Of course, both psychiatrists saw themselves as therapists rather than abduction researchers, and after a few weeks of double-team therapy from Naiman and Klein, Strieber dropped Naiman* and focused on Klein, going in for regression sessions accompanied by Hopkins.

At the first session with Klein, Strieber sat in a comfortable chair in Klein's office and Klein went through the trance induction routine, holding up a finger for Strieber to stare at, and then working Strieber gradually forward from the 1st of October to the

---

* In *Communion*, Strieber would omit any mention of his own regression sessions with Naiman.

4th, the night on which the incident had occurred. He asked Strieber what had happened after he had gone to sleep on the night of the 4th. Strieber said something about an object going past the big octagonal window at the top of the living-room; he could see the window from his bed. Something flew past the window. A big thing. He began to cry. It was a big light. And then there was something in the corner of the bedroom, something about three feet tall, wearing a hood or cloak or some sort of covering. Strieber opened his eyes, and Klein told him to close his eyes and to relax. Strieber saw the goblin in the cloak sweep mercilessly across the room at him, and the goblin stuck the wand in Strieber's forehead and Strieber started to scream like hell, sitting there in Klein's chair, and he opened his eyes again and now there was no doubt at all that he had screamed himself out of hypnosis. He recovered himself and then described in greater detail the creature that had come at him with the wand, and he was confused about whether or not he had screamed at the goblin, and Klein put him back into hypnosis and the goblin held the wand to his head and Strieber wept again and reported seeing pictures of the world blowing up, red fire in the middle and white smoke outside, and the goblin said, 'That's your home. That's your home. You know why this will happen.' Then Strieber saw his son in a green park and the goblin said he wouldn't hurt Strieber but then he took a needle and held it in front of Strieber's face and ignited its tip and there was a bang and a flash and Strieber started to think the house was burning down and he emerged spontaneously from hypnosis for the second time. After he collected himself, he explicated the imagery a little more for Klein and Hopkins: the park where he had seen his son represented death, and the goblin wand was perhaps stimulating and reading his mental images – images which he admitted were still recent from his work on *Warday* – rather than creating and implanting new images. Strieber wondered whether the goblin had done some kind of psychological test, hypnotizing him, using the CD-laser wand the way Klein used his mesmeric finger. Anyway, he wanted to go back under, to see how it all would end, and Klein put him under again and Strieber saw his kid sitting limply in a park, with dead eyes, and then he saw his father die, choking in an armchair while his mother watched, which was not the scene his mother had described to him, not at all – and Strieber spontaneously emerged from hypnosis for the third time.

Strieber later underwent hypnosis with Klein about the events of 26 December, and this time was hauled naked out of his bedroom by the blue meanies, and into the clearing in the woods and then into the messy chamber with the vaulted ceiling, where the air smelled dry and stuffy and now also like Cheddar cheese and sulphur, while the entities again smelled like cardboard and cinnamon and they zapped his head with the needle. Then a grunting yellow-brown female raped him with the scaly proctoscope, and told him, 'You are our chosen one.' Ever the sceptic, Strieber scoffed at this, and when she encouraged him to develop an erection, he begged her to be a dream. Then he tumbled backwards and found himself naked on the living-room couch in the house in the woods, and went upstairs and brushed his teeth and put on his blue pyjamas and went to bed.

That adventure was fairly tame, however, compared to some of the others that emerged in the hypnosis sessions. There was the time, for example, when Strieber had been in a spaceship and a group of soldiers in fatigues had lain comatose on tables, and his sister had been there, too, lying sprawled on a table in her nightie, while Strieber's father stood beside her wearing his own blue pyjamas, his arms dangling at his sides, a look of frozen surprise on his face. There was the time a group of 'tar babies' had come in and surrounded his own bed. There was the time when he had seen triangles and pyramids and leaping animals, and when the aliens had spoken certain words to him, and each word had evoked associated memories and thoughts and emotions, in such an exhausting manner that he had soon begged them to stop. There was the time he had driven into a sudden fog bank on an autumn afternoon and had been abducted by a group of entities including a bug-like woman who had evoked abstract expressions in his mind ... triangles ... circles ... squares ... and they had fitted together smoothly and had made him feel better.

Outside of the hypnosis sessions, back at the apartment in Manhattan or at the house in the woods upstate, Strieber continued to be plagued by strange occurrences. He awoke one night with paralysis and the sensation that some kind of probe was in his nose, crunching through his nasal cavity into his brain; he later developed a nosebleed. His wife and his son suffered from nosebleeds, too. Smells of cardboard and cheese and cinnamon began to erupt in his apartment. He awoke one morning with triangles etched on his forearm. He experienced episodes of missing time. Old memories spontaneously flooded back, memories of bright lights and grey monkeys and black cars and the Texas Tower massacre and exploded intestines* and exploding seltzer bottles and intermittent missing time, and a sinister Mr Peanut figure on a parade float and a skeleton on a motorcycle and a dash across rooftops in the King's Road, Chelsea while in film school and threats of bewitching if he left London, and getting strange telephone calls in New York and holding a conversation with a voice in his stereo speaker and fearing New York and moving to Connecticut, and then fearing Connecticut and moving back to New York.

With Budd Hopkins's help, Strieber quickly plugged into the ufological network, and after every new visitation or strange occurrence he would telephone someone such as David Jacobs, or the Center for UFO Studies (CUFOS) vice-president and journal editor Jerome Clark, or MUFON director Walt Andrus, or *MUFON UFO Journal* editor Dennis Stacy, to tell them what had happened and to plead with them to tell him what was going on.

Strieber simultaneously sought a medical diagnosis. Under the supervision of Klein and other psychiatrists, he took half a dozen psychological and IQ tests, and submitted to neurological examinations from CAT scans to MRIs to temporal lobe EEGs. There were a few unidentified bright objects (UBOs, in the medical lingo) on his MRI scans, but there was no evidence that they were related to his condition. Don Klein also didn't have any strong evidence that Strieber was psychotic, or that he had a mood disorder or personality disorder, and Klein said so in writing in response to Strieber's request. Nevertheless, once Strieber was reasonably able

---

* The Texas Tower incident was one in which a crazed gunman killed several people from a tower on the campus of the University of Texas at Austin. Strieber claimed to have memories of being present at the incident, and even remembered the smell of one victim's bullet-torn intestines.

to cope with his experiences, and no longer needed to come in for hypnotherapy, Klein seemed to decide that abduction research was not for him, and began referring abductees to other psychiatrists.

Don Klein, despite his scepticism about the abduction phenomenon, seemed to get along reasonably well with Strieber. The situation was reversed where Budd Hopkins was concerned. Hopkins believed that Strieber's experiences were essentially real, but between himself and the celebrity writer-abductee there developed an antagonism that would reverberate through ufology for the next several years.

A few weeks after their first meeting, according to Hopkins, Strieber informed him that the business about the right-wing southerners, the ones who had threatened his life and had threatened to kidnap his son and had chased him out of Texas – well, it wasn't actually true. He had more or less made it up, out of embarrassment over having to admit that he had motion-detectors and an Uzi at his cabin in the woods.

Hopkins didn't mind the fib so much; after all, intruder-phobia was fairly common among abductees, and if an abductee couldn't understand why he had this phobia, and was put on the spot about it, he might just make up a reason, to save face. But what bothered Hopkins was that Strieber had come up with the story so quickly, so glibly. If he had made that up, he could have made up anything. Or almost anything – for certain details of Strieber's experiences seemed to match details of other abduction experiences, experiences which, apparently, only Hopkins and some of his abductees knew about.

According to Hopkins, Strieber's emotional volatility also was hard to bear. One night, Hopkins threw a dinner party for Strieber and his wife, and invited some other abduction researchers and abductees, and their spouses. Earlier, Hopkins had told the researchers and the abductees that Strieber was a well-known writer whose prominence might help to encourage orthodox scientists to sit up and take notice of the abduction phenomenon. So they all came to the dinner party, and dinner was served and they were all sitting around the table and Strieber was holding forth on some subject or other, and suddenly Strieber said, 'I hope there are no reporters in this room.'

And the guests started to look around at one another, and Strieber explained that what he had been going on about, whatever it was, would be embarrassing if it were printed in the newspapers. And Hopkins and his guests protested mildly that Strieber needn't worry about reporters because they were all in this together, and anyway no one there was a reporter, but Strieber was still worried that there might be reporters around, incognito, and his tone was calm but just a bit eerie, and suddenly the storm burst forth and Strieber leapt out of his chair and pointed a finger down at the diner next to him –

'YOU ARE A REPORTER!'

And the poor guy, who was the husband of some poor abductee and worked the early-morning shift at some chemical factory in New Jersey, or somewhere equally unassuming and unjournalistic, cowered down in his chair beneath the horror-novel wrath of Whitley Strieber. *I – I'm not a reporter, I swear. I swear, man . . .*

But after a few more incidents like this, Strieber had made everyone around him a reporter, and Hopkins's circle began to hum and buzz with the tales of Whitley's alleged eccentricities. In one episode, according to Hopkins, he and Strieber went over to Strieber's apartment and as they entered the apartment house elevator on the ground floor, a man got in with them who looked at Strieber as if he wanted to kill him. Strieber put on a sheepish look and stared at the ceiling, and when the guy got out and the elevator continued its ascent, Hopkins asked Strieber what that had all been about. 'Oh, he doesn't like me,' Hopkins recalls Strieber responding. 'I play tricks on him.' And, according to Hopkins, Strieber proceeded to explain to Hopkins that when the tricksterish spirit moved him he would get up early in the morning and would head downstairs in the elevator to the lobby where all the tenants' morning newspapers had been left by the newspaper deliveryman, and would find this particular tenant's copy of the *New York Times*, take out a knife or a pair of scissors and cut out a face from a picture on the front page, or a word from a headline, or make some such irritating mutilation of his neighbour's newspaper.

The most famous story about Strieber was one originally told by the abductee Debbie Tomey; it concerned a time when Tomey had

come to Manhattan for a few days in early 1986. She had arrived
by bus from Indianapolis, for a few hypnosis sessions, and Hopkins
had put her up at his place. Strieber had phoned to say he wanted
to take her to lunch. She didn't have any money, but that was all
right, since it seemed that Strieber was buying. So Hopkins, who
had been paying for virtually all of her expenses, gave her the cab
fare and told the driver to take her to Strieber's address, and she
went to meet Strieber. According to the story told by Tomey and
Hopkins, Strieber saw Tomey and said, 'I've seen you before.'
Tomey asked where he had seen her, and Strieber said he couldn't
tell her, because it might be . . . disturbing for her if he did tell her.
Then Strieber took her to a nice restaurant, and when the waiter
came to take their order, he stipulated that separate bills be
brought. Tomey ordered a cup of soup, which was all she could
afford, and said she wasn't hungry. Strieber, digging his way
through a big meal, decided to let the cat out of the bag: he had
seen Debbie in a spaceship, during one of his abductions. Her head
had been on a shelf – just her head, although it had been alive, with
the eyeballs and the facial muscles still twitching.

Whitley, are you sure it wasn't just a dream? she protested. But
Strieber was dead sure he had seen her. It had to have been her,
couldn't have been anyone else. That face, those eyes, animated
and alive . . . It had all been real. Later, Tomey told Hopkins, 'I
never want to see that crazy son of a bitch again.'*

Even then, Hopkins might have been willing to walk the extra mile
with Strieber. He put up with all kinds of phobias and anxieties
and neuroses and strangeness on the part of abductees. Strieber
seemed worse than most, but one had to realize that Strieber's
problems arose from his experiences, and that once those experiences had been integrated and understood, he should become
emotionally stable again, or at least less unstable.

There was an insurmountable problem, however. Hopkins got
an inkling of it during Strieber's initial visits, when according to
Hopkins, Strieber complained that his writing career was going

---

* Strieber ignored my requests for an interview, but it is probably safe to assume that
he denies the truth of some or all of these stories.

nowhere, his last book had not done as well as he had hoped, he seemed to have reached a dead end . . .

Strieber soon proposed that he write a book about his experiences. Then not long afterwards, according to Hopkins, Strieber said he had decided against the idea. He wasn't sure he wanted to put his life, with all its weirdness, on public display. He wasn't sure any of his experiences were objectively real.* But eventually he worked himself back to liking the idea, and decided to see it through, and within a month or two of his first visit to Hopkins, he had a draft of the book ready. Initially he had wanted to give the book the Strieberesque horror-novel title of *Body Terror*, but as winter had turned to spring he had begun to interpret his experiences in a more positive light. Perhaps he was a chosen one after all. Perhaps, whether he liked it or not, he was an emissary from human civilization to an advanced but ancient otherworld . . . Perhaps they wanted something more from him than animal terror. As a matter of fact, in one of his most recent abductions, he had made the aliens vanish by the simple expedient of smiling at them.

One night in April 1986, according to the account in his book, Strieber was lying awake in bed beside his wife, thinking about the book and how he had thought of calling it *Body Terror*, when suddenly his wife, still asleep apparently, began to speak in a deep, basso-profundo voice . . .

'THE BOOK MUST NOT FRIGHTEN PEOPLE. YOU MUST CALL IT *COMMUNION*, BECAUSE THAT'S WHAT IT'S ALL ABOUT.'

The voice didn't seem in a mood to negotiate. And so the book was entitled *Communion*.

Strieber circulated drafts of the typescript to people such as Hopkins and Dave Jacobs and Jerome Clark and Dennis Stacy, and they made comments and sent the drafts back. Just about everyone had comments to make, but Hopkins was especially critical of the book. As far as he was concerned, some of Strieber's experiences had originated from Strieber the horror-novel writer, rather than Strieber the abductee. Some of it was just *too* fantastic, *too*

---

* This angst was echoed with Shaveresque overtones in Strieber's book: 'Do my memories come from my own life, or from other lives lived long ago . . .?'

dramatic. In certain places it fit the abduction paradigm, but in others it soared off into . . . well, for instance, according to Hopkins, in one early draft there was a passage in which a female alien grabbed Strieber's penis and led him from her spacecraft as if he were a dog on a leash. Hopkins always seemed to have one eye on what the psychologists and psychoanalysts and sociologists would think of abduction accounts, and he cringed to imagine what they would think of Strieber's. He urged Strieber to rewrite the book – or better yet, to slow down on it, to put it on the back burner, since Strieber himself was still in such a fragile state, and his recollections seemed so mercurial, so mutable. He should wait until the therapeutic process had had a chance to work.

Strieber considered Hopkins's criticisms to be a clumsy attempt at censorship, and would later argue that Hopkins was deliberately trying to obscure the real variety and strangeness of abduction accounts, by forcing them all into a rigid nuts-and-bolts *War of the Worlds* ufological framework. Hopkins's pressure to go slow on the book strained their relationship until it approached breaking point.

By the late spring of 1986 Strieber was offering the typescript of his book to literary agents, and soon found one who liked it, and this agent showed the typescript to some publishers and hardly needed to explain that if true this book would be the most important book of the century, and by the end of June Strieber had accepted a contract for one million dollars, film rights excluded, with his old friends at William Morrow.

Hopkins, of course, was by now finishing his second book, *Intruders*, which focused on the Debbie Tomey case and the alarming epidemic of foetus-snatchings that seemed to be occurring. Random House hadn't given him a million for it, but the advance was somewhere in the low six figures, and they wanted to publish it in the summer of 1987 – around the time Strieber's book was coming out. The original idea was that both Hopkins's and Strieber's books would come out simultaneously, and would create such an enormous stir that people would never be able to laugh at the subject of UFO abductions again. Hopkins had even toyed with the idea of a joint Random House–Morrow advertisement for both books. It would make publishing history . . .

However, it seems that Strieber soon decided that he didn't like the idea of a simultaneous publication. He began to telephone Hopkins, asking him to delay the publication of *Intruders* so that . . . well, so that *Intruders* wouldn't interfere with, or be swamped by, the wave that *Communion* created. Strieber's book was possibly going to be the most important book of the century, possibly the most important book of all time, and Hopkins as a gentleman and a scientist who would not wish to impede the progress of human knowledge should step aside, should get out of the fast lane and let Strieber pass. As a sign of his good faith, Strieber sent Hopkins an original Strieber blurb for the cover of *Intruders*.

Hopkins figured this was just Strieber wallowing in his emotional trauma as usual, not really meaning it, and he remained on speaking terms with him, until one day Hopkins received a call from a perplexed editor at Random House. Strieber, it seemed, had written to Random House and had given them the same story about how Strieber's book could be the book of the century and how Hopkins's *Intruders* might simply founder in its wake, spilling the seed on the sand, and delaying the progress of human knowledge and so on and so forth, and perhaps the good people at Random House could see the sense in delaying Hopkins's book even if Hopkins himself couldn't.

As a result, Hopkins broke off communications with Strieber, and Random House moved forward the publication date for *Intruders* by a few months. Then Morrow moved forward the date for Strieber's book. In the end, Strieber won the race, and eventually notched up sales of several million copies worldwide. The full title of his book, published in late January 1987, was: *Communion: A True Story*.

6

Klass

Philip Klass had one thing in common with Whitley Strieber. His father had been a lawyer. In fact, one day, when Klass was a boy growing up in Cedar Rapids, Iowa, his father took him down to the courthouse to see what a trial was like. The case involved a car accident, and seemed to hinge on the question of how fast one of the cars had been going before the accident. Young Klass watched each witness swear on the Bible to tell the truth, then listened as the witnesses for the plaintiff said the car had been travelling at between 50 and 60 miles per hour, while the witnesses for the defendant insisted that the car had been travelling at only about 10 to 15 miles per hour. Klass never became a lawyer like his father, but the visit to the courtroom taught him a valuable lesson about the softness of eyewitness evidence.

It was not immediately clear, however, that young Klass would ever have a chance to make use of this lawyerly lesson. He was into electronics and engineering. He loved to tinker with shortwave radios and other gadgets. When a drugstore down the street was burgled, he rigged up an electric alarm and strung the wires along the roofs of the intervening street-front houses to his own bedroom, where he would be awakened should another burglary occur. None did, and finally the drugstore owner, annoyed at the mess of wires emerging from his shop, took the whole thing down – and was promptly robbed again.

Eventually Klass entered Iowa State University and took a degree in electrical engineering. He spent the forties in upstate New York, working in the avionics division of General Electric (avionics is a general term for aircraft electronic devices such as altimeters and air-speed indicators and radio-direction finders). Although as a boy in the early thirties he had won a prize ride in an autogyro – the spindly precursor of the helicopter – he hadn't been naturally drawn to aviation. GE put him there when it assigned him to a war-effort job writing the instruction manual for the remote-control gun turret system on the B-29 bomber.

In the early fifties, Klass quit GE to become the avionics editor at a new magazine, *Aviation Week* (later *Aviation Week & Space Technology*), which covered the civilian and defence aerospace industries. By this time, Klass had heard reports of flying discs and flying saucers, but he had never been impressed enough to look further. When strange lights appeared over Washington, DC, in July 1952, were seen by hundreds of witnesses, and were tracked by civilian and defence radar systems, Klass simply reported the findings of a Civil Aviation Authority commission, which attributed the visual and radar sightings to mirages caused by atmospheric temperature inversions.*

The years went by, and Klass covered the avionics beat in Washington, DC, and went to conferences and interviewed military brass and industry officials, and racked up several journalistic awards, and in 1966 there was another major UFO wave. It was in all of the papers – and so were the UFO buffs, who now, to Klass's dismay, were beginning to be taken seriously. One day in the spring of 1966, talking to a friend about a forthcoming military electronics conference to be held in Washington, Klass heard that the conference would feature an evening session on flying saucers, open to the public.

Now, the conference was being sponsored by the local chapter of IEEE, the big electrical engineering society, and Klass was a member of this chapter of IEEE, and hearing about this evening session on flying saucers, Klass had a dark vision . . . of some UFO buff standing up in the audience at question time, and talking about this UFO case and that UFO case, and the scientists and engineers on the rostrum, not being too impressed but also not wishing to be rude, responding blandly that it was all very interesting

* The news of the Washington UFO sightings briefly overshadowed the Democratic National Convention which was then taking place, and the temperature-inversion explanation was disputed by some air traffic controllers and meteorologists. A few days after the last sightings, the INS wire service reported that USAF pilots around the country had been instructed to 'shoot down' any UFOs that refused to land.

and, no, they couldn't explain it, and the next day, the headlines would read:

SCIENTISTS AT LOCAL CONFERENCE
UNABLE TO EXPLAIN UFO REPORTS

So Klass wrote to the board of the Washington IEEE chapter, and complained that the flying saucer-night gimmick would only bring discredit upon the organization. The board invited him to come and talk it over, and so Klass sat down with them, and was surprised to learn that quite a few of them thought there might be something to this whole UFO business after all. However, collectively the board agreed with some of Klass's points, and decided to focus the evening session of the conference on *identified* flying objects instead, such as weather balloons and satellites, and in view of Klass's interest in the subject, they invited him to speak. Klass said OK.

To begin his preparations, he decided, he would go out and buy a book on UFOs. At the time he was dating a correspondent for one of the Paris dailies, and one day, poring through the newspapers for story ideas, she came across a full-column review, in the *Wall Street Journal*, of a book by John Fuller called *Incident at Exeter*. Fuller, then an editor at the *Saturday Review*, had gone up to Exeter, New Hampshire, to investigate a rash of flying saucer sightings. Many of the sightings had occurred near power lines, and Fuller wondered whether the UFOs might somehow have been drawing power from such lines. Anyway, Klass's girlfriend told him about the book, and Klass went out and bought it, and had worked his way through a few chapters when . . . he became convinced that there really was something to this UFO phenomenon. It didn't seem possible that all of these witnesses in New Hampshire could be lying.

However, Klass was far from buying the ET hypothesis. In fact, the descriptions of balls of light hovering over power lines reminded him of ball lightning. A few years before, he had written a story about the phenomenon for *Aviation Week*. Atmospheric physicists believed it to be some kind of plasma, a plasma being a gas in which the outer electrons have been stripped from a significant percentage of the atoms, typically causing the gas to glow and buzz. A gas could be turned into a plasma by subjecting it to a high-strength electric field, such as existed around power lines. In fact, if you looked closely at some power lines at night, you would see them glowing. This type of plasma was known as a coronal discharge. A number of scientists believed that ball lightning formed in a similar manner – from local pockets of high electric field strength, which one might expect near lightning strikes. Some scientists also had had the idea of making ball lightning, or a related kind of atmospheric plasma, by focusing several radar beams* at a certain point in the air, plasmifying the air at that point into an electric fireball, and then moving the beams upwards rapidly to blast an enemy aircraft or an incoming nuclear warhead.

Anyway, by the time he had finished reading Fuller's book, Klass was convinced that the Exeter sightings had been of ball lightning, or of some other kind of atmospheric plasma. But shortly thereafter he learned that IEEE headquarters in New York had heard about the planned 'identified flying objects' session at the autumn conference in Washington, and had frowned on it. The new session topic would be 'Vietnam – The World's Electronic Proving Ground'.

Alas, Klass now had a theory and nowhere to publish it. He thought about it for a while, and then decided that he might write a review of Fuller's book for the *Washington Post*, inserting what he knew about plasmas and ball lightning. But before he could moonlight like that he needed permission from the managing editor at *Aviation Week*, Bob Hotz, so he went in and asked Bob Hotz, and Hotz said why not just write it up in *Aviation Week*? Well, Klass could now do research on the magazine's time, so he made some calls, spoke to people up in Exeter, and electric power experts at General Electric and Westinghouse, and learned that the air around power lines was more likely to become ionized (a) when the lines were near the ocean, because airborne sea-salt was then deposited on the insulators and intensified the electric field at

---

* Electromagnetic waves such as radar waves are so called because they consist of varying electric fields and varying magnetic fields. A high-strength radar beam therefore contains a high-strength electric field, and where several beams intersect, the field strength can be much more intense.

certain points, and (b) when the weather had been dry, and the salt deposits consequently hadn't been washed off. Klass quickly determined that Exeter, New Hampshire was ten miles from the ocean, and that the summer of the sightings had been one of the driest in years. QED.

Klass's analysis of the Exeter case was published in an August issue of *Aviation Week*, and for a few days thereafter was widely, and for the most part sympathetically, reported in the popular press. The ufology community, and John Fuller in particular, was less sympathetic, heavily criticizing Klass for seeming to dismiss the phenomenon as so much plasma-hot air. By November, though, Klass had put together a proposal for a book about plasma UFOs, and several New York publishers were interested. Bennett Cerf, the CEO at Random House, was particularly keen, and invited Klass up to New York for Thanksgiving dinner, with Frank Sinatra and some other friends, and Klass gave an after-dinner speech on UFOs and how there was nothing extraterrestrial about them, and in 1968 Random House published Klass's book: *UFOs – Identified*, and Klass became ufological enemy number one.

Of course, Klass didn't think that all UFOs were random atmospheric plasmas, or satellites, or shooting stars, or Venus. A good deal, he argued, were the product of hoax or fantasy. Deciding to dig into the 1964 Socorro case, for example, in which the landing of an egg-shaped craft in New Mexico had been reported by a highway patrolman named Lonnie Zamora, Klass went to Socorro and interviewed Zamora and several of his friends and associates and fellow-townspeople. Talking to Zamora and his associates, and comparing some of their later accounts, Klass found a number of apparent inconsistencies. Then some townspeople hinted to him that the flying saucer story had been rigged as a publicity stunt, meant to bring commerce to a dying town. Klass decided that the whole thing had been a hoax.

The Hill case, which broke in *Look* magazine when Klass was still trying to sell his book proposal, was for Klass a case of fantasy whipped up by greed, with perhaps a touch of plasma physics to keep things interesting. After reading the story in *Look*, he phoned Benjamin Simon, the psychiatrist who had hypnotized the Hills, and eventually interviewed him at length while Simon was at a psychiatry conference in Washington. According to Klass, Simon told him that in his opinion, Betty Hill had dreamed the abduction scenario, had passed the dream information to Barney, and then both Betty and Barney had re-lived the dream under hypnosis. Simon also told him that before the *Look* story broke, one of the magazine's editors had come up to Boston for an interview with him. The editor's first question: did Simon really think that the Hills had been abducted by aliens? 'Absolutely not!' Simon had responded, and at the end of the interview, the editor had confessed his own scepticism: 'Doctor, if you had replied to my first question by saying that you really believed that the Hills had been abducted, I would have put on my hat and taken the next flight back to New York.' Yet the editor and his colleagues had gone on to buy a big advertisement in the *New York Times*, promoting the *Look* story as a report of a genuine UFO abduction. The Hills' 40 per cent share of the magazine, book, and film rights had eventually amounted to more than a quarter of a million dollars. When the dust had settled, Simon had suggested to Klass that they collaborate on the 'true story' of the case – although Klass had doubted that further debunking was necessary; he figured that the Hills had seen a star or a power-line associated plasmoid, had been mesmerized by it into an amnesic trance, and then later had subconsciously filled in the mnemonic gap with a scenario originating from Betty's imaginative nightmares.

For his next book, *UFOs Explained*, Klass investigated the 1973 Pascagoula case, where Charles Hickson and Calvin Parker claimed to have encountered the lobster-clawed, cone-eared, elephant-skinned aliens. He quickly dismissed it as a hoax: Charley Hickson, for example, 'had been fired from his previous job for improperly obtaining money from persons who worked under his direction'. And although Hickson had passed a lie-detector test shortly after the alleged experience, the test had been administered by a young and inexperienced polygrapher. When Hickson was asked by ufo-logists to take a test administered by a more experienced polygrapher just before a UFO conference in 1975, he agreed, then appeared to develop cold feet at the last minute. Parker, according to Klass, had claimed to experience a disabling nervous breakdown just before his own scheduled test, although he had recovered enough to appear on a talk show a week later. According to Klass, Hickson's lawyer, acting as his agent, had set the opening bids on film rights at $1 million.

The Travis Walton case of 1975, argued Klass, was an even more clear-cut case of hoaxing: firstly, it had occurred just two weeks after the broadcast of *The UFO Incident*, the TV dramatization of the Hills' encounter, starring James Earl Jones and Estelle Parsons, which among other things had depicted Parsons in helpless agony as a giant laparoscope needle was jammed into her lower abdomen. Secondly, Walton and his family had long been UFO buffs, and Walton had assured his mother, shortly before the incident, that if he were ever abducted by aliens, she shouldn't worry for him, because he would soon return safe and sound, as he did – groggy but otherwise in good shape. Thirdly, Walton and his family had once lived in a cabin near the abduction site, and members of the family reportedly had played repeated pranks on their landlords, who lived miles away, phoning them and telling them such things as that their cattle had all been killed, just to get a rise out of them; the cabin-owner's daughter-in-law told Klass that she believed Walton had hoaxed the abduction. Fourthly, Walton and Charles Rogers (the brother of Walton's woodcutting crew-chief, Mike Rogers) had broken into a company office one night five years before, had stolen cheques, and then had forged them; both had served two years' probation for the incident. Fifthly, Walton's woodcutting team had been hopelessly behind on a major job for the US Forest Service, and had desperately needed an 'Act of God' to excuse their failure, without which excuse they would be in default of their contract, and Walton's crew-chief might be barred from future Forest Service contracts. Finally, although Walton had taken and passed a polygraph test paid for by the UFO group APRO and the *National Enquirer*, the administration of the test was later evaluated by an experienced polygrapher to have been deeply flawed; moreover, Walton had earlier taken a test, sponsored by the same organizations but administered by one of the best polygraphers in Arizona – who had concluded that Walton had engaged in 'gross deception', and that he had even resorted to such tricks as holding his breath to regulate his respiration rate. Both

APRO and the *National Enquirer* had covered up this earlier failure, and the *Enquirer* had eventually paid Walton and his woodcutting colleagues $5,000 for the rights to their story. Walton had later done a book deal, and by 1988 had done a movie deal.

Of course, none of Klass's arguments appeared to make a significant impact on the public's perception of the UFO phenomenon, and this was increasingly the case as time went by, thanks to a curious ideological stratification that seemed to have begun in the late 1960s. Before then, in the first three decades since the Arnold flying saucer sighting, ufology had received high-profile academic and government attention, and had been debated seriously at virtually all levels of American culture, from *Look* to *Aviation Week* to the halls of the Air Force and CIA. In fact, around the time that the Hill case had hit the news in 1966, the Air Force had commissioned a special report on the subject from a team led by Edward U. Condon, an eminent physicist at the University of Colorado. The body of Condon's massive report, compiled by three dozen different researchers and eventually delivered in late 1968, made clear that despite obvious hoaxes and misidentifications there were still quite a tantalizing number of cases which remained unexplained, many of these having been reported by highly trained witnesses such as aeroplane pilots and astronauts.

However, Condon's preambulatory conclusion to the report, which was all that most journalists were willing to stick around for, essentially dismissed UFOs as unworthy of further scientific investigation.* With that, and with the passing of the 1964–7 UFO waves, there seemed to be nothing to prevent the subject from nose-diving downmarket, into the realm of supermarket tabloids and Spielberg movies, where the wildest ufological claims were accepted and critical thinking was a sin. At higher levels of culture, the debate had arrived at a different dogma: UFOs were hoaxes, hallucinations, weather balloons, and Venus after a few drinks; they were for low-rent people who bought tabloids and mistook Spielberg movies for reality.

---

* 'Our general conclusion,' wrote Condon in the second paragraph of the report, 'is that nothing has come from the study of UFOs in the past twenty-one years that has added to scientific knowledge. Careful consideration of the record as it is available to us leads us to conclude that further extensive study of UFOs probably cannot be justified in the expectation that science will be advanced thereby.'

This stratification did little to reduce the overall level of UFO enthusiasm; in fact, ufology's fall from high-culture and scientific orthodoxy was cushioned by an almost explosive expansion in low-culture interest in the subject, as shown by Whitley Strieber's colossal financial success, and by films such as *ET*, which at the time of writing, a decade after its release, still stands as the greatest box-office draw of all time. However, this cultural change meant that books of Klass's genre – books which sought to explain UFO cases in prosaic terms, and which generally disparaged UFO researchers – had almost nowhere to go. The believers wouldn't want to read such books because they were believers and wanted to continue believing, and the non-believers wouldn't want to read such books because their views on the subject were orthodox, and therefore required no further reinforcement. Klass's third book, in 1983, somewhat plaintively entitled *UFOs – The Public Deceived*, was not released by a major publisher, and Klass privately announced that it would be his last major contribution to the UFO debate.

The Public Deceived was published by Prometheus Books, of Buffalo, New York. Prometheus was in effect the book-publishing organ of the Committee for the Scientific Investigation of Claims of the Paranormal, better known as CSICOP – the mortal enemy of unorthodoxy wherever it dared to raise its head.

CSICOP had been an outgrowth of the American Humanist Association, through its journal, the *Humanist*. Humanists were existentialists who looked on the bright side; they believed that God was dead but that Man had a great future all the same – he had only to run faster, to stretch his arms out farther, to throw off the chains of superstition and mysticism and religion and magic . . . In 1975, the *Humanist*'s editor, Paul Kurtz, a philosophy professor at the State University of New York in Buffalo, published a statement objecting to the claims of astrology (which had inspired a certain amount of low-culture enthusiasm during the sixties) and obtained co-signatures from 186 scientists, including a fair number of Nobel Prize winners. The media attention to the venture inspired Kurtz to form a distinct group whose purpose would be to zap the pretensions of astrologers and other proponents of the paranormal; and in due course Kurtz assembled a committee that included the psychologists B. F. Skinner and Ray Hyman, the astronomers George Abell, Carl Sagan, and Dennis Rawlins, the Houdini-style stage magician James Randi, and the science writers Martin Gardner, Isaac Asimov, Kendrick Frazier, and . . . Philip Klass.

The problems started right away, however. Co-chairman Marcello Truzzi, a sociologist at Eastern Michigan who was supposed to edit the CSICOP journal, took a softer line than Kurtz on the paranormal, and as a result was more or less forced to resign. Then CSICOP attacked the claims of Michel and Françoise Gauquelin, a husband-and-wife team of researchers who had been arguing that the astronomical position of the planet Mars at the time of an individual's birth correlated with that individual's chances of becoming an outstanding athlete. CSICOP challenged the Gauquelins to duplicate their results with a new sample. The Gauquelins complied, and their new results seemed to confirm the old ones. But Kurtz would have none of it; he and some other members of CSICOP culled the new sample, for various reasons which seemed plausible to them at the time, until the statistical power of the results was no longer significant. The upshot was uproar within CSICOP, more resignations, and the organization's withdrawal from any direct involvement in research; thenceforward, they would merely criticize, praise, or publish the work of others – perhaps knowing that otherwise they were likely to get their fingers burned.

So CSICOP, through Prometheus, published Klass's third book. After that there seemed to be a lull. Perhaps it had to do with the Reagan-era economic boom, or the alternative attractions of the fast-growing New Age movement, but in any case UFO enthusiasm, which had been widespread during the wave of 1973–4, and had experienced an additional spasm or two after *Close Encounters* in 1979 and *ET* in 1983, seemed to just peter out by the mid 1980s.

Then in early 1987 Whitley Strieber's book came out, and a month later Budd Hopkins's book came out, and UFO abductions became . . . very big . . . and Klass's phone began to ring constantly, with producers and assistant producers and researchers wanting to know whether he would be willing to appear on something such as Oprah or Donahue or *Sonja Live* or Geraldo or Joan Rivers or Sally Jessy Raphael or the *Today Show* or the Morton Downey

Jr show, opposite Hopkins or Strieber or some other proponent of the reality of abductions.

So Klass hit the talk show circuit, and did his best to debunk the claims of Strieber and Hopkins and the abductees. One of the first stops was Oprah. Oprah seemed very uncertain about the whole abduction business. She would roll her eyes a little, or her voice would sink down into that deadly Oprah deadpan, whenever she mentioned the words 'abducted by aliens'. In any case, she had two of Hopkins's abductees on the show, Connie and Dorothy. Connie began by telling the story about how, although single, she had had a great life as a marketing executive for a TV station in Kansas City, and how one night, about 3 a.m. on a Saturday morning actually, she had been closing the curtain in front of her living-room picture window and a big light had moved into view with a helicopter sound, and it had been a spaceship, about twenty-five feet in diameter, and it had teleported her through the picture window and then she had been up next to the ship, peering through a porthole from the outside, and the next thing she knew it was two hours later and she was sitting up in bed hugging her knees and terrified out of her wits. She hadn't remembered anything about being on board the craft, not even under hypnosis, although she did remember seeing through the porthole a three-and-a-half-foot-tall being, dark olive green, almost *black* – 'Awww right!' said Oprah, pouncing on the word black. 'We're in charge in outer space!'

And it became clear that Oprah was taking none of this too seriously. After a commercial break, Hopkins and Klass came on. Hopkins decried the climate of ridicule that had arisen around the abduction phenomenon, and as an example discussed the New York police officer he knew who had been abducted and, during the abduction, had had his uniform and gunbelt removed. How, in the present climate of scientific ridicule, could this New York police officer tell his superiors that he had been abducted by aliens and expect ever to get a promotion? Oprah turned to Klass and invited him to ridicule the entire subject. Klass declined to do so, but gently implied that the abductees were fantasy-prone people and that their fantasies were being stoked by people like Hopkins. Oprah perfunctorily protested that there must be aliens out there somewhere in the galaxy, and Klass said yes, OK, but not aliens who come down to earth and rape people, you wouldn't like it if aliens raped your daughter, Oprah, and there was a brief argument between Klass and Hopkins about whether the aliens ever raped people, and Hopkins said he didn't know of any such thing, but Klass cited the case of the thirteen-year-old girl from *Missing Time* who had had an immaculate conception via an alien in her bedroom, and why hadn't the FBI been contacted, and Hopkins pointed out that when the thirteen-year-old abductee had been hypnotically regressed it had emerged that the procedure had really occurred in a spaceship, on a table, and the girl had been inseminated artificially, by a needle, and that was why her hymen had not been ruptured, and it was very different from rape, and after a commercial break, during which Hopkins and Klass had a long wrangle about the FBI and whether they should be called in, it was time to go to the phones, and a young woman called in with a lengthy story about meeting an angelic being in a spaceship in the parking lot of the San Antonio airport, and as Hopkins's smile gradually froze into a grimace, and Oprah rolled her eyes and dropped her voice, Klass laughed his resonant, rolling, smoke-cured laugh.

Other talk show hosts were more receptive to the abduction phenomenon. Hopkins and another one of his abductees, a well-spoken Washington, DC lawyer named Mike Shea, went on the Charlie Rose show, and Shea, with his agnosticism about everything but the idea that he had seen a UFO and had experienced missing time, was utterly convincing. Strieber was similarly impressive on the *Tonight Show* with Johnny Carson. As the weeks went by, and Strieber's book soared to the top of the bestseller lists, and Hopkins and his abductees toured the talk show circuit, now specifying that they would not, repeat not, appear opposite Philip Klass the despicable sceptic from CSICOP, it became clear at CSICOP headquarters that a more substantial counter-attack against the abduction forces was in order. Paul Kurtz got on the phone to Klass and asked him to come out of retirement to write book number four, this time exclusively on abductions. Klass winced at the prospect of spending six months or whatever, researching a book that hardly anyone would buy, when what he really wanted

to write was a book about the Star Wars missile-defence programme, or the demise of tactical fighter aircraft; but duty called,
and in the end he said he would do it.

Most of the earlier abduction cases Klass had debunked hadn't
relied upon the use of hypnosis; even the Hills' abduction scenario
had first emerged in Betty's dreams, which she had then discussed
with Barney and others. The emphasis on hypnosis by Budd
Hopkins and David Jacobs and other abduction researchers caught
Klass's attention right away, and one of the first things he did was
to dig out a review article, 'The Use and Misuse of Hypnosis in
Court', which had been published in the *International Journal of
Clinical and Experimental Hypnosis* in 1979. The paper's author,
Martin Orne, a professor of psychiatry at the University of
Pennsylvania, and a recognized expert on hypnosis, had argued that
regression hypnosis was just not very reliable in recovering factual
information. Orne cited a number of previously published studies.
In one, subjects under apparently deep hypnosis were able wilfully
to lie. In another, subjects were regressed back to elementary
school days, and vividly recalled the classmates sitting next to them
– many of whom, according to a subsequent check of school
records, should not have been there. According to Orne, information obtained from hypnotized subjects engaging in 'free narrative
recall' (i.e. without prompting from the hypnotist) was generally
more factual, but there was also a lot less of it. In general, only
questions from the hypnotist could elicit a complete narrative
recollection; the problem was that such questions – even if they
were not leading questions – encouraged extensive confabulation.
Sometimes even free narrative recall produced what appeared to be
pure confabulation, as would happen, for example, when a subject
was regressed back into his crib, into the maternity ward, back up
into the warm bath of his mother's womb, and out the other side of
the space-time discontinuum to . . . a past life . . . where he would
turn out to have been Galileo, or a knight of the Round Table, or a
famous Lemurian artist . . . There was such a thing as hypnotic
progression, too, under which the subject would go forward in
time, to become President, or a star-hopping astronaut. The point
was that the human subconscious, when no longer suppressed by

ordinary consciousness, could become a great spraying fountain of information, in which memories situated more or less factually in place and time were mixed with other memories from other places, other times . . . a nightmare, a newspaper story, a scene from a movie, a vignette from a book . . .

Orne warned in particular that 'if the hypnotist has beliefs about what actually occurred, it is exceedingly difficult for him to prevent himself from inadvertently guiding the subject's recall, so that [the subject] will eventually "remember" what he, the hypnotist, believes actually happened.' Orne suggested that the hypnotist be informed of the subject under investigation only in writing, and that all communication between hypnotist and subject be minimized prior to hypnosis. Obviously, to Klass, the UFO abduction researchers were violating these strictures left and right.

Klass also found ammunition amid the early abduction literature. In 1977, the ufologists Alvin Lawson, John De Herrera, and Bill McCall had run an experiment to see whether ordinary imaginative people could make up plausible abduction stories under hypnosis. Lawson, a lecturer in the English department of California State University at Long Beach, advertised in the student newspaper for creative, imaginative types. UFO buffs or people who had had sightings were weeded out, and the remaining eight subjects were put under hypnosis by McCall, who was a physician and clinical hypnotist with earlier abduction research experience. The subjects were each asked to imagine and then to narrate an episode in which they had seen a UFO, had been taken aboard, and had been given a physical examination. Lawson and his colleagues compared the narratives with those from four published and unpublished abduction cases, and, as they reported at two ufology conferences in the summer of 1977, they had found 'no substantive differences' among the accounts. Indeed, they had been astonished by the subjects' 'ease and eagerness of narrative invention', which had required relatively little prompting; and which had reproduced 'many presumably obscure "patterns" from the UFO literature . . .' After criticism from other ufologists, Lawson and his colleagues acknowledged that their study did not, of course, disprove the claims of abductees, many of whom bore scars or had remembered UFOs which had been independently witnessed; and they revised their paper accordingly, but they continued to express surprise at how easily and convincingly their own experimental abduction accounts had been manufactured – by people who, unlike ordinary abductees, had been selected for their *lack* of prior knowledge about the subject.

Finally, Klass found the Slater study. In 1981, in the wake of *Missing Time*'s publication, the Fund for UFO Research had commissioned a psychological profile of nine of Budd Hopkins's abductees. A New York clinical psychologist, Elizabeth Slater, had been paid by FUFOR to evaluate the abductees' similarities and differences, with respect to each other and to normal, sane individuals. Slater was not told that her subjects had claimed to experience abductions by aliens. FUFOR and Hopkins expected, of course, that the study would prove their hypothesis: that UFO abductees were, except for their peculiar experiences, psychologically normal.

But Slater's findings were somewhat less straightforward. In fact, she found that the subjects were somewhat distinctive, tending to exhibit high intelligence, high creativity, lowered self-esteem, emotional immaturity, egocentricity, sexual identity confusion, mild paranoia, and a tendency, under stress, to slip into 'more or less transient psychotic experiences involving a loss of reality testing along with confused and disordered thinking that can be bizarre'. In short, they were the kind of people Slater often treated in her practice as a psychotherapist.

But then Hopkins told Slater that the people had been UFO abductees, and he gave her *Missing Time* to read, and afterwards Slater seemed to change her mind slightly, writing in an addendum to the report that in her opinion the psychopathology she had seen was *not* sufficient to explain the claimed missing time and abduction accounts – which she implied could only have been fabricated by pathological liars or paranoid schizophrenics.

Klass, however, sent the report to several other psychologists, who wrote back that the abduction accounts could very easily have been fabricated by personalities as fantasy-prone as those in the study were deemed to have been, particularly after reinforcement by Hopkins and other researchers. It was unnecessary that their psychopathology be as dramatic as compulsive lying or paranoid schizophrenia.

But what if the abductees' psychological eccentricity, however major or minor, could be attributed to the abduction experience itself – that is, as an effect rather than a cause? Slater suggested that if the subjects had actually experienced the things they recalled under hypnosis, then like rape victims they would probably carry 'social stigmatization', which would lead to 'a deep sense of shame, secretiveness, and social alienation'.

To which Klass responded: then why are so many abductees appearing on the talk show circuit?

Klass hadn't been to a ufology conference since 1975. In fact, since an incident surrounding a conference in Nebraska in 1982, he had been rather unwelcome on the ufological scene . According to the story told by ufologists, the incident had begun with a phone call from Klass to an official at the University of Nebraska; Klass had informed the official that the UFO enthusiasts who were about to use one of the university's hired rooms might reasonably be considered politically subversive, given their beliefs about government cover-ups and conspiracies and so on. Klass later denied that he had said this, but in any case, after a long wrangle with Klass regarding the leaked memorandum of his conversation with them, the university decided that the better part of valour lay in refusing permission for any further UFO conferences on the campus.

Even so, there had been a certain amount of water under the bridge since 1982; and since a MUFON conference was a public event, and the annual MUFON conference of 1987 was to be held irresistibly close to Klass's home in Washington, on a weekend in late June, when a great many abductees and abduction researchers would be there, Klass figured he might be able to do some valuable research for his book. So one evening he drove up to the conference hall at American University, where the session was being held. First he was buttonholed by some people who wanted to argue about the MJ-12 papers, a series of documents which a ufologist named Bill Moore had recently claimed to have received from an anonymous source; the papers purported to describe a secret organization of high-level government officials, the 'Majestic 12' (like the *Magnificent Seven* but dressed in pin-stripe suits), which had been formed during the Truman administration and whose purpose was to study UFOs while simultaneously suppressing the truth about them – a truth which if it got out would threaten public order and create mass hysteria. Anyway, the necessity of a brief sermon on how MJ-12 had to be a hoax delayed Klass, and he arrived at the abduction session a few minutes late. The conference hall was packed. A row of abductees sat up on the dais. Debbie Tomey was there, and Charley Hickson, and Strieber, and some other abductees that Klass had never seen or heard about before. The abductees were speaking in turn, giving brief testimonials, and Klass looked around but there weren't any seats, except on some steps up close to the dais. So he sat down there, like the proverbial spectre at the feast, and soon Strieber's turn came, and Strieber – Well, Strieber apparently had wanted to deliver his own major presentation, as his book had made the greatest impact on public consciousness, but he and Hopkins were still more or less at each other's throats, and the ufology community had sided with Hopkins, and so Strieber had been allotted a mere few minutes, along with the other abductees. Strieber's turn came and he began to tell of the slings and arrows of the media and the sceptics, and his voice took on a dramatic tone; he cited the fact that he had taken a lie detector test and had passed it, and his eyes moved over to Klass sitting below him on the steps, and he pointed to Klass, who was so close he was practically on the stage, and said, 'You called me a liar!' And Klass, who had been trying to look as demure and harmless and reasonable as possible, shot a pleading look at Strieber and said, 'I did not!'

After the session was over and the crowd was milling out of the conference hall, Klass went up to Strieber, who was with his son, Andrew. Klass said, what's this all about, Whitley? When did I ever call you a liar? And Strieber replied to the effect that Klass had called him a liar on some talk show that had aired in New York. And Klass didn't remember any such talk show, but then he recalled that a crew had come down from a New York television station to his house and had taped an interview – although he couldn't remember having said that Strieber was a liar. Whitley, said Klass, you send me a transcript of the show and if I called you a liar, I will issue a public apology. Strieber said OK, and they parted amicably, and Klass figured, rightly it turned out, that that would be the last time he would ever hear such an accusation from Strieber in public.

Klass liked to keep things amicable with people when he was speaking to them in person, and it must have given him a particularly warm, forbidden feeling to be amicable there in the camp of the enemy. No one threw anything at him, or spat, or hurled insults; in fact, several people approached him and asked if he would pose with them for photographs. He was a novelty item, and at the age of sixty-eight he had that harmless, grandfatherly look that could induce the hardest ufologist to smile and shake his hand in greeting.

Another thing that helped Klass to fit in among ufologists, or at least made them more curious about him, was that there seemed to be two of him. The first Philip Klass wrote for staid, solid *Aviation Week*, and defended orthodoxy against the heresy of ufology. The second Philip Klass wrote wild science fiction and fantasy stories, under the pen-name William Tenn. You could look it up, in the science fiction writers' anthologies: William Tenn was really Philip Klass, who also wrote for *Aviation Week*. It was the strangest thing.

There was no disputing that Klass had written good stories, however, and most of them had a dry irony reminiscent of some of Woody Allen's early work. Altogether Klass had written more than fifty stories between 1946 and the late 1960s, for pulps such as *Galaxy Science Fiction*, *Planet Stories*, *If*, *Future SF*, *Fantastic Mysteries*, *Fantastic Adventures*, and *Fantastic Universe*, the latter three being Ray Palmer creations owned by Ziff-Davis. As William Tenn, Klass had never reached the celebrity of Richard Shaver, but his prose was well put together; in fact, his style was generally much more mature than those of the space operas preferred by Shaver fans.

Oddly enough, Klass's stories, most of which had been written long before the Hill case brought the alien abduction phenomenon to public attention, were absolutely full of future dystopias, alien invasions and abductions, mutant breeding programmes, and time warps. In 'Of Men and Monsters', humans live in burrows and are used as laboratory animals by invading aliens who regularly vivisect them and steal their children; the oppressed humans' only hope lies in stowing away aboard alien ships like rats, colonizing other planets and living off alien detritus. In 'The Liberation of Earth', warring alien forces repeatedly attack and liberate Earth from other alien forces, leaving the planet a smoking ruin. At one point, the wormlike Troxxt land in Australia and the Ukraine, and set about stealing humans:

> They erected a dome-like fort around each ship . . . captured the few courageous individuals who had ventured close to their landing sites, and disappeared back into the dark craft with their squirming prizes.

'The Flat-Eyed Monster', written in the early sixties, came even closer to the modern alien abduction motifs, and might have inspired a few 'Far Side' comic strips as well. In the story, a college professor falls asleep one night in his bachelor apartment, then awakens with a strange tingling sensation and floats off his bed and through the window and up and away into the sky where he loses consciousness, regaining it on a white table under a vaulted domed ceiling from which the usual dental and ray-gun apparatuses hang down over him. On either side of him perch slime-grey, tentacled aliens with multiple bulging eyes. The aliens, who call themselves flefnobes, confer telepathically over the professor (who fearfully avoids their horrific glances) and conclude that he is nothing but a miserable flat-eyed monster. At one point one of the flefnobes expresses a philosophical disquiet about the abduction and examination of such a creature:

> I believe that there are mysteries that flefnobe was never meant to examine. Monsters as awful-looking as this – no slime on the skin, only two eyes and both of them flat, unable or unwilling to *pmbff*, an almost complete absence of tentacles – a creature of this sort should have been left undisturbed on its own hellish planet.

One of Klass's weirdest stories was 'Wednesday's Child', in which a man meets a pretty but odd young woman who has no navel, who gets appendicitis and grows a new appendix every year, and who loses her old teeth and grows a new set every five years.

He impregnates her, and in childbirth she loses her personality and transfers it to the newborn child, who greets her father with, 'Oh Darling, the strangest thing has happened!'

'The Discovery of Morniel Mathaway' involved a time twist, and seemed to have some strange connections both to Richard Shaver's Mutan Mion, and to one of the other Klass's future ufological adversaries. A down-and-out abstract artist in Greenwich Village, Morniel Mathaway,* is sitting in his draughty studio talking to a down-and-out anti-imagist poet, when the wall starts to ripple and a man in a purple box materializes and announces that he has come from the year AD 2487. His name is Glescu. He has won a great Nobel-type prize, awarded only every fifty years because of the colossal energy required by the prize itself: travel to the time of the prize-winner's choice. Glescu is an art critic, and has travelled here to Greenwich Village in the 1950s to find the great artist Morniel Mathaway – whose work will eventually revolutionize all of painting, sculpture, architecture, design, culture, etc. He asks Mathaway to show him some of his work; Mathaway complies, but Glescu is horrified at the artist's obvious lack of talent. Finally Glescu shows Mathaway a future photograph of one of his great early works; Mathaway, knowing that he will never be capable of such a work, gets his poet friend to divert Glescu for a moment, then steals the book and the time machine and goes back to the future, to the fame and fortune that surely await him. Glescu, stranded in Greenwich Village, resigns himself to mid twentieth-century life, adopts Mathaway's beatnik painter identity, and begins to turn out the revolutionary stuff that in time will create the Mathaway legend.

Yes, it was very strange that Philip Klass had written all this. The man seemed to have a hidden side – dark or bright depending on your point of view – a split personality, almost, in which the fantastic side would let off the hot steam, the mythopoeic, cosmogenic urges, which had been pent up by the sceptical side. But what if this split personality actually resided in two separate individuals? What if there really *were* two Philip Klasses, both

---

* 'He'd come to New York from Pittsburgh, Pennsylvania, a tall, awkward boy who didn't like to shave and believed he could paint . . . Recently he had developed his own technique which he called smudge-on-smudge.'

about the same age, both writers and science buffs, both concerned with themes of alien invasion – except that one of them had skipped aimlessly through the pastures of fiction, while the other had soberly guarded the iron curtain of non-fiction? Was it possible? Klass was a rare name, but perhaps the anthology writers had got it wrong . . .

One day in the early fifties, just after Klass had begun to work for *Aviation Week*, he walked into a Bloomingdales department store and applied for a credit line. A large woman behind the counter asked him if by any chance he had ever worn a beard.

'Well, no,' said Klass.

'Have you ever lived in Greenwich Village?' asked the Bloomingdales woman.

'No, I haven't,' said Klass.

Bloomingdales gave him the credit, but Klass had had his first glimpse of his alter ago, his dark, bearded, beatnik twin.

Some time later, Klass received a telephone call from a fellow who asked, 'Is this the Philip Klass I was in the Navy with?' 'I was never in the Navy,' said Klass. The fellow on the other end of the line sounded relieved: 'I didn't think the Philip Klass I knew would have a job at *Aviation Week*.'

Eventually, Klass tracked his dark twin down, and began a file on him labelled . . . 'The Other Philip Klass'. The other Philip Klass was, like his creation Morniel Mathaway, a bearded beatnik bachelor, living in Greenwich Village. Although much later he would go on to become a distinguished English professor at Pennsylvania State University, he had gone from a youthful stint in the Navy during the war to write science fiction and fantasy stories, and to study ancient Greek, supporting himself variously as a waiter, a cruise ship purser, a cooking-appliance salesman in a department store, a television comic, a tropical fish nursemaid, and a door-to-door market researcher, among other professional personae.

Having established the existence of the second Klass, the first Klass wrote a formal letter to the editor of *Aviation Week*, preemptively making it clear that Philip Klass the avionics writer was an entity distinct and separate from Philip Klass the fantasy writer who sometimes went by the pseudonym William Tenn. To underscore his uniqueness, he changed his *Aviation Week* byline from Philip Klass to Philip J. Klass.

But through the years the confusion continued. Once he received a phone call at his office from a woman curious to know the meaning of a particularly opaque passage in this or that science fiction story. Another time he received a manuscript, for a work of fiction, in the mail for review, despite having confined his reading, for the past three or four decades, strictly to non-fiction. Yet another time, he received a letter from a woman in New York who seemed to believe that she had once been his girlfriend and wanted to know if he, Phil Klass, was still available . . . The crowning blow came one evening in Washington, DC, when Klass attended an organizational meeting of a local CSICOP offshoot, the National Capital Area Skeptics. He was one of the featured speakers, and after his speech one of the sceptics approached him and asked for his autograph. 'Certainly,' said Klass, pleased at his apparent celebrity, but as he reached for his pen the sceptic added: 'I've been reading your science fiction stuff for years!'

7

Old Hag and the Amygdala

And suddenly there was a terrible roar all around us and the
sky was full of what looked like huge bats, all swooping and
screeching and diving around the car . . .

– Hunter S. Thompson, *Fear and Loathing in Las Vegas*

One afternoon back in the early 1980s, the astronomer and ufologist
Allen Hynek was sitting at his home in Illinois when a call came in
from one of the network late-night TV news-talk shows. The
assistant producer or whoever was on the phone explained that
they wanted to do a show about UFOs; could Professor Hynek
oblige them with his presence that night at the nearest network
studio?

Hynek responded warily, wanting to know who else would be
appearing on the show. The producer said she thought Philip Klass
would probably appear, to put forward the sceptical point of view.
Hynek said that in that case, he had better things to do.

With Hynek at his home in Illinois that day was the ufologist
Jenny Randles, a former high-school science teacher in Manchester,
England, who had risen to become the director of investigations for
BUFORA – the British UFO Research Association – the best-
known and perhaps best-organized of the British UFO enthusiasts'
groups. Randles had enormous respect for Hynek, whom she
considered to be a kind of founding father of respectable ufology,
yet she couldn't understand why he should be so skittish about
appearing on television with Klass. She reminded him gently that
he was supposed to be a scientist, engaged in the great struggle of
scientific ideas. To shy away from a fight would be to admit defeat
in advance. If he turned up, on the other hand, his logical, rational

arguments with Klass couldn't help but persuade the audience that UFOs were something worth studying.

'But you can't argue rationally and logically with this man,' complained Hynek. 'It can't be done.'

Randles had heard that sort of thing before, from other American ufologists. They seemed to her to have a tremendous fear of the man from *Aviation Week* – fear not only of Klass's rhetorical abuse, but of the rational and logical power of some of his arguments, despite his alleged irrationality and illogicality. As far as Randles was concerned, for example, Klass's critiques of abduction research, and of the abduction phenomenon, were for the most part valid and useful, and should have been made by ufologists themselves.

Randles was one of a growing number of researchers, especially European researchers, whose beliefs about the UFO phenomenon existed in a kind of nether world – between nuts-and-bolts American-style ufology on the one hand, according to which the phenomenon was the result of aliens flying around in high-tech spaceships, and on the other hand a CSICOP scepticism which rejected virtually all UFO reports as hoaxes or psychotic delusions, and seemed to deny the possibility not only of extraterrestrial visitation, but of anything paranormal or supernatural. She didn't rule out the possibility of nuts-and-bolts spaceships, or of hoaxes, but she seemed more interested in other explanations for the strange things that zoomed quietly around in the skies and occasionally seemed to land and disgorge variform humanoid entities.

In retrospect, British ufologists would see that close-encounter cases from the fifties, sixties, and early seventies had had all the hallmarks of abduction cases, but it was only with a wave of CE3 and CE4 cases in 1976 – which British ufologists later would dub the 'Year of the Humanoids' – that Randles and her colleagues began to recognize the abduction phenomenon as a distinct one. The first case Randles investigated that year had to do with a young ambulance driver in Keighley, West Yorkshire. He had been lying in bed one night when several tall, slender, grey-skinned, and large-headed beings had appeared in his bedroom. One of them presented a U-shaped piece of metal tubing, and explained, telepathically, that the tubing was a part of their spacecraft that required repair. The aliens and the ambulance driver then beamed up through the ceiling into the spacecraft, which was shaped like a bathtub, and inside the craft the ambulance driver was examined by some strange eyelike device and was given a certain amount of information pertaining to world peace and nuclear disarmament and so on. He awakened in his bed again, with enough recollection of the incident for no hypnosis to be needed.

The idiosyncratically odd shape of the spacecraft, its occupants' unlikely need for human help, and their clichéd prophecies convinced Randles that the young man's experience had been the product of his central nervous system. Another woman she interviewed had told her a similar story about having been awakened, one night when she had been five years old, by a noise outside the house and the apparition beside her bed of a thirty-inch-tall big-eyed grey alien – who had disappeared when her screams brought her father rushing into the room. Other cases which came to her attention had similar features. There was the case of Gaynor Sunderland, a young English girl who seemed unusually prone to bedroom encounters with tall blond aliens; during one such encounter, Gaynor's mother observed her daughter lying unconscious in bed. There was also the case of Jose Alvaro, a Brazilian who was observed by several witnesses to be in an apparent trance state, flat on his back beside a road, during an interval in which, he later claimed, he had had the usual experiences with alien abductors.

And then there was the Maureen Puddy case, from the early seventies in south-east Australia. At the time of the case, Puddy had been a twenty-seven-year-old housewife, with an invalid husband and two children. One day in June 1972, her son had hurt his leg badly in an accident and had had to be taken to hospital by helicopter. Driving to visit her son in the hospital one evening, along the Mooraduc road between Frankston and Dromana south-west of Melbourne, Maureen had seen a strange blue light in the sky. At first she thought it was a helicopter, but then, according to her story, it resolved into a spaceship shaped like two saucers atop one another. It made a faint humming noise. It was about a hundred feet across and thirty to forty feet high. It chased her down the road and she reported her experience to the police. One evening about three weeks later, this time driving back from the hospital, Puddy saw a blue glow in the sky. The blue glow came down and dragged her car on to the shoulder of the road, bathing her in blue light. It was just above her car; she could see the rim of the craft through the top of her car windshield. She had a sensation of low pressure within the car. Then a voice explained to her telepathically that 'All your tests will be negative' and that she should tell the media of her experience.

She did tell the media, but they declined to take her seriously. Local UFO groups took her seriously, however, and in early 1973 two investigators, Judith Magee and Paul Norman, were summoned to meet her on the road where she had had her two previous experiences. She arrived in a panic, claiming that on her way to the meeting she had been visited by an alien in a gold-foil suit who had materialized inside her car. The three then went back to the place where Mrs Puddy said the materialization had occurred, and sat in her car together to wait for something to happen. Within minutes Mrs Puddy pointed to a spot in front of the car and exclaimed, 'There he is! Can't you see him?' Magee and Norman explained that, alas, they could not see him, and then Norman got out of the car and walked towards the place where the alien apparently was standing. Mrs Puddy reported that the alien stepped aside to let Norman pass. Then the alien disappeared behind bushes, and Mrs Puddy screamed that she had been kidnapped. She went on to describe, as she sat in the car with Magee and Norman, the interior of the alien spaceship, and at one point mentioned that the alien had asked her to close her eyes. She then appeared, to Magee and Norman, to relax into a trance state, and began describing the spaceship and its inhabitants as if she were undergoing hypnotic regression. Finally, she said, 'He's gone. I can tell. It feels different.' And she returned to normal consciousness within the car. Mrs Puddy was widowed soon thereafter, and moved out of the state.

The Aveley case was a good deal less straightforward. It had happened one night in October 1974, near the Essex town of Aveley. John and Susan Day had been driving home from a relative's house with their three young children when they had seen a blue light in the sky. The light seemed to be following them. It crossed the road ahead of them and then disappeared. Then the car radio began to blare and smoke, and as they rounded a bend in the road they entered a strangely luminous green mist; the car was jerked around but then suddenly the mist was gone and they were a half-mile or so further along the road. When they arrived home, at what should have been about 10 p.m., the television programme they had been rushing home to see was long over; they were confronted with an off-air test pattern on their TV screen, and several hours of missing time. They reported it to a local UFO research group, who wrote up a report concerning the mist and the light but forgot to note the missing time. The case seemed to drift into oblivion, but as the months went by the family continued to be plagued by strange experiences. They had visions of strange beings, and nightmares of stranger ones. Their house became haunted by poltergeists. John and Susan began to believe that strange men were following them, and John believed that the police were harassing him. John and Susan stopped drinking, smoking, and eating meat. They became obsessed with environmental issues. John had a nervous breakdown, and afterwards began writing poetry. Eventually a small team of experienced UFO researchers, known as the UFO Investigators' Network, recognized the symptoms of the alien abduction syndrome and decided to revisit the case. By extensive questioning of the family, several times using regression hypnosis on the mother and father, the ufologists Barry King and Andy Collins came up with an account of a classic abduction scenario, in which John and Susan apparently had been targeted by a group of aliens consisting of tall, fair-skinned humanoids in silver suits and helmets, and smaller, bat-like creatures who performed the medical examinations.

King and Collins weren't sure what to make of the case. The light and the mist on the road, the paranormal phenomena inside the house, and the apparent participation of both John and Susan (the children had apparently slept through the encounter), indicated that something more than a solitary dream-like vision had occurred, even if the family members' behavioural changes (John Day later divorced Susan and moved to a hermitic rural cottage) were similar to those which followed the more ordinary bedroom visitations. There was also the fact that John and Susan Day, under hypnosis, not only re-experienced their ordeal, but experienced it from a new angle: from above they saw *themselves* sitting in a car (a blue car, although theirs was white) as if they were watching from the aliens' vantage point. This kind of dissociative vision, which happened to many people and did not necessarily involve UFOs or alien encounters, was just beginning to be familiar to psychologists as an 'out-of-body experience', or OBE.

Another clue came from one of the hypnosis sessions with Mrs Day in 1978. Andy Collins, who had picked up hypnotism during the investigation the year before, took the mother into a trance, and then directed her back to one of the episodes when she had been on board the aliens' spaceship. At one point Collins handed the questioning over to Jenny Randles. Randles asked the woman why she thought the aliens might be there. What were they up to? The woman paused for a few moments and then said that she had asked the aliens that particular question and the aliens had responded that they were from a particular stellar system in another part of the galaxy, and we humans were their children, part of a genetic experiment they had carried out over 10,000 years ago, and they had been watching us ever since, and were concerned that we not make as much of a mess out of our planet as they had done with theirs, although they wished to avoid direct, overt, disruptive contact with an alien civilization, and therefore they had to go about their work indirectly, at night and in secret, taking individual abductees up into their ships and checking out their genotypes and phenotypes and driving home the necessity of world peace and a clean environment.

It was pretty standard visionary stuff, but what really caught Randles's attention was that the woman had said that *she* had asked the aliens the very question that Randles had wanted her to ask. As the questioning went on, it became clear that the woman had not asked the aliens these questions unprompted, during the previously reported abduction. She was passing the questions to the aliens *then and there*, while under hypnosis. Randles would ask a question, and Mrs Day would be silent for a while as she mentally relayed the question to the aliens, and then she would speak up and relay the aliens' answer back to Randles. The question and answer relays were the ongoing, dynamic product of Mrs Day's fecund brain and Jenny Randles's prompting questions.

Over the years, Randles tried this experiment on three other hypnotized abductees, and two of them began the same real-time confabulatory dialogue with the aliens. They weren't deceiving her intentionally, of course; they were so far into their trances that they no longer recognized the boundary between fantasy and reality. For them that boundary might have been blurred to begin with, even before they went into a trance – although it seemed to her that a lot of abductees, when asked directly, drew a strong distinction between what they could remember consciously, and what they had remembered under hypnotic prompting. Alan Godfrey, a Yorkshire policeman who had seen a UFO and experienced missing time on a road in Todmorden, between Leeds and Manchester, in 1980, was asked by Randles some years later whether he really believed he had been abducted. Godfrey responded, according to Randles, that he was convinced that the thing he had seen on the road that night was real. 'If I'd had a rock and had thrown it, I'd have hit it; it was there. There is no doubt in my mind.' But as for what he remembered later under hypnosis, he couldn't say for certain whether it was real or fantasy. He acknowledged to Randles that in the six months between his experience and his first hypnosis sessions, he had read books about UFOs. He hadn't been able to resist; he had wanted to know what had happened to other UFO witnesses under similar circumstances. He admitted to Randles that the abduction sequence he had remembered under hypnosis could possibly have come from those books. 'All I was doing under hypnosis,' she says he told her, 'was describing images that were coming into my mind from somewhere.'

Of course, long before this conversation with Alan Godfrey, Randles had become convinced that hypnosis was the wrong tool to use in abduction research: not only did it bring forth data that, in her opinion, were to an uncertain extent confabulated, and therefore useless; it also tended to steer the abductee towards a certain scenario, depending on the beliefs of the hypnotist, and therefore had the potential to cause enormous psychological damage – particularly when it convinced someone, erroneously, that a terrible and traumatic thing had happened, such as that she had been impregnated by aliens, or had had her baby snatched.

Interestingly, in her public pronouncements and writings Randles was often much more ambivalent about the use of hypnosis, and for example would cite Eddie Bullard's data as an illustration that hypnosis wasn't entirely to blame for the contents of abduction accounts. This may in part have been because Randles diplomatically wished to avoid appearing to attack the more prominent regression hypnosis proponents, such as Budd Hopkins and Dave Jacobs, whom she would later describe in her book, *Abduction*, as, respectively, 'one of the kindest, most affable men one could wish to meet ... a superb professional artist ...' and 'a remarkably astute man, an incisive historian whose recent conversion to the study of abductions is a great bonus'. Even so, in 1987, when the hoopla began over the books by Whitley Strieber and Budd Hopkins, Randles pushed a measure through BUFORA imposing a five-year moratorium on the use of hypnosis in abduction cases.

In any case, Randles was far from being a complete sceptic about abductions. It was clear to her, especially when close-encounters clustered in certain areas, or during certain periods of time, or were supported by UFO reports from independent witnesses, that something was going on. Most abductees really seemed to have undergone some kind of traumatic or otherwise life-changing experience. And the aliens, aside from some notable variations – from the blond and benign to the blue and mean – seemed remarkably consistent in their appearance and behaviour. Where was this imagery coming from, if it was not part of our here-and-now world of reality? Randles proposed, among other more prosaic theories, that alien civilizations might actually be the originators of abduction imagery; they might be beaming telepathic imagery to suitably receptive humans – mediums, to use an older term* – in such a way that these humans would believe that they had actually experienced alien encounters, and would therefore take seriously the messages of nuclear doom and environmental destruction whose transmission was, presumably, the aliens' primary objective.

Other British researchers, most notably the anomaly-hunter Hilary Evans, eschewed such exotic explanations and concentrated

---

* Following the claimed travels to Mars by the nineteenth-century medium Helene Smith, it had been suggested by spiritualists that 'astral travel' or 'psychic visitation' could be used by humans to meet other species on other planets, and vice versa.

on the fact that some people tended to have these kinds of experiences and some didn't. To Evans, it seemed clear that abduction stories were basically vivid fantasies experienced in an altered state of consciousness, with similarities to other departures from ordinary reality. Since the early 1980s, a series of psychological studies had demonstrated what mental health professionals and armchair sceptics had long suspected: the existence of a 'fantasy-prone personality'. FPPs, as they had come to be known, typically had higher than average intelligence and creativity, were highly hypnotizable, and had a profoundly active fantasy life which occasionally would become indistinguishable from reality. As children, they had imaginary playmates. They saw ghosts and monsters. They were surrounded by poltergeists. They could read minds. Their dreams foretold the future. They had out-of-body experiences. They seemed to have extraordinary recall, even of events from their early infancy, although sometimes they also suffered partial, and apparently inexplicable amnesias. Many claimed to have suffered trauma or abuse in childhood. This latter feature suggested to investigating psychologists that the fantasy-prone personality could arise – among other environmental or genetic reasons – from the chronic use of dissociation as a defence against severe stress. At one end of the spectrum would lie those whose fantasy-proneness was relatively minor, perhaps even beneficial if their livelihoods depended upon imagination and creativity; at the other end would lie those with debilitating ailments known as the dissociative disorders.

The term 'dissociation' is simply a label for what happens when one or more mental processes are split off from the rest, resulting in hypnotic trances, hallucinations, psychosomatic ('hysterical') illnesses, and so on. An example of ordinary dissociation would be the trance-like state that most people experience while watching television. Pathological dissociations would include chronic self-hypnosis, amnesic somnambulatory fugues, hysterical aches, pains, eating disorders, allergies, and even the manifestation of multiple, distinct personalities each with its own constellation of likes, dislikes, and abilities.

Individuals with dissociative disorders, the most extreme of which is multiple personality disorder, are visionaries *par excellence*, their alternate-reality experiences often seeming to serve as a form of therapy. Hilary Evans liked to cite the case of a twenty-three-year-old Boston woman, Christine Beauchamp, who had been treated by the trail-blazing psychiatrist Morton Prince around the turn of the century. Prince, in his book *The Dissociation of a Personality*, had noted that:

> Miss Beauchamp as a child frequently had visions of the Madonna and Christ, and used to believe that she had actually seen them. It was her custom when in trouble, if it was only a matter of her school lessons, or something that she had lost, to resort to prayer. Then she would be apt to have a vision of Christ. The vision never spoke, but sometimes made signs to her, and the expression of his face made her feel that all was well. After the vision passed, she felt that her difficulties were removed, and if it was a bothersome lesson which she had been unable to understand, it all became intelligible at once. Or, if it was something that she had lost, she at once went to the spot where it was. On one occasion when she had lost a key, her vision of Christ led her down the street into a field where under a tree she found the key. She constantly used to have the sense of presence of someone (Christ, or the Madonna, or a Saint) near her, and on the occasion of the visions it seemed simply that their person had become visible.

Out of this fantasy-flooded childhood Christine eventually developed several separate personalities, but not all of them were as benign as her childhood companions had been. Sometimes they fought it out among themselves, and the results were physically evident. Christine confided to Dr Prince that 'Sally', an alter personality, 'always treated my body as if it were not even remotely connected with herself, cutting, scratching, and bruising it in a way so shocking that it is hard to believe'. On one occasion, according to Christine, Sally caused her to see and feel that her feet had been amputated. Sally, for her part, admitted to Dr Prince that she sometimes manipulated Christine: 'I can make her not see things, or see things.' The point was that, for a mind with dissociative tendencies, the boundary between one personality and another, between ordinary reality and an alternate state, was easily crossed.

Of course the most interesting altered states, from the point of view of ufologists, were those connected with UFO sightings. Both the Aveley case and the Todmorden case were classic examples: a person or persons had encountered a strange light or a flying saucer or a mist on the road, and then had apparently experienced a brief period of amnesia. Only under hypnosis, or in retrospective nightmares where the mind made a similar attempt to fill in the temporal gap, had any details about an abduction emerged. Perhaps those details had been mere hallucinatory fantasy, as in the cases of Gaynor Sunderland, Jose Alvaro, and Maureen Puddy. Perhaps a distant observer, watching the scene through a telescope, would have seen only a car approaching a strange object or mist or lightform on a road; the car would pull over, slow to a stop on the roadside, and remain there – its occupants in some kind of trance – until the object or the mist or the lightform drifted away or disappeared, and the driver regained full consciousness.

But how, or why, would a lightform, or a flying saucer, or a strange mist induce such an altered state? And where would it come from in the first place?

Paul Devereux, a British paranormal researcher, was one of the first to take a crack at such questions. Since the late 1970s, Devereux had been pushing an idea similar to Philip Klass's – namely, that most if not all of the UFOs which did not have obvious prosaic explanations were not structured craft or flying saucers or even anything solid, but rather were 'earthlights', little electromagnetic tempests caused by natural processes. Devereux had an idea what these natural ufogenous processes were: tectonic stresses within the earth. One piece of evidence came from earthquake lore; electromagnetic interference with radios and televisions, to say nothing of effects on the behaviour of animals, was well known to be common immediately prior to and during major earthquakes. UFOs also were often reported to cause such interference. Moreover, before and during earthquakes it was not uncommon to see strange aurora-type light displays in the atmosphere, or balls of light bubbling out of the ground.

Devereux mapped out the tectonic fault lines in Britain, and found that they seemed to correspond to areas of high UFO prevalence. Which made it seem likely that ordinary UFO lightforms had the same source as earthquake-related lightforms; the presence of UFO-type activity even during seismically quiet periods suggested that ordinary UFOs, or earthlights, were caused by tectonic processes which on occasion could be too subtle to manifest as surface tremors. As for the precise mechanism by which seismic processes generated these earthlights, Devereux wasn't sure, but over the years he looked at a number of possibilities. The first was piezoelectricity, the phenomenon by which certain mineral crystals under pressure or strain would generate electric fields, which at great enough intensities could ionize the air, creating luminescent bubbles of plasma. The attraction of the piezoluminescence idea was that the actual motion of rock along a fault line would be less important than the strain built up along the fault. At a certain critical point, the fault rock would no longer be able to stand the strain and would begin to crush and buckle and slide, causing an earthquake; but such an event was fairly rare, at least on a large scale, and therefore was less likely to be responsible for UFO-type lightforms than were the random rises and falls of tectonic strain which could occur without any seismographic murmurs at all, or at least not immediate ones.

The problem was, however, that piezoelectrically generated fields should occur only around certain types of rock, especially quartz-bearing rock; moreover, conductive groundwater should for the most part confine any generated electric fields beneath the earth's surface anyway. Exploring alternatives to piezoelectricity, Devereux during the early 1980s became interested in rock-crush luminescence. A number of geophysicists were working on the phenomenon, and in 1983 Devereux and his colleagues did their own experiments, photographing the little blue and orange lightforms that formed around fracturing granite. Unfortunately, they didn't have the equipment to do much more than photograph the lightforms, but in 1986, Brian Brady and Glen Rowell at the US Bureau of Mines published a paper in *Nature* describing some new rock-crush experiments performed under various conditions with different rocks, and filmed with image-intensifiers and spectroscopes. Spectroscopic analysis of the miniature lightforms emitted by the rocks indicated that they were associated with ambient air molecules rather than rock molecules, but didn't give off microwaves, and therefore, for various complex reasons, probably weren't plasmas. The lightforms also didn't seem to have anything to do with piezoluminescence, since they also formed around fracturing basalt, and basalt didn't have the atomic structure that seemed to be necessary for piezoelectric phenomena. Brady and Rowell suggested, citing some earlier work by physicist Stuart Hoenig at the University of Arizona, that the rock fracture must have been giving off showers of electrons which excited the surrounding air molecules, causing them to give off photons of visible light. Unfortunately, 'exoelectron excitation', as it was called, was something that could only have effect in the very near vicinity of whatever was giving off the electrons. It wasn't too plausible as a mechanism for generating UFOs thousands of feet above the earth's surface – unless, as Devereux and others began to speculate, the charges generated by the electron bombardment were somehow conducted to the surface, perhaps by underground streams and thin films of water between rocks.

Well, in any case, the idea was that something within the earth was producing light phenomena in the atmosphere. These light phenomena would swerve and swoop crazily according to the invisible electromagnetic topography of the atmosphere, and would be caused by something that could also make radios and televisions buzz and hum, compasses spin, and animals and humans howl and hallucinate. During the daytime, an earthlight would be less visible, but its outer surface, perhaps being an interface between two dynamically distinct types of air (for example, ionized plasma and ordinary air) might not only emit light but reflect it, giving the impression of a solid, metallic object.

A researcher named Michael Persinger was taking a similar approach to the UFO problem. In fact, Persinger, a psychology professor at Laurentian University in Ontario, had independently put forward his own tectonic-strain hypothesis for UFO experiences as far back as 1976, and by the late 1980s had developed a fairly comprehensive theory, with a substantial body of supporting evidence, to explain why UFOs – and a lot of other things – caused some people to believe that they had been abducted by aliens.

Persinger was shaping up to be quite a spoil-sport. His work seemed to suggest that not only alien abductions but a whole range of anomalous occurrences, from angelic visitations to demonic possessions to OBEs, were merely the results of electrical misfirings within the parts of the brain known as the temporal lobes.

Persinger's scientific odyssey had begun when he was still a teenage undergraduate at the University of Wisconsin. He had initially been interested in the psycho-chemistry of human behaviour, but he couldn't help confronting the fact that researchers in a given discipline tended to deal more or less exclusively with their own phenomenological stratum, ignoring every other level of investigation. Nuclear physicists studied quarks and quanta; chemists studied molecules; biologists studied cells; and so on. Persinger was attracted by the idea that there might be a phenomenon which could cross all of these different disciplines, something that could affect not only quarks and quanta but entire organisms, even entire societies. Electricity and magnetism seemed to fit the bill. Persinger had taken courses in physics and electronics, and he knew that if one bundled up a bunch of separate wires, each wire carrying its own electrical current, and subjected the bundle to a changing magnetic field, then by Faraday's Law and Lenz's Law and the Biot–Savart Law and all the other rules governing interactions between electricity and magnetism,* all of the currents in the bundle would change. The same should be true of human brains – intensely electrical devices with billions of neural circuits – bathed in the earth's magnetic field. Magnetic fields, which by their nature could penetrate where electric fields and ionizing radiation could not, might be the fundamental, discipline-crossing phenomenon he had sought.

Unfortunately, there had already been several studies performed to examine the effects of magnetic fields upon animals and humans, and most had concluded that there were no effects, at least not substantial ones. But Persinger wasn't too impressed with these

---

* These laws can be summarized roughly as: (1) a changing magnetic field induces an electric current in conductors within the field, or changes the existing currents within those conductors: (2) a changing electric field, for example that caused by an electric current in a conductor, generates a surrounding magnetic field, or alters the existing magnetic field.

studies, and for his undergraduate thesis, and later for his MA thesis at the University of Tennessee, he subjected prenatal and newborn mice to rotating magnetic fields, and found changes in the production of melatonin, an important brain hormone which (in humans) helps to regulate the sleep-wake cycle as well as moods. As the years went by, his experiments continued, other investigators adding their own positive results to his own, and it began to seem clear that exogenous magnetic fields, however subtle their apparent action, could have a substantial, perhaps even harmful, effect on biological systems.

Persinger's interest in UFOs also had originated in his undergraduate years. One day he had read somewhere in a pulp paperback about a 'dārk day' that had occurred on 19 May 1780, on the north-east coast of the US. The sky had gone black at ten o'clock in the morning, and all manner of apocalyptic terrors had been set loose among the population. The University of Wisconsin had a good collection of early American newspapers, from which it became clear to Persinger, digging through them, that the 'dark day' really had taken place. Even so, no modern scientist had so much as attempted to come to grips with such a weird phenomenon. Persinger could just about understand why, having taken a few courses in the history and philosophy of science, and having read about paradigms and dominant scientific ideologies and how scientists tended to exclude from their view the things that didn't fit into those ideologies ... Still, it bothered him. If such a phenomenon existed, then someone should attempt to explain it. He began to delve into the books of Charles Fort, the turn-of-the-century journalist who, after inheriting a modest fortune, had spent much of the rest of his life sitting in the New York Public Library in Manhattan and the British Library in London, sifting through old newspapers and scientific journals, searching for reports of things that didn't fit the conventional scholarly view of the universe and human existence. Persinger's interest might have seemed odd, but in fact there were a lot of people out there who for some reason or other had become hooked on the books of Charles Fort and had begun to track down anomalous phenomena themselves. Such people were called Forteans.

Persinger became a Fortean, too, and being an experimentalist, devoted to quantitative analysis, he decided to note down every one of the 6,000-odd anomalous phenomena that Fort had recorded, plotting them geographically and by year. Persinger spent most of his nights as a master's degree student, there in Knoxville, Tennessee in the late 1960s, plotting Fort's reports of anomalous phenomena. He did some more work on the data during his PhD years at the University of Manitoba, but it wasn't until he arrived at Laurentian University in 1971, as a twenty-six-year-old assistant professor, that he was able to get his hands on a computer that could help him analyse all of his Fortean data. Persinger put all the data into the computer, an old IBM 36040, and ran some statistical analyses to see if he could match the reports of strange occurrences with some external, global variable, something that involved the release of an anomalously high amount of energy – such as tornadoes, or hurricanes, or meteorite impacts, or . . . earthquakes.

The computer analysis indicated what Persinger had already suspected from reading Fort's books, namely that there was a close correlation between earthquakes and strange phenomena, especially strange luminous phenomena. Persinger was also able to show, from a time-series analysis of the data, that it appeared that UFO flaps tended to *precede* periods of intense seismic activity by about six months or so. In other words, whatever caused UFOs seemed somehow to be related to the precursory processes, deep within the earth, which gave rise to earthquakes. In 1976, Persinger wrote a paper for a mainstream experimental psychology journal, *Perceptual and Motor Skills*, outlining his hypothesis that tectonic stresses and strains before earthquakes could give rise to airborne luminous electromagnetic phenomena. His idea, supported and elaborated over the next decade, was that seismic activity, through piezoelectricity or any other underground mechanism, could generate short-lived but extremely intense electric and magnetic fields in highly localized areas. He called these short-lived electromagnetic storms 'transients', and suggested that they could not only ignite plasma-type fireballs in the sky, but could also, by inducing rogue electrical currents within the brain, wreak hallucinatory havoc on the perceptions of nearby humans.

Of course, to say that UFO-related magnetic fields could induce rogue currents in the brain was to beg a very large question. Why would something that scrambled the entire brain cause an ordinary human – say, fishing on the banks of the Pascagoula River on a pleasant autumn evening – to believe that he had been abducted and subjected to medical examination by extraterrestrial monsters?

This is where the temporal lobes came in. Situated below and on either side of the frontal lobes, their functions included some of the processing of incoming and outgoing sounds and speech. Through their associated structures, the hippocampus and the amygdala, the temporal lobes enabled memory and evaluation, the experience of images, the experience of dreams. When the hippocampus of a living person was touched in the right places by a neurologist's probe, the person could experience a flood of images and memories, either 'real' or fantastic and dream-like. The amygdala, for its part, helped to coordinate the experience of emotion, and its connections to the frontal lobes and other areas of the brain ensured that emotions were tied to memory and the sense of the self.

The hippocampus and the amygdala and the other structures of the temporal lobes were also very 'labile' – their neurons, by comparison with other neurons in the brain, were easy to stimulate with mechanical probes or with electrical currents or current-inducing magnetic fields. Given a stimulus to the entire brain, Persinger believed the temporal lobe was likely to be affected first. And once stimulated, temporal lobe neurons tended to keep firing long after their initial stimulus had been removed. Which made it easy for them to 'learn' to react to certain stimuli, and also made them relatively prone to have 'seizures' – in other words, to fire all at once. According to Persinger, everyone once in a while had a minor temporal lobe seizure, or a transient episode of abnormal temporal lobe activity, and it seldom meant that one would lapse into a trance and roll around on the ground and have a fit; but something would happen, and that something was very interesting. Depending on which neurons, and how many of them, were involved, temporal lobe transients often resulted in experiences such as the sense of levitation, the sense of leaving one's body, the sense of *déjà vu*, the feeling of paralysis, the hearing of voices within one's head, the sense of anxiety or panic or that something isn't right, the smelling of odd odours, strange sensations around the genitals, the anal sphincter, and the base of the spine, erotic experiences (though for some reason less often in men), the sense of another's presence, the perception of shadowy figures, and of course a great variety of very real-seeming visual, auditory, and tactile hallucinations.

Just as importantly, temporal lobe transients could be followed by amnesia, a sense of missing time, a sense that something profound had happened, a sense that all of the chaotic events of one's life now fit a purposive pattern, a sense that one now had a special destiny, a sense of communion with the world or the universe, and a desire to spread the word. Such 'religious conversion' symptoms, which often resulted in profound lifestyle changes for the individual in question, suggested that the momentary chaos of the seizure or other abnormal neurological activity had helped to bring about a fundamental neural rewiring – somewhat analogous, ironically, to the tectonic revision enabled by an earthquake.

Persinger believed that temporal lobe transients, or neurological processes which had the same effect on consciousness, memory, and fantasy, probably underlay some of the phenomena observed during dissociation. The relationship was not straightforward, since people who were prone to dissociation did not always display electroencephalographic (EEG) abnormalities, even when they were in a trance state. However, the fact that many dissociative people did seem to have clinically detectable EEG abnormalities suggested to Persinger that some temporal-lobe-related neurological process was at work, perhaps one which could exist beneath the detection threshold of clinical instruments such as EEGs. Indeed, Persinger believed that most temporal lobe transients occurred routinely, on a small scale, and inconsequentially, for example during dreams or daydreams. Others, though, could be large enough to cause people to lapse into deep trances, resulting afterwards in anything from severe psychological trauma to religious fanaticism to insanity. Moreover, temporal lobe lability varied from person to person. Those on the low end of the scale only had temporal lobe seizures during dreams, and perhaps dreamed infrequently and unmemorably; while those on the high end suffered from a debilitating and clinically recognizable syndrome known as temporal lobe epilepsy. Most people fell into the low range, and the more labile their temporal lobes, the more creative and intuitive they tended to be. A greater than average temporal lobe lability made for good poets and writers and aesthetes. It also, however, tended to cause anxiety, emotional instability, paranoia, panic, and manic-depression, although even people with frequent temporal-lobe-related experiences might appear clinically normal.

Persinger had been following trends in ufology since the 1960s, and the alien abduction experience struck him as being very similar to some of the experiences reported by patients with temporal lobe epilepsy. He and his colleagues had performed a number of experiments involving the application of magnetic fields to people's brains, using electromagnets buried in helmets and so on, and he had found that under certain conditions, involving very low frequencies of induced current within the brain, people with an already high degree of temporal lobe lability could be induced to have out-of-body journeys, partial amnesia, and other types of temporal lobe experiences. By the time he had finished reading Whitley Strieber's *Communion* in 1987, Persinger had developed a general theory for UFO encounters, which went something like this.

Stresses and strains along tectonic faults underground occasionally would give rise to highly localized areas of intense low-frequency electric and magnetic fields. These might ignite aerial lightforms, which then would glow and buzz and zoom around. Persons in the distance, out of range of the intense magnetic fields, would see only a strange lightform, or lightforms, their perception having been unaltered. Persons closer to the transient area, if their temporal lobes were sufficiently labile, would begin to have their perception altered according to the dictates of culture and belief, and perhaps also according to obscure neurophysiological factors; they would begin to discern structure within the lightforms – perhaps portholes or antennae. Persons even closer would see not strange lightforms but clearly structured spacecraft. They might even lapse into unconsciousness as the ambient magnetic fields caused dream-like seizures within their temporal lobes. The imagery experienced would tend to be the imagery which for cultural or idiosyncratic reasons was expected, just as Joan of Arc saw angels, and the faithful at Fatima saw the Virgin Mary, and the 1896–7 contactees saw dirigibles, or dragons, or men from Mars. And as so often happens in dreams, the imagery would also reflect physiological sensations which were occurring at the same time – perhaps those caused by the intense fields within the transient – such as tingling, burning, strange smells, strange sounds, floating, and paralysis. Physical after-effects, such as scarring or bruising or pain, might result from psychosomatic responses, perhaps mediated by the immune system, to the vividly imagined assaults.

Of course, at close proximity to the lightform, other effects would also be likely to occur; there might be ionizing X-ray and gamma radiation given off by the extremely energetic lightform; the close-encounter victim might therefore suffer afterwards from radiation sickness. Ultraviolet radiation given off by associated lightforms might also cause severe skin and retinal burns. At closer range, the energy from the lightform might be intense enough to burn the encounter-victim to death.*

Persinger was primarily interested in the neurocognitive effects, however, and here his theory became fairly detailed. The 'sense of presence' and the experience of aliens, he speculated, might result from transient, perhaps seizure-related differences in electrical activity between the left and right temporal lobes, allowing material from the right side of the brain – including subconscious, cryptomnesic material stored incidentally during a variety of sleeping and waking states – to intrude fantastically upon the left side, the command side, where the normal sense of 'self' resided. Other effects, such as sensations of floating or the perception of bright lights or the attribution of intense significance to geometric shapes such as triangles, would probably be related to specific functional areas of the temporal lobe. In a paper published in *Perceptual and Motor Skills* in 1989, Persinger dealt with *Communion* in a few swift neurological strokes:

> Whitley Strieber's fundamentally aversive sensations associated with intense smells, hypervigilance, and anal sphincter images should reflect anomalous activity within the anterior parahippocampal gyrus with special involvement of the amygdaloid complex and adjacent uncus.

---

* A number of authors, including Jenny Randles, have suggested that this theory might apply to some cases of spontaneous human combustion.

For another abductee, Persinger was able to apply his theory more directly:

> ... in one case investigated by this researcher, a 35-year-old woman reported that she was visited by creatures who surrounded her bed during the night and intermittently carried her away. She could only sense their presence because they vibrated so quickly and reflected light strangely. They were 'felt' to be small creatures with large heads and infant-like eyes.
>
> The creatures seemed obsessed with her sexual organs and tried to operate on her. Wheals and later warts were reported around the pubic area and on the left hand. Except for a mild elevation on the hypomania and F (validity) scales of the MMPI [Minnesota Multiphasic Personality Inventory], she responded as a normal, middle-aged female. The only remarkable feature was her enhanced suggestibility, an early history of sexual abuse, and a recent episode with cocaine about six months before the incident. The visitors disappeared with carbamazepine, a drug that is specific to complex partial epilepsy and hypomania. Although this treatment may not be beneficial for all such cases, it emphasizes the importance of understanding the neuropsychological mechanisms.

Well, so much for UFO abductions. As for UFO abduction researchers, Persinger noted that access to the scenarios generated and stored during UFO-encounter experiences might be difficult because they would have been stored in areas of memory not usually accessible in the normal, conscious, waking state. They might be accessible only through dreams or through the induced altered state of hypnosis, although both the dream-state and the hypnotic state, being similar to the state experienced during the close-encounter, might involve the generation of just as much imagery as – if not more imagery than – that generated during the original encounter. Which was another way of saying what a lot of other critics of abduction research had been saying: that a person's recollection of a UFO encounter could not only be facilitated by subsequent dreams and hypnosis, it could be created by them.

In fact, argued Persinger, the underlying temporal-lobe-related microseizures which brought about visitor experiences and other kinds of altered states could be triggered by any number of conditions. Malnourishment, fatigue, anxiety, fear, anger, bereavement, and other emotions could release stress hormones such as ACTH (adrenocorticotrophic hormone) which were known to have a powerful effect on the temporal lobes. Hypoxia, such as that brought about by asphyxiation or high altitudes (where mystics traditionally received their wisdom from above), could also induce transient imbalances between left and right temporal lobe activity as could sensory deprivation, ritual music or dance, psychedelic drugs, suggestion, and the most common cause of out-of-body experiences – the altered state brought about by general anaesthetics during surgery.

Other more ordinary psychological conditions could facilitate entry into the hallucinatory state, for example the 'highway hypnosis' brought about by an extended automobile journey, or the altered states between sleep and full consciousness, often experienced in bed. In fact, highway and bedroom encounters accounted for a remarkably large proportion of supernatural-type folklore.

One good example of a bedroom visitor was the Old Hag of Newfoundland and the Canadian maritime provinces. David Hufford, a folklorist at the University of Pennsylvania, had recorded the accounts of hundreds of Old Hag victims in the late 1970s. Typically, the victim would wake in the middle of the night with a sense of creeping paralysis, an eerie sense that something wasn't right. He would then see the Old Hag standing beside the bed, or perhaps lying on top of him, pinning his arms down, exhaling horribly into his face. 'You knew that I would come,' one Hag was said to have rasped to her victim.

Creeping paralysis, and the sense that something wasn't right, were primary symptoms of the onset of the temporal-lobe-related altered state. This altered state, according to Hufford's Old Hag research, seemed to occur most often when the experiencer was sleeping on his back. Hufford himself seemed to draw few conclusions from this, but to anyone seeking a physiological trigger for the Old Hag experience, or for any other such experience, it was easy to hypothesize that sleeping on one's back, perhaps by altering the pattern of blood-flow in the brain, could facilitate abnormalities in temporal lobe activity.

The Hag could also be summoned, in a susceptible individual, by mere suggestion. In one case Hufford studied, a young woman was apparently threatened with 'hagging' by a man whose attentions she had spurned. One night shortly thereafter the woman awoke with the Hag astride her, cackling haggishly. Persinger's and other researchers' data suggested that fantasy-prone individuals or those with temporal lobe instability were very susceptible to this kind of suggestion.

According to this emerging 'psychosocial' view of UFO abductions, however, many abduction experiences would be more or less spontaneous, and although the abductee would be receptive to some imagery provided by researchers and by the modern ufological lore, the basic form and sequence of her story would be relatively inelastic, having been shaped by thousands of years of cultural and neurophysiological evolution. As researchers such as Jacques Vallée had been arguing since the sixties, UFO abduction stories were similar to folkloric stories of fairies, goblins, dwarves, elves, angels, and baby-snatching demons. Going back even further, the UFO abduction – when stripped down to its essential motifs – bore a remarkable resemblance to the magical transformative journey of the shaman.

'The shaman,' according to Joseph Campbell's *Historical Atlas of World Mythology*, 'is a particular type of medicine man, whose powers both to cause illness and to heal the sick, to communicate with the world beyond, to foresee the future, and to influence both the weather and the movements of animals, are believed to be derived from his intercourse with envisioned spirits; this intercourse having been established ... by way of a severe psychological breakdown of the greatest stress and even danger to life. The extraordinary uniformity in far-separated parts of the earth of the images and stages of this "shamanic crisis" suggest that they may represent the archetypes of a psychological exaltation, related on the one hand to schizophrenia and on the other to the ecstasies of the yogis, saints, and dervishes of the high religions. Moreover, the typical way of functioning of the shaman everywhere is by passing into a state either of trance or of semitrance, and thus abstracted, performing his mysterious work.'

The word 'shaman' comes from the 'saman' of the Tungus, a tribe of Siberian hunters and herdsmen who, when they were visited by researchers in the early part of this century, represented one of the few remaining anthropological laboratories for the study of pre-agrarian society. In such societies, the shaman appears to have played a central role for thousands of years, and the instinct to become a shaman – to overcome affliction by spirits or poverty or general bad luck by reaching a valuable *modus vivendi* with the spirit world – must therefore have become deeply entrenched in the human psyche, to the extent that it continually manifested in certain individuals even after, as Campbell and others have argued, the rise of agrarian societies with their relatively complex, group-oriented religious structures signalled the end of shamanism as the primary form of religious expression.

Now of course, as was certainly evident to Campbell, agrarian culture is almost everywhere being eclipsed by industrial and post-industrial culture, in which social complexity has spawned not communalism, but an extraordinary individualism. The highly ritualized religions mediated by highly organized priesthoods now seem to be giving way to much more individualistic, idiosyncratic modes of religious life – in which gurus, mystics, prophets, mediums, channellers, dowsers, healers, fortune-tellers, self-help psychoanalysts, and similar shamanic figures again play a central role.

Among the old-style cultures, new shamans were selected in a number of ways: for example, if their father or grandfather had been a shaman; or if they spontaneously manifested the symptoms of a shamanic possession and trance, usually at a fairly young age. In some cultures, epileptics and others who suffered frequent convulsions or seizures or hallucinatory episodes as children were marked for a life of otherworldly intercourse; in fact, for these individuals shamanism (which might now be diagnosed as schizophrenia or perhaps multiple personality disorder) could be interpreted as an adaptive, socially tailored form of mental instability. In other cultures, the tendency to drift abstractedly into song was the sure sign of the shamanic call. In still other cultures, including many American Indian tribes, a visionary experience was encouraged in all young males by fasting and perhaps a brief but stressful exile alone in the wilderness.

The shamanic journey was a trip out of the body and into the world of spirits. The spirits could be represented as wolves, or deer, or human ancestors, or giants, or lovely women, or as virtually any type of creature, but in general they took the young shaman from wherever he was – the wilderness, the ceremonial lodge, his bed – to an otherworldly place and gave him otherworldly wisdom, after which he was returned to his earthly body, exhausted but wiser. His initial experience – his initiation into the mysteries of shamanism – would involve the most stress, but also the most imparted wisdom. In many cases, the process of imparting wisdom was physical and extremely painful, involving the dismemberment and re-assembly of the shaman's body – after which he would have new and mysterious skills. Joseph Campbell gives an example of shamanic initiation which recalls the bloody procedures undergone by abductees, the scars they bear afterwards as a sign of their experiences, and the mysterious alien practice of placing implants within abductees' bodies.

> Spencer and Gillen have reported that in Australia, among the Aranda, those transformed into medicine men are supposed to have had magic crystals introduced into their bodies either by spirits of the Dream Time or by other medicine men. There is a cave near Alice Springs that is supposed to be occupied by such spirits, and when a man feels that he is capable of enduring their transformation, he goes alone to its entrance and lies down there to sleep. At break of day one of the spirits, coming to the mouth of the cave and finding him there, hurls at him an invisible lance that strikes and penetrates his neck from behind, goes through his tongue, and leaves there an actual hole large enough to admit the little finger. A second lance goes through his head from ear to ear and, falling dead, he is carried deep into the cave, which is supposed to run to a spot beneath the Edith Range some ten miles distant. There the spirit removes his internal organs and implants an entirely

new set, along with a supply of magical stones, after which the man returns to life, but in a condition of insanity. He is led back to his village by the spirit, who is invisible to all but the most gifted medicine men and to dogs, and after a certain number of days, the man paints himself in a certain way, and the state of insanity ends. For a year, he does not practise but consults with other medicine men and acquires from them their secrets, 'which consist', state Spencer and Gillen, 'principally in the ability to hide about his person and to produce at will small quartz pebbles or bits of stick; and, of hardly less importance than this sleight of hand, the power of looking preternaturally solemn as if he were the possessor of knowledge quite hidden from ordinary men'. If during this period the hole in the tongue closes, his virtues have departed and he will not practise. Otherwise, so long as the stones remain inside him, he is able to project them, either to heal or to injure. How the hole in the tongue is really made, Spencer and Gillen remark, it is impossible to say, but it is always present in the genuine medicine man.

The author Holger Kalweit, in his book *Dreamtime and Inner Space*, provides a similar example of the shaman's torturous journey, this time from the lore of the Siberian Buryat tribes:

Among the Buryat the shamanic apprentice is visited by the Utcha, his shamanic ancestors. They take his soul to heaven and place it before the assembly of the Saatjani, who torment him in a horrible fashion, poking around his belly with knives, cutting whole chunks of flesh off him, and throwing them about. During these tortures the shaman can hear his heart beat, but his breath subsides and his skin becomes dark blue. The spirits cook his flesh to 'ripen' it. The initiate acquires his inner knowledge during this procedure and thus becomes conversant with the rules of shamanic wisdom.

And then, of course, there were the caves. The caves, leading labyrinthically deep within the earth, featured in the origin myths and the shamanic lore of numerous palaeolithic-type societies. This wasn't especially surprising, since archaeological evidence, including dozens of cave paintings, suggested that many palaeolithic societies had spent the last ice age – which ended about 12,000 to 15,000 years ago – housed within caves. During the day, it seems, the men would venture forth to hunt woolly mammoths and fend off sabre-tooth tigers and so on, and the women would tend the children and perhaps uproot a few semi-edible tubers or berries, and at night everyone would retire to the caves, and the women would cook and the men would sit around talking and . . . some of them would descend deep within the caves, thousands of feet down, and would beat their drums and begin to shamanize. Now, some of the great anthropologists of recent years, and especially myth and religion specialists such as Joseph Campbell, had an ongoing dispute with sociobiologists and others who argued that primitive human society could be described reasonably well in terms of biological economics, with evolutionary fitness the primary unit of currency. In the stereotyped sociobiological view, a certain amount of energy would be expended on hunting, a certain amount on gathering, a certain amount on mate selection and reproduction and child-rearing and so on, all of it determined by the laws of neo-Darwinism and the selfish gene. But how, wondered Campbell, could the sociobiologists explain, in terms of biological economics, why a grown man – who might otherwise have been hunting, or sleeping, or impregnating a female, or raiding a neighbouring cave – would haul himself several strenuous thousands of feet beneath the earth for the purpose of beating a drum and going into a trance, and along the way perhaps sacrificing a few animals and eating some foul-tasting mushrooms and painting a few hallucinatory tableaux on the wall? Why did he feel the need to do those things, and why in a dank blackness half a mile inside the earth?

For Campbell, the answer was obvious. The caves were a metaphorical, sense-depriving path to the wondrous depths of the human unconscious – depths which existed across space and time and culture. 'Whatever the inward darkness may have been to which the shamans of those caves descended in their trances, the same must be within ourselves, nightly visited in sleep. Moreover, in parts of the world marginal to contemporary civilization, the beat of the shaman's drum may still be heard, transporting spirits in flight to regions known to our own visionaries and to men and women gone mad.' Reading that passage, especially the last part, one can't help but think that somewhere in his literary odyssey through myths and rites and arts and dreams, Joseph Campbell had encountered Richard Shaver.

In some primitive societies, shamans were more or less uniformly benevolent towards other members of their tribe, and worked together peacefully with other shamans; in other societies, shamans murdered and plundered without compunction, and engaged in constant, malicious rivalries with those who shared their vocation. Similarly, in some shamanic traditions the spirits of the otherworld were generous and kind, while in other traditions the spirits were bloodthirsty mutilators, intent on imparting more pain than gain.

The same spread of attributes characterized the abduction lore. Oprah's caller from San Antonio, the one who had met the angel in the airport parking lot, had apparently experienced no horror whatsoever. She had experienced only pleasure and consciousness-raising. Budd Hopkins's abductees, on the other hand, seemed to experience no enlightenment and no pleasure; they seemed to receive only terror and trauma from the aliens.

In fact, by the late 1980s it was becoming clear that most abduction stories included measures of both trauma and enlightenment, with perhaps a greater emphasis on the latter. The abductees in the orbit of the Wyoming psychologist Leo Sprinkle, who had been doing abduction research longer than anyone else,* seemed more or less consistently to come up with stories involving a small amount of stress and pain, and a large measure of environmental and spiritual consciousness-raising. The Hopkins camp liked to explain Sprinkle's results by reference to his own New Age beliefs. Sprinkle, who felt that he himself might be an abductee, argued that the aliens were guiding humanity gently through a programme of spiritual and technological enlightenment. Hopkins and his colleagues

---

* Sprinkle had worked briefly with the Condon Report team, hypnotically regressing Nebraska highway patrolman Herb Schirmer after his close-encounter in 1967, in order, as the Report put it, to assess the value of hypnotic regression in retrieving hidden memories. Unlike Sprinkle, the Condon group concluded that hypnosis had been useless in this case.

generally disparaged the enlightenment experience as alien deception or as abductees' wishful thinking. But even David Jacobs, especially in his early cases, had seen examples of the enlightenment motif, and of course Strieber's story, along with several of his earlier works, was self-consciously full of shamanic striving for enlightenment and apotheosis. Among researchers more receptive to progressive, New Age themes in the abduction accounts, it was said that Budd Hopkins was suppressing evidence for the positive nature of the aliens' programme.

Phil Klass, surveying both sides of the argument, advised prospective abductees that if they felt they really must see a ufologist, they should go to Sprinkle rather than Hopkins, because with Sprinkle, at least, the experience would be less painful.

One question remained for the psychosocialists, however, and that was the question of imagery. Where did the actual abduction scenes come from? What was the source of the images which seemed to emerge again and again, under hypnosis or by conscious recollection?

Most psychosocialists seemed to venture, at least tentatively, that the basic themes of the abduction story came from deep within the mind, i.e. from the neurological library of ancient motifs shared by all humans and expressed in dreams, hallucinations, shamanistic journeys and similar phenomena. These themes were then dressed in more contemporary and idiosyncratic imagery which had come from movies, television, books, childhood experiences, fantasies, and overheard conversations – especially anything having to do with the ufological lore.

The only problem was that, at least according to Hopkins and Jacobs and other nuts-and-boltsers, abduction images sometimes matched at the smallest level of detail – the gassy whiteness of the spaceship's atmosphere, the vagueness of its exits and entrances, the strange symbols on the wall by the examination table, the greasy sheen on the bulbous forehead of the little grey as he wielded the speculum ... How was it that these details could match, not only for individuals who had been abducted at the same time, but for those whose abductions had occurred years and miles apart? Of course, in some cases, the answer was that even these minor details had been previously published. BUFORA researchers in 1988 investigated a case in which a woman claimed that she had been floated from her bed to a field nearby and thence into a spaceship that smelled of cinnamon, where leathery-skinned aliens had done the usual gynaecological examination and had inserted a tube into her arm, which still had little marks when she showed it to Randles two days later. The cinnamon smell and the leathery skin of the aliens were very precise recollections, but on the very night that the woman had experienced her abduction, British TV had broadcast an episode of the American soap opera *Dynasty* depicting the abduction of one of its characters by leathery-skinned aliens, and her examination within a spacecraft whose interior smelled of cinnamon. The cinnamon and the leather-skin motifs, of course, had appeared earlier that year in Strieber's *Communion*.

Many of the big cases seemed susceptible to this kind of analysis. The ufologist Martin Kottmeyer, for example, noted that quite a few of the motifs found in the Hill case had appeared previously in the sci-fi lore. The 1953 film *Invaders from Mars* had featured big-nosed mongoloidish aliens who abduct a woman, bring her into their ship, place her on an examination table, and implant a tracking device into her neck with a large needle. In *Killers from Space*, released in 1954, an injured air force pilot is abducted and taken to an underground alien base, where bug-eyed aliens heal him and then hypnotize him, giving him post-hypnotic suggestions to make him their unwitting agent. The 1960s television serial *The Outer Limits* had featured, in one episode, aliens who spoke through their big, wide, wraparound-type eyes; it had been broadcast less than two weeks before the hypnosis session in which Barney Hill had told Dr Simon that the aliens had wraparound eyes through which they seemed to be talking to him. Some psychosocialists noted that the standard ufological motifs had been around for decades before any of the first big cases. The French sociologist Bertrand Meheust, for example, dug up a science fiction short story, 'Hodomur, Man of Infinity', which had been published in 1934 by a man named Ege Tilms. In the story, a Mr Belans is walking through an area near Brabant, in Belgium, where wheatfield crop circles had been reported; he notices a man dressed in black waiting expectantly beneath a tree. Belans waits, too, and after a while is overcome by drowsiness; he hears a buzzing noise, sees a light, and watches a UFO land in a nearby field. Following the strange man into the spacecraft, Belans encounters a tall alien who telepathically explains to him that his race does not wish, through open contact with Earth people, to hasten human cultural evolution. Belans is returned to Earth with amnesia and a sense of missing time.

Of course, to say that abductees drew their experiences from a mixture of archetypal and cultural sources was something like saying that they were victims of contagious hysteria – of which there had been numerous and startling examples throughout history. Epidemics in which sufferers helplessly and publicly danced themselves to exhaustion swept certain southern European cities during the Middle Ages. For some reason, perhaps having to do with excess stress or hardship, women and the deeply religious seemed particularly susceptible to this kind of social suggestion, and epidemics of sexual oppression by the devil – who would sometimes have regular, violent, but addictively satisfying intercourse with his oppressees – were surprisingly common among cloistered nuns.

Such hysterias were by no means confined to unenlightened eras. In 1944, a case occurred which had similarities both to ancient hysterias and – in its themes of bedroom intrusion and paralysis – to the more modern Old Hag and abduction syndromes. In the small town of Mattoon, Illinois, a woman living alone with her two children telephoned the police one night to report that a tall, shadowy intruder had entered her bedroom and had sprayed a paralysing nerve gas in her face. The police were unable to find the culprit, but, via the local press, warned other residents to be on the look-out for this mysterious assailant. Within weeks, attacks of the 'gasser' had become common in formerly sleepy Mattoon, and had drawn the attention of the national and international media. The gasser had an uncanny ability to enter people's bedrooms without warning – one woman claimed that her dog must have been gassed, since he hadn't raised an alarm – and although local vigilante groups occasionally fired rifles and handguns at shadowy figures seen fleeing houses, no shot hit its mark. Chemists puzzled over the apparent existence of a gas which could work so quickly and specifically, without leaving traces, and local doctors were puzzled, too. Upon examining the gasser's victims, they could find nothing but the symptoms of hysteria. Eventually, the diagnosis of hysteria was applied to the whole town, and the Mattoon Gasser departed as mysteriously as he had come. The episode entered the sociology and social-psychology textbooks, with standard sociological and psychological explanations to the effect that it had all been caused by anxiety over the war.

Well, all right, retorted the nuts-and-bolts abduction researchers; suppose the abduction phenomenon were simply a case of contagious hysteria, in which certain people, for physiological or psychological reasons or whatever, experienced temporal lobe seizures and paralyses and archetypal bedroom visitations, episodes upon which the imagery of grey, gynaecologically minded aliens was superimposed, via mass culture and the ufological lore, down to the most obscure, apparently inconsequential details, by the all-absorbing right hemisphere of the brain. But if that were all there were to abductions, how could one explain the repetition, in these abduction accounts, of details which had never been published, which had never appeared in popular or ufological literature, but which nevertheless were confirmed again and again by abductees who had never met one another?

Some psychosocialists suggested that abduction researchers such as Hopkins and Jacobs might accidentally have let slip such details clearly enough that they could be incorporated, consciously or unconsciously, in a subsequent account by a different abductee. But Hopkins and Jacobs contended that they regularly buried such material in their files, retrieving it only when they found a match; it was impossible, they argued, that an abductee whose story was still under investigation would ever have access to a previous abductee's detailed descriptions of her experience.

For a small but vocal segment of the psychosocial confederation, however, such things were not impossible at all, even with the information tucked away in files: abductees, like others with right-brain types, could read minds, especially when they had been placed in the altered state of a hypnotic trance. According to this view, they obtained the crucial details of their abduction experiences simply by listening, unconsciousely of course, to the conscious or unconscious thoughts of the researchers who attended to them. In fact, to the proponents of the psi school of abduction research – 'psi' being a slang term for parapsychological phenomena such as ESP, precognition, and psychokinesis – the idea that mind-reading could be facilitated by a deep hypnotic trance was old hat. Hilary Evans liked to cite examples of this kind of thing from the early literature on hypnosis, which was then known as mesmerism or 'animal magnetism'. He particularly liked the following excerpt from a letter received in the mid nineteenth century from a Mr Gilmour by William Gregory, and printed in his *Letters to a Candid Inquirer on Animal Magnetism*:

> Following the directions of the Revd Mr Townsend, I asked one of my servants, Vera, age 18, if she was willing to be mesmerized. She had never heard of mesmerism before this, but consented. After my first successful trial, I mesmerized her every night. She became more and more susceptible; at last I could throw her into the mesmeric trance in 40 seconds . . . [In the winter of 1844, during a dinner party] We requested Vera to visit [clairvoyantly] the house of Mrs Palmer, one of the ladies present. This house was in Greenock, distant from my cottage about a mile and a quarter. She saw her servant in the kitchen, but said that another woman was with her. On being pressed to look earnestly at the woman, she said it was Caroline Menzies. This, Mrs Palmer declared to be true. We then asked her to see if any person was in Mrs Palmer's parlour, when she said that Miss Laing was there, a young lady from Edinburgh, who was boarding with Mrs Palmer at the time; that she was crying, and that a letter was in her hand.
>
> On the party breaking up, I walked into Greenock with the ladies and gentlemen, in order to see if she was right. It was true. Miss Laing had received a letter by that evening's post from her father in Edinburgh, stating that her mother was not expected to live.

Alvin Lawson and colleagues, who had compared false and genuine abduction stories, had also performed a side-experiment to test the psi hypothesis; Bill McCall, the psychologist who had performed hypnosis on the abduction-imagining subjects, had concentrated mentally on various abduction-type images during the hypnosis sessions, to see if any of the imagery appeared in the abduction accounts. None did, but McCall and the others noticed that the accounts seemed to contain not only abduction imagery but the very syntax of image descriptions from some standard reference sheets McCall and the others had with them during the sessions. Moreover, some of the scenarios described by the imaginary abductees bore remarkable syntactical and visual similarities (a) to obscure accounts from the ufological lore with which McCall and his colleagues were already familiar, and (b) to accounts which had been previously thought up by other imaginary abductees in the study. McCall and the others suspected that a surprising number of the fake abductees had been reading their minds – only at a less conscious level than they had anticipated.

While Hopkins and Jacobs and the nuts-and-boltsers concentrated on the similarities among the various abduction accounts, proponents of the psi school concentrated on the various manifestations of paranormal activity which, though apparently unrelated to UFOs, seemed to plague UFO abductees throughout their lives, sometimes even preceding their first abductions. Abductees seemed almost uniformly to remember incidents featuring ESP, clairvoyance, OBE-type 'astral travel', psychokinesis, poltergeist phenomena, interference with electrical equipment, and brief visual or auditory hallucinations (a demonic face, a disembodied voice) that might occasionally be perceptible by others. Such individuals would be able to experience abduction scenarios sensually indistinguishable from reality, to such an extent that they would be able to manifest marks and scars as if the scenarios had really occurred. Parapsychologists, religious historians, and even many medical researchers had long been reporting these kinds of bizarre mind-over-matter psychosomatisms. The stigmata of the saints were only the best known examples of the genre; others included the man with multiple personalities all but one of whom suffered from allergies to citrus fruit; the somnambulist army officer who manifested rope-marks on his flesh while hypnotically reliving an earlier episode when he had been tied down in bed; the man alone in the jungle, who desperately needed to feed his child and promptly began lactating; the schizophrenic whose abdomen distended dramatically, despite no change in diet, after he expressed the desire to become pregnant; the much more common cases in which women developed false pregnancies (pseudocyesis); and of course the everyday cases, familiar to dermatologists, where mere suggestion could conjure or banish a wart.

But what of shared experiences, in which two or more persons had seen or heard or felt or smelled or tasted something which, according to the psychosocialists, wasn't really there? Actually, this kind of thing was covered, to a certain extent, by orthodox notions of hysteria and *folie à deux*, which referred to the occasional dominance of one fertile imagination, or social suggestion, over subservient and suggestible minds. And even where orthodoxy left off, the psi school were happy to leap in. The literature on demonology, ghosts, and sorcery was full of examples where different people had experienced the same imagery, despite that imagery being non-photogenic. The mechanism was unknown but it seemed clear, from anecdotal evidence as well as from parapsychological 'remote-viewing' experiments, that two persons with sufficient empathy and/or psychic ability could communicate information to one another through unconscious telepathy, perhaps involving the same dominant-subordinate principle as that involved in mass hysteria. In cases where two or more people 'experienced' a close-encounter, telepathic transmission of imagery might be facilitated by the altered-state inducing factors which had triggered the encounter in the first place. Some of the psi school people even wondered whether an ethereal entity conjured up by one person's mind could actually *physically affect* someone else, as in that fabulous science-fiction movie from the 1950s, *Forbidden Planet*, where the gigantic subterranean computer on Altair IV could transform the secret thoughts of Walter Pidgeon's id into an invisible monster that tore people apart.

According to the psi school, UFO abductees were people whose electromagnetic or crisis-induced or spontaneous altered-state experiences had been made to conform to the abduction lore by archetypal or cultural imagery, and by abduction researchers, harbouring their own stereotyped imagery, who remained blithely ignorant of the damage they were inflicting on their subjects' pliant minds. At the same time, of course, those minds, being eager to please, or perhaps being simply perverse, would invent evidence to confirm every hypothesis the abduction researcher put forward, even those which had barely formed in the researcher's mind. With its inbuilt circularity – its 'positive feedback', to use an electronics term – the abductee-investigator relationship would be like a machine gone out of control, feeding on itself, spinning faster and faster, spiralling endlessly away from reality.

Old John Keel had seen all of this before. He had been a newspaper columnist, radio personality, and magazine feature writer back in the fifties and sixties, respected as a mainstream journalist but something of a cult figure among fans of weird phenomena. In the 1950s, he had travelled around Egypt and India and the Far East, chasing mummies and levitating yogis and Indian rope tricks and Hindu monsters and various other oriental manifestations of the paranormal, and writing it all up in a book called *Jadoo*. He had burst on to the ufological scene in the mid 1960s with a series of articles in *Flying Saucer Review*, the thesis of which was that flying saucers were not nuts-and-bolts spacecraft from other planets, but belonged instead to the same mystical, quasi-physical, and probably ineffable realm as ghosts and vampires and demons and angels and so on. One of the things that had helped to solidify Keel's views on the matter was a wave of strange events along a certain stretch of the Ohio River, between the autumn of 1966 and the autumn of 1967. The events, as reported anyway, included UFO sightings, power failures, alien encounters and abductions, harassment of UFO witnesses by strange, almost-human impostors, and – perhaps most sensationally – appearances of a terrifying winged humanoid which subsequently became known as the Mothman.

The Mothman, according to Keel's researches, seemed to have antecedents in mythology, folklore, and even relatively modern newspaper reports. Hindu deities like Krishna and Vishnu flew around on the back of a giant bird called a Garuda, whose counterpart in certain North American Indian mythologies was the Thunderbird. Mexican mythology included winged men-beasts called *ikals*, who lived in caves and occasionally ventured out to kidnap humans. A bat-winged man-beast was occasionally seen disporting in the air over Coney Island, New York during 1877–80; the *New York Times* of 12 September 1880 reported that 'many reputable persons' had seen him pass overhead at an altitude of about 1,000 feet, apparently headed for New Jersey. There were sightings of winged man-beasts, or just unusual winged beasts, reported in California in 1905, in Siberia in 1908, in California again in 1946, throughout the United States in 1948,* in Texas in 1953, in Florida and New York and West Virginia in 1961, and of course in the event in Kent, England, in 1963, when a bat-man had been seen near a UFO.

The 1966–7 Mothman sightings had begun in the Ohio River valley in the same area as the sightings of 1961, around the West Virginia town of Point Pleasant (a couple of hours downstream from Wheeling, where Budd Hopkins grew up). One night at a deserted high-explosives manufacturing facility outside town, a place where young people liked to park at night, two teenage couples were driving around in a 1957 Chevy looking for friends when they saw two large red eyes reflecting their car headlights. The eyes belonged to a tall, bat-winged humanoid which unfolded its wings, rose into the air, and easily kept pace with the terrified teenagers as they sped from the area. The creature's wings seemed to be more for show than for locomotion, since it moved without flapping them. It also seemed to screech at them, loud enough to be heard over the roar of the Chevy's engine. Eventually the thing abandoned the chase, and the teenagers made it to the local police station. They persuaded one of the local sheriff's deputies to come out with them to see the thing, and since he knew them and their families, and believed that they must have seen something, he followed them back to the area in a patrol car. He noticed nothing unusual, but then he switched on his radio and

---

* In May of that year, two laundry workers reported seeing three 'birdmen' circling over Longview, Washington. One of the laundry workers, a Mrs Viola Johnson, told reporters: 'They wore dark, drab, flying suits. I couldn't make out their arms but I could see their legs dangling down and they kept moving their heads like they were looking around. I couldn't tell if they had goggles on but their heads looked like they had helmets on.' Hang-gliders, of course, would not be developed for some decades.

heard a tremendous electronic wail, drowning out the voice of his dispatcher.

Sightings of the Mothman continued in the area, and at night the old explosives manufacturing facility would be crowded with curious locals, Forteans, vigilantes, and reporters. But soon the focus of the town's attention began to shift towards UFOs. They were appearing almost every night, flying with their garishly bright coloured lights along the river and buzzing the gawkers parked along the banks. John Keel would often drive up to a secluded hilltop with Mary Hyre, a local newspaper reporter, and on a given night they might see dozens of strange lights flying around in the sky, in a manner very reminiscent of the old 1896–7 airship reports. The lights would bob up and down as if attached to the body of a huge bird, and Keel often noticed that the lights seemed to be attached to large dark masses. When Keel would flash a powerful flashlight at them, they would seem to signal back. And like the old airships, the objects would occasionally shine down searchlight-type beams; people caught in the beams tended to develop mysterious sunburns and cases of conjunctivitis, as if they had been blasted with ultraviolet radiation.

All kinds of other light phenomena occurred, such as the strange purple aurora Keel and Hyre saw lighting up a nearby forest one night; but the main attractions were the UFO-type lights in the sky. Wherever they landed, or briefly alighted, strange things would happen. Television sets would blow. Radios would blare static. Animals would be found dead, with strange mutilations or highly localized charring. Circles of charred earth or ground vegetation would also be found. People would develop severe headaches, and inexplicable amnesias with a sense of missing time. They would have odd dreams involving giant eyes floating over their house. They would wake up in the night hearing voices on the radio, when all nearby radios were turned off. They would see strange people outside, although no footprints would be found later. They would have the urge to prophesy, and messages concerning future events would come to them as if out of the blue – messages which sometimes bore remarkable similarities to messages which had been published, obscurely, by contactee-types hundreds of years before. They would hear strange beeping noises, like the ones Betty and

Barney Hill – whose 1961 experiences had just been published – had heard. Their telephones would ring strangely, and on the other end would be only the beeping noises, or strange voices speaking rapidly in a language that might have been Spanish. Locked doors would open themselves spontaneously. Very odd men would arrive on their doorsteps asking questions about UFOs and ufologists. These men tended to have high cheekbones, pointed chins, oriental eyes, and olive or deeply tanned complexions. Their fingers were too long. They would be dressed strangely, in archaic fashions or in black suits* or in clothes that would not come into style until years later. They walked oddly, as if unused to it. They were conversationally inept, and seemed to take an inordinate interest in ordinary everyday objects, like table knives and forks, as if they couldn't understand what they were. Like the fairies in Celtic mythology, they liked to collect trivial objects from people, pens or old magazines or whatever. They drove around in black Cadillacs whose licence plate numbers, as reported by witnesses, didn't exist on police records. Sometimes they arrived in nondescript panel trucks, or in cars that, despite being ten or twenty years old, seemed to be in mint condition inside and out.

People in the area began to report contacts with other strange entities. A man named Woodrow Derenberger, who lived about fifty miles upriver from Point Pleasant, claimed that while he had been driving one evening on Interstate 77, his truck had been forced off the road by a strange bulging object that had then disgorged a six-foot tall grinning humanoid. The humanoid had dark hair combed straight back. He wore a dark topcoat and walked with his arms crossed, his hands tucked under his armpits – presumably so Derenberger wouldn't see his unusually long fingers. Under the topcoat, Derenberger saw what looked like a green metallic suit. The humanoid told Derenberger telepathically not to be afraid. His name, he said, was Cold. His little ship rose above the interstate highway about forty or fifty feet to let the traffic go past, and as it

---

* Harassment of researchers by apparent humans dressed uniformly in black suits had been a feature of ufology since the 1950s, and the term 'Men in Black' (MIBs for short) had come to refer to anyone strange or impostor-like who visited or otherwise made themselves known to ufologists.

did Cold chatted telepathically with Derenberger, asking where he lived and so on, and reassuring Derenberger that he meant no harm. Eventually, the ship came down and Cold flew off. Derenberger went home in a distraught state, and his wife persuaded him to call the police. The police took his story seriously, and after it was broadcast over the local and national news, several witnesses came forward to say that on the night of the apparent encounter they had seen a truck like Derenberger's sitting on the side of Interstate 77, its driver apparently engrossed in conversation with a man in a dark topcoat. In Point Pleasant, a man told Mary Hyre that he and a companion had had a virtually identical experience on the same stretch of Interstate 77, and on the same night. Derenberger began to have frequent visits from Cold, and also strange telephone calls, and beeps, and voices, and poltergeists, and Men in Black, and of course dozens of visits and calls from mundane reporters and cranks.

As the months went by, Keel got to know many people who fitted this general pattern, in the Point Pleasant area and elsewhere around the country. Anticipating Budd Hopkins by nearly a decade, he hypothesized that for every contactee* who was willing to talk to ufologists or the press, there were thousands who kept silent. It was not difficult to understand why they would want to keep silent. A Long Island radio journalist named Jaye Paro told Keel that she had been walking near her house one evening when a black Cadillac pulled up beside her. A well-dressed man in the back asked her to get in. He said he was a friend of a friend. She got in, and was quickly mesmerized by a series of lights on the dashboard panel. The interior of the Cadillac had an antiseptic smell. The Cadillac drove along back roads and finally ended up in a secluded area where a man with a doctor's bag got into the Cadillac and waved an object under Jaye's nose, causing her to lose her will. The men asked her a series of questions the purpose of which she couldn't fathom, and then they took her home.

Keel wasn't sure what to make of it all. Could these well-dressed un-men perhaps be real people, perhaps part of some secret

---

* Keel made no distinction between contactees and abductees, and at one stage in the 1960s promoted the general term 'UFO percipients'.

organization? There was ample reason to think so. At one point Point Pleasant had been crawling with crewcut FBI types, and UFO witnesses were always reporting strange inquiries from military officials. The government obviously took an interest in the area's strange goings-on. Also, on several occasions the un-men had been seen by multiple witnesses, either up close, or on roadsides, fooling around with telephone wires. They had walked into Mary Hyre's office dozens of times, in full view of the other newspaper staff.

But eventually Keel seemed to decide that the un-men – at least the ones who fitted the usual pattern* – were from some other level of existence. His theory went something like this: the lights in the sky and the Mothmen and the un-men were simply forms of energy which had been shaped to fit human perception. They were like the *tulpas* – 'thought-forms' – which witches and shamans and mediums always seemed to be conjuring up in their seances, except that they had been shaped not by humans but by some external intelligence. This external intelligence could manifest itself in other ways, too. One night Keel was walking around the old high-explosives facility near Point Pleasant when he was suddenly gripped by terror. He continued to walk and noticed that the terror stopped abruptly at a certain point. He retraced his steps and the terror began again. Almost anticipating Persinger, he attributed the transient 'zone of fear' to 'a beam of ultrasonic waves'. He also decided that the light phenomena and the Mothmen and the un-men were somehow related to the electromagnetic spectrum, only a part of the spectrum which humans could not normally experience, and that somehow these strange phenomena could trigger, in certain susceptible people, extraordinary experiences involving neurological changes and psychic side-effects which could lead anywhere from insanity to shamanic glory.

For Keel, the Parker–Hickson case in Pascagoula in 1973 was typical. The two men had been fishing when a strange flickering lightform had come along the river. Hickson, who apparently had long been something of a psychic – he had reported episodes of

---

* One reported harasser, with incongruously Nabokovian overtones, was a man who wore a fright wig and drove a red Ford Galaxy. Keel later speculated that he might have been a member of an occult group which somehow fed off the local UFO hysteria.

clairvoyance, and had claimed that watches would stop working properly once placed around his wrist – had seen a spaceship with lobster-claw aliens. Parker, being less gifted neurologically, had merely passed out, and later had spent a great deal of time being treated for mental illness. Parker had taken the road towards insanity, Hickson towards shamanic glory.

Yet even those taking the shamanic path would often be a bit deranged. Their triggering encounter would open up a Pandora's box of uncontrollable and traumatic experiences, from strange wounds to weird apocalyptic prophecies to strictures regarding dietary changes to harassments by the various agents – un-men, poltergeists, Mothmen, aliens – of the phenomenon-controlling intelligence.

One of the most unnerving things, as far as Keel was concerned, was that once he got close to the contactees, they – or their controlling intelligence – would begin to read his mind and play games with him. The un-men would turn up at houses where he had been, and would begin to ask odd questions about him, or would plant false stories about him. Sometimes, according to Keel, they would telephone houses or hotels where he was *about* to visit, even if he had chosen the place at random, on the spur of the moment. They would telephone Keel's friends and tell ridiculous stories, all the while perfectly mimicking his voice. His mail would disappear, or would be inexplicably diverted to distant cities. At home, his phone would ring oddly, and upon picking it up he would hear the strange beeping noise, or speeded-up Spanish gibberish. Sometimes the same thing would happen to UFO witnesses as soon as Keel set foot in their houses. Telephone conversations between Keel and other investigators or contactees would be interrupted by strange static or gibberish whenever he ventured on to certain topics – such as the Pope. Sometimes Keel would get a call from a contactee and she would say that one of the aliens or un-men wanted to speak to him, and the alien or the un-man would come on the line and Keel would ask it obscure questions such as where had his mother's father been born, or where had he misplaced a stopwatch, and effortlessly the entity would come up with the right answer.

But all of that paled in comparison with another game the

intelligence played. Something would happen to the contactees which would lead Keel to develop some new theory about the phenomenon – say, that it had connections with the vampire lore. No sooner would he set the thought down in his notebook or wherever than he would get a report of a spaceship chasing a Red Cross bloodmobile. It was frighteningly bizarre ... On one occasion, Keel noticed that two of his female contactees had both been born on 6 September. Suddenly he was deluged with female contactees who claimed to have been born on 6 September. Another time, he began to toy with the idea that the aliens were reptilian; almost immediately he received a report from a contactee who told him that one of the aliens had come into her house and had gone into the refrigerator and had begun to suck the contents of eggs, as if the alien were some kind of snake.

Yet another time, Keel's contactees all phoned him, one after the other, with variations on the theme of having been taken to a big red glass hospital where, together with long lines of other humans, they had been waited on by alien doctors. The alien doctors had impregnated them, as the contactees' mothers had been impregnated by alien doctors a generation before. The aliens were developing a hybrid race. Several contactees reported that, subsequently, they had mysteriously become pregnant. Keel decided that this alien impregnation theme, which he knew had ample precedents in the fairy lore, the demonological lore, and even the Bible, was just another game. And abruptly the game ended. The contactees became un-pregnant, and diverting new themes appeared in their accounts.

As time went on and the contactees or their controlling intelligences tapped deeper into Keel's mind, he would only have to think momentarily of some new idea about the contactee experience, and his phone would ring with some confirmatory information from one of the contactees. The contactees were always trying to convince him, in accordance with his hypotheses of the moment, that their experiences were the result of some real, outside force. They would send him physical evidence; one contactee, a Long Island woman named Jane, claimed to have received a metal disc from one of her alien contacts, an entity named Lia. Jane sent the disc to Keel, and miraculously – for these things usually seemed to disappear in the mail – Keel received it. It looked to him like one of those cheap discs people used for noting inoculation records on dog collars. Unimpressed, he sent it back to Jane, and when she received it, she said, it was bent, charred black, and smelled like rotten eggs. Another time, Jane presented Keel with a pill. She said that Apol had given it to her. Keel had it analysed, and it turned out to be a sulfa drug pill, commonly prescribed to women for urinary infections.

The aliens seemed to go to extraordinary lengths to draw the attentions of investigators to their contactees. One night, Jane said, she awoke to find that all the gas jets on her kitchen oven had been turned on, and that the house was filling with fumes. The same night another contactee reported the same experience. An elderly contactee on Long Island reported that strange fires had been started on his farm. Several contactees, like the participants in the New England witchcraft hysteria three centuries before, were asked by their alien entities to sign contracts giving the aliens their souls; Keel was pressed into service to argue the entities out of this idea.

Keel, an amateur hypnotist, sometimes tried to hypnotize contactees in order to figure out what had happened to them during their frequent episodes of alien contact or missing time. One time he went to see Jane, and putting her into a trance, began to ask her about Apol. Jane answered a few questions and then Apol seized control of Jane and began to talk about Marilyn Monroe and Robert Kennedy. He said that Kennedy was in grave danger. He made some specific predictions about impending plane crashes, too. Keel asked Apol where he was speaking from, and Apol replied that he was calling from his Cadillac, parked nearby. All the while, Jane's phone was ringing. Keel would answer it but the line would always be dead. Eventually he regained control of Jane and brought her out of the trance. According to Keel, the plane crashes soon occurred, just as Apol had said they would.

Other predictions Keel received from contactees had to do with the deaths of famous journalists, or of Martin Luther King,* or of

* Keel says that at one point he was warned that King would be shot in the throat on a certain date. He says he tried to warn King, but unsuccessfully – although nothing happened, until several months later, in April 1968, when King *was* killed by a bullet to the throat.

the Pope, or of dozens of people in some horrific but unspecified disaster along the Ohio River. Some contactees were sure that the world was going to end, and that the chosen few would first be taken to UFO bases in underground caves, and thence to orbiting spaceships. At one point, word went around among the contactees that Keel himself had been killed, in a cave, the victim of a mine collapse. Then, towards the autumn of 1967, the contactees began to speak of a tremendous electromagnetic shut-down, as in *The Day the Earth Stood Still*, which would shortly affect the entire world. It would happen on 15 December at the moment President Johnson performed the annual ceremony of switching on the White House Christmas tree lights. They were sure of it.

On 15 December 1967, Keel and several friends sat at his New York apartment watching television. Keel had his candles and flashlights ready. He wasn't even sheepish about it. He was sure that the big blackout was about to occur. Shortly before 6 p.m., President Johnson delivered a brief speech and then threw the switch lighting up the Christmas tree. The lights came on and there was no blackout. Then the news anchor interrupted to announce that there had been a disaster on the Ohio River. A bridge laden with rush-hour traffic had collapsed, killing dozens. The bridge was, of course, at Point Pleasant.

Keel eventually decided, although he shied away from overtly religious language, that contactees were possessed by some exogenous intelligent entity. This entity could make the contactee go into a trance in which (a) he would think that he had been visited by aliens, but (b) he would really have gone off on odd journeys, to do various bizarre errands on behalf of the controlling intelligence. As Keel would put it in his book, *The Mothman Prophecies*:

> . . . his body proceeds on to, say, Point A where he picks up a letter or object left there by another contactee. He carries the letter or object to Point B and deposits it. Later he has no memory of these actions. Meanwhile some poor slob with the wrong aura, like myself, receives a phone call advising him to proceed to Point B where he will find something left for him by the space people. In short, all physical evidence and

manifestations are produced by human beings. They dig holes in fields, rifle mailboxes, and who knows what else.

Actually, Keel suspected that he knew what else. The contactees possessed by this outside entity, he believed, would hear voices telling them to commit crimes. Political assassins would almost always fall into this category. So, apparently, would milder voice-hearing criminals such as Richard Shaver.

As for the controlling intelligence, the fact that it was constantly playing tricks and laying traps, manipulating people into believing that they knew the future and then duping them with some false or misleading prophecy – causing them to do pointlessly silly things like camping out on mountaintops waiting for global power failures or other forms of apocalypse – convinced Keel that it was either malevolent, or insane. Or both.

8

Blue Beams, Blue Meanies

When pressed, Budd Hopkins and David Jacobs and the other nuts-and-bolts ufologists were usually willing to concede a few points in the psychosocialists' favour. Alien abduction accounts did have some motifs in common with Mothman encounters and Old Hag stories and shamanic journeys and OBEs and other strange tales from the paranormal. And perhaps some people who claimed to be abductees were not actually abductees but were rather the victims of some kind of hysterical contagion – something that counselling and carbamazepine might cure. And perhaps some researchers questioned their hypnotized subjects in ways that encouraged confabulation.

Nevertheless, Hopkins and Jacobs and the others felt that the abduction phenomenon was solid and real at its core. Folklorist Eddie Bullard's data, after all, had already demonstrated that abduction accounts tended not to vary much with the competence of the hypnotist; therefore, it seemed, the practice of hypnosis was not at fault. Moreover, the postulation of a largely subclinical continuum of 'temporal lobe lability' to explain odd experiences such as abductions was largely based on reports of such experiences by clinically normal people; Persinger and other such researchers did not *know* that such experiences always stemmed from temporal lobe lability. In fact, reports of such experiences might alternatively be seen as evidence for how widespread the abduction phenomenon had become.

And finally, when one got right down to it, the similarities between abduction accounts and other folklore-type stories were really only superficial. Eddie Bullard had shown in his FUFOR study that the abduction lore, despite variations here and there, seemed to have its own repeating patterns, its own internal logic.

Trying to link abduction stories to fairy tales and the shamanic lore, on the basis of a few superficial similarities, was for Hopkins an example of 'stewpot thinking'. The psychosocialists, according to Hopkins, were just throwing everything into the theoretical stewpot, mixing it all together, making stew instead of good science. Good scientists didn't make judgements about a phenomenon on the basis of superficial similarities it might have to other phenomena. They investigated the phenomenon itself, and listened to what it was telling them. They let Nature speak.

However, despite Hopkins's opposition to comparisons and parallel-drawing, he couldn't resist citing the connections, as far as societal resistance was concerned, between the alien abduction syndrome and another syndrome which was now accepted as being relatively widespread: childhood sexual abuse. Back in the nineteenth century, when Sigmund Freud had been exploring the childhood memories of neurotic Viennese, he had been surprised to discover that a high percentage of his patients reported memories, under hypnosis or other forms of questioning, of events which seemed to indicate some kind of sexual abuse by a parent or other adult figure. Freud eventually decided that if his patients were telling the truth, then child abuse was epidemic in good, staid, civilized Vienna. Which suggested that his patients couldn't be telling the truth. Which suggested that the sexual imagery had another meaning. Which led Freud to postulate the Oedipus Complex and a sex-drenched general theory of psychological development and psychoanalysis – which then went on to fertilize the minds of psychologists until late in the following century. By the eighties, of course, it seemed obvious not only to psychologists but to anyone who read the newspapers that childhood sexual abuse *was* epidemic, and probably had been back in Freud's day. Thanks to Freud's obtuseness, it had taken humanity an extra hundred years to recognize this. And thanks to the obtuseness of the Klasses and the psychosocialists, the alien abduction phenomenon might go unrecognized for a similar period – only in this particular controversy, involving an abusive interaction between planetary cultures rather than intraplanetary age-groups, the stakes were potentially much higher.

What Hopkins couldn't get over was that the psychosocialists would dismiss even the physical evidence of alien abductions: the scars which seemed to turn up all over abductees' bodies. The idea that they were merely the result of some kind of psychosomatic stigmata-type process seemed to him to be utterly far-fetched. Stigmata happened to people who were obviously and profoundly obsessed. But abductees weren't like that. They didn't like the continual hassle of being abducted and biopsied and impregnated or whatever. If they were obsessed by anything, it was the hope of living a normal life again. Sometimes they wouldn't even notice their scars until a researcher pointed them out to them. Sometimes similar scars would turn up on their children, even their infant children who could not possibly have been capable of creating psychosomatic injuries.

And then of course there were the multiple abductions, such as the Hill case, or the Kent, Connecticut case, or even the Aveley case. If you put these people on the witness stand in a courtroom, for any other matter, their testimony would collectively convince a jury. Why try to debunk them with explanations which depended on telepathic mass-hallucination, or *Forbidden Planet* id-monsters – mechanisms which were just as exotic and outrageous as those they were meant to defend against?

All of this added up to a conviction that the simplest explanation was the best one: something real and physical and alien was happening to abductees. But even so, Hopkins and the others would have liked to see some alien artefacts, or perhaps photographic evidence that nuts-and-bolts spacecraft were zooming into abductees' backyards in the dead of night. They couldn't help but acknowledge that the continual absence of such evidence, even as the number of abduction accounts recorded by ufologists climbed into the thousands in the late 1980s, was bothersome. If the aliens were so clever at hiding their work, why were abductees able to remember anything at all? Surely, with so many alien spacecraft swooping about crowded residential areas, someone, somewhere, on some lucky night, would be able to photograph something . . .

November 11, 1987. On the bestseller shelves across America, black-eyed aliens still stared out from the jacket covers of Strieber's *Communion* and Hopkins's *Intruders*, but the abduction mania which had gripped the nation had begun to wane. Hopkins and Strieber no longer made regular talk-show appearances. The American collective consciousness had turned to the approaching presidential primaries, the booming stock market, the looming deficit, perestroika, the Iran-Contra scandal ... And yet, in the sleepy suburban groves of Gulf Breeze, on the Florida panhandle near Pensacola, a building contractor named Ed Walters was about to grab hold of the *Zeitgeist* for ufology once again.

According to Walters, it was about five o'clock in the afternoon on 11 November – Veterans Day in the US – when his odyssey began. The sun was setting in the south-west beneath a scattered cloud cover, and Walters was sitting in his office at the front of his house. His teenage son Dan was watching the wide-screen television in another room, his twelve-year-old daughter Laura was over at a friend's house, and his wife, Frances, had just gone out to the store for something. As darkness fell Walters looked out of the window to the west and noticed a peculiar bluish-grey light peeking through the branches of a pine tree in the front yard. The light seemed to be coming from a large object gliding slowly over the houses across the street. The odd thing was, it wasn't making any noise. Walters went to the front door of the house and looked out. The bright object was still there. It was very strange. It wasn't a helicopter, or one of the jets from the nearby naval air station. It almost looked like ... yes ... it had to be ... It was an honest-to-god *spaceship* – almost as if it had flown off the set of a Spielberg movie.

Better call the police, thought Walters. But before he could dial 911, it occurred to him that perhaps the police received calls like this all the time ... from lunatics, or from people who were seeing Venus, or a plane with its landing lights on, or whatever. He needed proof before he went to the police. Proof ... such as a photograph. Walters grabbed the old Polaroid camera he used for photographing construction sites, and went back outside. As he stepped out on to the front porch, the ship emerged from behind the pine tree, and Walters snapped his first photograph. The thing appeared huge now. It was cylindrical, and seemed to be about sixty feet in diameter, and about thirty-five feet from its domed top to the bright, throbbing, ring-like exhaust port at its bottom. There seemed to be windows and portholes, and a series of parallel lines, like racing stripes, around the ship's outer edge – although these would fail to show up on the Polaroid photographs which by now lay in a trail from Ed Walters's front door to the street. Over this street the ship loomed – zapping Ed Walters and his Polaroid camera with a paralysing blue beam.

The blue beam ... At the recent MUFON conference, a young New York artist on the abduction panel, Peter Robbins, had spoken about being paralysed by a blue beam out in front of his house on Long Island in the early 1960s. The saucers had just come right in over the neighbourhood, and Peter and his sister had been playing in the front yard and Peter had turned to run inside to tell his mother that three or four silver flying saucers were hovering over the Greenbergs' house across the street, and then ... everything ... slowed ... down ... and ... everything ... was ... blue ... and by the time he regained consciousness a half-hour later his sister had had her first of many abductions and his mother and the Greenbergs across the street were none the wiser ...

But now Walters stood motionless in the blue beam in front of his own suburban house at dusk on Veterans Day, 1987. The beam seemed to lift him up and press him down simultaneously. He couldn't raise his arms to take another picture. The pressure was terrific. He couldn't scream. He could hardly breathe. He felt a sharp pain in his forebrain, near the back of his right eye socket. He felt his feet leaving the ground. A deep, computer-like voice in his head said, 'We will not harm you.' He screamed – a dream-like blue-beam scream, that never makes enough noise to rouse anybody – and the voice said, 'Calm down.' He semi-screamed again, 'Put me down!' but the blue beam continued to lift him off the pavement. A smell like ammonia laced with ... cinnamon ... scorched his sinuses.

The aliens grew annoyed at his resistance. 'Stop it,' said the Voice. 'Aagghh!' screamed Walters. He was blacking out. A strange hum filled his head, followed by a female-sounding voice, followed by a rapid series of images of dogs. He now seemed to be about four feet off the ground.

Oooofff! He hit the pavement suddenly, fell forward on to his knees. From above in the sky came the reassuring sound of a passing plane, headed for the Naval Air Station. Walters rolled over on to his back in the street, gulping air. That plane ... if it hadn't flown by just then, the blue beam might have taken him all the way up. He might have been abducted. No one would believe him, of course – except that he had the photographs.

Walters was working his way back towards the front door, picking up the photographs where his Polaroid in its frenzy had ejaculated them out on to the lawn, when his wife Frances drove up. He took her inside and explained what had happened – she could smell the alienesque ammonia-cinnamon smell all over him – and then explained the story to the kids, and they understood, although they were a little bit afraid, and within a few days Walters had dropped off the photographs at the offices of the local paper, the *Gulf Breeze Sentinel*. He explained to the editor that the photos had been taken by a friend, a Mr X who desired no publicity and who had merely seen the UFO one night during dinner and had gone outside to photograph it. Walters figured that the Mr X cover story might shield himself and his family from any ridicule, and as an extra precaution he left out the blue-beam business. Anyway, the *Sentinel* ran the photos, which showed a sort of crown-shaped object with dark portholes, a glowing bauble on top, and a gleaming ring at the bottom where the star-drive mechanism was. The photographs caused quite a stir around Gulf Breeze, and over the next six months the ufology community and the national media got wind of them, too.

During this period the UFO visitations continued, of course. On the afternoon of 20 November Walters heard the blue-beam humming sound again, and then something that sounded like a blast of air, and a voice speaking in a foreign language, African-sounding, and after this continued for a while – Frances and the kids having left the house for various reasons – he went outside with his camera and watched a star-like object fall towards him and heard the female voice commanding him to step forward for his abduction and then a male voice commanding him in Spanish – *los fotos son prohibido* – that photographs were prohibited. He continued to resist and eventually the aliens began to flash telepathic images of naked women of all shapes, colours, and sizes. Walters wasn't impressed, though. He shot some more Polaroid photos of the ship as it hovered over the trees in the backyard, and with a threatening telepathic 'We will come for you' the aliens zoomed aloft again, out of sight.

On 2 December the aliens came again, announcing themselves telepathically in Ed Walters's head by a cacophony of alien voices and the crying of abducted babies who, it seemed from the telepathic stream of consciousness that was invading his, were being malnourished by an exclusive diet of bananas at the hands of their captors. The ship hovered over the swimming-pool in the Walters's backyard, and left after Ed, now also armed with a .32 calibre hand-gun, took some more photos of it. The ship came back a few minutes later. Ed opened the bedroom curtains and saw, on the adjacent porch overlooking the pool, a four-foot-tall humanoid wearing some kind of metal suit and wielding a magic wand. Ed screamed and fell backwards, and the alien watched him with what looked like calm curiosity. Walters set aside his camera and gun and gave chase, but the blue beam struck again, and Ed might have been abducted had not Frances pulled him out of the beam in the nick of time.

The aliens returned again on 5 December, now addressing Ed as 'Zehaas'. 'We will not harm you . . . Zehaas,' they said to him telepathically. 'Zehaas, we have come for you.'

Ed and Frances and even some of their friends saw UFOs on 17 December, 23 December, 27 December, 28 December, 12 January, 16 January, 21 January, 24 January, 26 January, 7 February, 26 February, 8 March, 17 March, 20 March, and 1 May. By the time the aliens made their twentieth and final visit, the Ed Walters photographs and abduction stories had become the talk of ufology, not to mention the publishing world. To most people, Walters himself remained pseudonymous, known first as 'Mr X', and then as 'Mr Ed'.* But to New York editors and agents, and to the top echelons of ufology, Walters's true identity was much better known. Investigators from MUFON were heavily involved in the case; Budd Hopkins had been down to interview Ed and the family personally, and to talk to other people in the Gulf Breeze com-munity, which by the spring of 1988 was in a frenzy of ufophobia. Just about everyone had seen something unusual flying around the skies, and abduction reports were coming in thick and fast.

*

---

* *Mr Ed* was also the name of a popular 1960s television sit-com, the eponymous star of which was a wisecracking horse.

It was somewhat ironic that the Gulf Breeze story had generated so much excitement, because the story bore some strong similarities – in its details as well as in the broader themes – to Strieber's *Communion* escapades, which American ufologists didn't seem to like very much. One of the reasons they didn't like it was that Budd Hopkins, who didn't like Strieber, now wielded a major influence within the mainstream ufology organizations, MUFON and CUFOS. By the end of 1987, Hopkins and Strieber were almost as volatile a mixture as Hopkins and Klass. On a talk show in Dallas one day, Strieber was asked if it were true that he had once told Debbie Tomey he had seen her head on a shelf in a spaceship. Strieber responded that he had never said such a thing to Debbie Tomey; Budd Hopkins, he said, had fabricated the tale to discredit him.

Well, Hopkins heard about it, and he phoned Tomey, and she signed an affidavit stating that Strieber had said he had seen her head on a spaceship's shelf, and there was talk of cranking up a lawsuit against Strieber, but Hopkins's lawyer advised him that the American legal system being what it was, and libel damages being difficult to extract, and so on and so forth, his best option was simply to hit back through the media – and in due course it became well known to those in any way connected to alien abduction research that in the opinion of Budd Hopkins, Whitley Strieber was mentally unstable.

The Hopkins–Strieber feud was just one aspect of the resistance to Strieber, however. Michael Swords, an associate professor of natural sciences at Western Michigan University, and fairly mainstream as ufologists went, wrote a long analysis of *Communion* for *MUFON UFO Journal* in the spring of 1987. He took care not to come to any definitive conclusions, but it was pretty clear that doubts about Strieber's veracity, or at least about the objective reality of his experiences, had inspired him to write. One of the things he noted was that almost none of Strieber's stories of being abducted had been corroborated in any substantial way by his wife, Anne, his son Andrew, or anyone else such as Annie Gottlieb ('Sarah' in the movie) or Jacques Sandulescu ('Alex'). Besides Whitley, only his wife had undergone regression hypnosis, and as Swords argued, she hadn't been able to remember much of anything – unless it was something that Whitley had told her himself, and that she had later visualized in her mind's eye. Swords ventured the suggestion that, among other possibilities, Strieber's experience had constituted a vivid but dissociative altered state, triggered by stress and anxiety and fed by the horror and occult imagery with which his life had been filled. Strieber's wife, according to this hypothesis, understood his mild pathology and avoided challenging it for fear of forcing her husband's fragile mind past the breaking point. Strieber's son, it almost went without saying, was like most children too suggestible to be able to provide an independent verification of his father's claimed experiences.

Strieber didn't like this. He wrote an 'open letter' to Swords in *MUFON UFO Journal*, suggesting that Swords, like Hopkins and Jacobs and other ufological critics of *Communion*, couldn't handle the book because it didn't fit their neat, narrow categories of how UFO abductions should proceed. Strieber's case was messy; his life had been filled with incomprehensibly weird and dream-like yet undeniably vivid incidents, many of them having nothing to do with UFOs. Other abductees had had similar experiences, but somehow under hypnosis with someone like Hopkins they would always find that these experiences had actually been screen memories, masking the predictable and quite comprehensible activities of the little grey gynaecologists.

To Strieber, ufologists tended to proceed from the assumption that all abductions were neutral or negative experiences occurring at the hands of clinically detached aliens who flew around in nuts-and-bolts flying saucers with a mission to create a hybrid race of grey-humans. Ufologists tended to resist resisted the shamanic, mystical, visionary interpretation – a positive interpretation. They seemed unable to cope with the idea that the visitors – whether they came from outer space or from within the earth or from some other dimension – might always be incomprehensible to humankind but might somehow, through all the stress and uncertainty, promote our spiritual growth.

However, as far as Hopkins and Swords and the others were concerned, Strieber's emphasis on growth and transformation and prophecy and *rapprochement* with the greys and blue meanies and other alien creatures was starting to sound not only like the Leo Sprinkle brand of New Age abductionology, but like the old contactee stories – stories told by George Adamski and Truman Bethurum and Orfeo Angelucci and other people who hobnobbed happily with the Space Brothers in such places as the Greyhound Bus terminal in downtown Los Angeles. In fact, an editor at Morrow, a respected former *Newsweek* reporter named Bruce Lee, was now claiming to have seen the aliens in a bookstore in uptown Manhattan . . .

It had been a cold Saturday in February 1987, just after *Communion* had been released, and Lee and his wife had been walking along Lexington Avenue and had gone into the bookshop to see how some of the books he had edited were being displayed for buyers. He had been standing there towards the back of the store when a couple came in and headed straight for the rack where *Communion* was displayed. The couple were both quite short, and were heavily bundled up against the cold, with wool hats and long scarves and gloves and boots. They each grabbed a copy of *Communion* and, despite the encumbrances of their gloves, began flipping through the book rapidly. It didn't seem possible that they could be reading so quickly, and yet they were shaking their heads and saying such things as 'Oh, he's got this wrong,' and 'Oh, he's got that wrong.' Perhaps strangest of all, their accents sounded upper East Side Jewish. Lee walked over and introduced himself, explaining that he worked for *Communion*'s publisher, and was interested to know what errors might be contained in the book, and the woman looked up at him . . .

She had on large sunglasses which, with her scarf and hat, obscured virtually all of her face. And yet through the sunglasses Lee could see a pair of enormous dark eyes. *Jesus!* Lee had been raised on a farm, and those eyes reminded him of the eyes of a rabid dog. They seemed to be telling him to get the hell out of there. The hair on Lee's neck stood up, and he said a hasty goodbye. He grabbed his wife and went off to a bar and soaked his shock in Margaritas.

Except for the apparent malevolence of the encounter – and as Strieber had hinted in *Communion*, such malevolence might simply be the product of human xenophobia – Lee's encounter was similar to the old contactee stories. To Hopkins and Jacobs and the nuts-and-boltsers of mainstream ufology, contactees were the kiss of death. Maybe not all of the contactees had been hoaxers, but certainly none of their experiences – which had tended to be bizarre, idiosyncratically dream-like, and obviously wish-fulfilling – had been objectively real. The distinction between the old and discredited contactee experience and the new and still-viable abductee experience had to be maintained at all costs. If ufology slipped back into contacteeism, it would be lost for ever. Strieber's story, therefore, should be considered interesting, but unreliable.

Strieber by this time was working on book number two, *Transformation: the Breakthrough*. Its narrative took up pretty much where *Communion* had left off, but unlike *Communion* it put a heavy emphasis on the weirder, more shamanic aspects of Strieber's experiences, and in its pages Strieber seemed concerned to represent his graduation from a distraught, stressed, half-psychotic abductee to a coping, prophetic, and spiritually elevated contactee – although just what had abducted or contacted him was still not clear.

According to Strieber, in late March 1986, not long after he had begun hypnosis with Donald Klein, and around the time he had been finishing *Communion*, he had begun to fantasize, with fairly intricate elaborations, that the aliens, or visitors, or whatever, were here to start a happy and peaceful and benevolent empire, a New World Order. On the night of 1 April, at the cabin in the woods, the fantasy seemed to materialize when Strieber awoke inside a greyish-tan corridor of a spaceship. Two of the overall-wearing blue meanies walked in front of him. They were leading him somewhere. 'You're *blue*!' Strieber exclaimed. One of them looked back at him and grimaced a little and fluttered his blue eyelids a little and said, 'We used to be like your blacks but we decided this was better.' Shamefaced, Strieber realized that all along, despite marching for civil rights and condemning bigotry wherever he had seen it, he had been a secret racist.

The blue meanies led on, past large drawers with knobs on them, into a round room with louvred windows. A group of entities in white uniforms sat around a table. The entities' skin looked termite-white, with an insectoid translucence, but otherwise the place – especially the louvred windows and the white uniforms – reminded Strieber of a British regimental dining-room in India, in the golden age of the Raj.

Strieber, involuntarily recalling an old prep-school habit, snapped to attention. One of the termite officers came over and wanted to know why the old British Empire had collapsed. So Strieber delivered a lengthy lecture to the gathered regimental officers on the subject of economic interrelationships and racial exploitation and how the passion for independence followed inevitably from an increase in living standards. The termite officers waited until he had finished and then began telepathically to mock his grandiloquence. The blue meanies at the door motioned to him and took him back down the corridor and with a prideful flourish opened one of the drawers wherein lay stacks of inert and cellophane-wrapped blue-meanie bodies. Then Strieber woke up.

The next night, Strieber woke from sleep again and, as had become his habit, went downstairs to watch his son sleep. But although neither the motion-sensitive floodlights at the front of the house nor the motion-sensitive burglar alarm had been tripped, his son had disappeared. Strieber checked all over the house – quietly, so as not to awaken his wife, in case it was only a false alarm – and finally went outside. Strieber beheld a giant dark spaceship blotting out the stars, and also some blue-meanie-sized shapes hovering over the road. 'Can you go back upstairs by yourself or do you want us to help you?' asked a voice.

Strieber anguished and agonized for a while but then complied with the implicit command, going back inside and falling asleep instantly, awakening in the morning to the sound of his son's footsteps coming up the stairs. Andrew did this just about every morning, and today he seemed his usual self, as if nothing at all had happened. But later in the day, according to Strieber's account, Andrew began to say some very unusual things indeed . . . 'Y'know, I've been thinking,' he said to his father when they were out on the sundeck. 'Reality is God's dream.' Then later he said, 'The unconscious mind is like the universe out beyond the quasars. It's a place we want to go to find out what's there.'

A week or so later, just before dawn one morning in the apartment in Manhattan, Strieber felt himself suffused by a golden light, and then was flying over some lovely but apparently unearthly city, miles and miles of it, over thousands of buildings and street corners and sports stadia and all of it devoid of life. He awoke, briefly, to the sounds of his wife sighing and morning traffic whirring and honking on the street below, but then closed his eyes again and resumed the journey over the vivid but evidently abandoned city. The streets were paved with golden blocks and the stonework on the buildings was magnificent. It was all very realistic and he wondered whether it might be one of those lost cities, a repository of ancient wisdom ... One particular building had a red stripe below the black-louvred top floor windows, and for some reason when Strieber looked at the building the phrase 'a place where the truth is known' went through his head. He swooped down low to see if anyone was inside the building, but behind the louvres there was only a fleeting shadow, a column of light in the dusty air, an empty room, a pang of sadness ...

Strieber's visitations and adventures continued throughout 1986 and 1987. As he spent more and more time reading the works of Gurdjieff and Ouspensky and other mystics, and poring through old prophecies, and attending New Age-type conferences and conclaves, he saw that his experiences were of a frankly shamanic character, and when he wasn't being instructed by the visitors about the ozone layer or nuclear winter, or making out-of-body excursions through space and time, or having precognitive visions of disasters such as Chernobyl, he was becoming the focus of a number of strange poltergeist-like effects in the apartment in Manhattan and at the cabin in the woods upstate. Radios would turn themselves off when he walked past. Strange knocking sounds would frighten him and his family. But it was all right, because he was learning to live with it, and to live with the visitors, the modern materialization of the fairies, angels, demons, and miscellaneous spirits of yore. He was learning a lot, and they were teaching him.

And so, like many before him, Whitley Strieber shook the dust of ufology from his feet and entered the promised land of the New Age. There he was, quite naturally, regarded as a heroic figure, an oppressed prophet, a Job and a Jeremiah wrapped into one.

Ufologists such as Budd Hopkins were happy to be rid of him. Not that Strieber had presented a major challenge, for by now, in the late 1980s, mainstream nuts-and-bolts ufology was steaming along as strongly as ever. Ed Walters and the blue-beam exhibitionists of Gulf Breeze appeared to have finally disproved Carl Jung's remark that 'UFOs are somehow not photogenic.' Half a dozen authors, apparently having tracked down further witnesses to the 1947 Roswell saucer-crash episode, were at work on books about it. Petitions were being made to Congress to lift the lid on the government's UFO cover-up. Ufologists were again advancing on the gates of high culture.

And this time abduction research was in the vanguard. Two of ufology's most influential figures, MUFON director Walt Andrus, and CUFOS vice-president and journal editor Jerome Clark, stood squarely behind Hopkins and Jacobs and their research. Other abduction researchers in the Hopkins–Jacobs mould were entering the scene, such as the psychologists John Carpenter in St Louis, and Susan Fox in New York. Ron Westrum, a sociologist colleague of Michael Swords at Western Michigan University, was writing about the eerie parallels between the medical profession's resistance to UFO abductions and its earlier resistance to childhood sexual abuse. Some of Hopkins's abductees had even believed that their own childhood abductions had been incidents of sexual abuse, until Hopkins peeled away the screen memories under hypnosis. Hopkins was also invoking parallels between abductions and the Jewish Holocaust, which like child abuse had been denied for a long time despite overwhelming evidence of its existence.

Dave Jacobs had a contract with Simon & Schuster for his own abductions book, *Secret Life*, the first major work on the subject by an academic. His abductee circle had grown to include several dozen individuals from all walks of life, and their accounts seemed to correspond quite well with those from Hopkins's abductees: rape-like sexual encounters with the aliens were followed months later by foetus-snatchings and, years later, by presentations of hybrid babies. Men would have sperm samples taken, and would awaken with bruises around their genitals. The aliens also seemed intent upon studying the psychology of abductees, often putting them in contrived situations to study their reactions, or staring at them intently in a process which Jacobs began to call Mindscan. Actual physical evidence of what had happened, however, remained tantalizingly out of reach. The abductees would report all kinds of stains and gooey substances that the aliens had left behind, either on themselves or on their abducted children, but there was never enough to perform a proper analysis, and anyway what would such an analysis search for? Jacobs also began to set up video cameras in the bedrooms of some of those abductees who were abducted frequently, instructing each abductee to turn on the camera before going to bed at night. Sometimes, with the video camera on, the abductee would go for weeks without an abduction, but eventually she would develop the compulsion to turn the video camera off, or the power would mysteriously go out, and an abduction would then take place.

Jacobs had more success with another new investigative approach. To prove that hypnosis wasn't causing confabulation in abduction accounts, he developed a non-hypnotic questioning technique, 'facilitated recall', in which he would simply bring the abductee mnemonically to the point where her missing time began, questioning her again and again about what she had seen or felt . . . until she broke through and with the aid of his careful questioning was able to remember most if not all of the abduction episode. Sometimes people would telephone him long-distance, distraught over a recent episode, and wanting his help, and he would start the facilitated recall process and within a few minutes the abductee would remember that, yes, there had been an odd blue light over the house, and a deer had stared at her from the window, and before the abductee started to panic over the phone from the flow of traumatic memory, Jacobs would terminate his questions, having satisfied himself, without the need for a face-to-face meeting, that the incident was worth further investigation.

Budd Hopkins was working on book number three, *A Crack in the Universe*, with a New York writer and editor named Penelope Franklin. As planned, it would be an extensive study of the various ways in which abductees coped with the trauma of their experiences. And speaking of coping, in the wake of *Intruders* Hopkins was receiving dozens of letters every day from apparent abductees. There was no way he could deal with all of them satisfactorily. It was becoming clear that some kind of organization was necessary to help train abduction researcher-therapists around the country and to match them with abductees. Already an informal network of psychiatrists, therapists, gynaecologists, radiologists, neurosurgeons, and hypnotist-ufologists had sprung up around the country and across the border in Canada. Abduction research and therapy was becoming a serious medico-scientific enterprise. Who would lead this enterprise?

One day in April 1988, Hopkins received a telephone call from a woman in the town of Dobbs Ferry, in Westchester County, New York. Her name (pseudonymized here) was Mina Hobart, and she was a psychiatrist. On reading *Intruders*, she had experienced an unsettling sense of *déjà vu*. It was possible that she had been abducted at some time in her life. Could Hopkins help her to investigate her past? Hopkins invited her over for a session, and two days later she underwent hypnosis on his couch. More sessions followed, at Hopkins's studio, and then at Dave Jacobs's home in Philadelphia when Hopkins and his wife, April, went away to Cape Cod for the summer. It became clear that Mina had indeed been abducted. But by the end of the summer, Mina had begun to shift her role from that of an abductee to that of a researcher. She was a psychiatrist, after all; she had an MD, with training in hypnosis. She could make a contribution by regressing abductees herself. Hopkins gave her his blessing, plugged her into the abduction research network, and began to refer some of his own abductees to her. By the end of the year, Mina had not only established her own modest circle of abductees, she had begun to organize a scientific gathering on the subject.

Mina's conference on Treatment and Research of Experienced Anomalous Trauma (TREAT) was held in mid May 1989, in a hotel in Fairfield, Connecticut. Everybody who was anybody in abduction research was there – psychologists and psychotherapists and psychiatrists and sociologists and journalists and, of course, ufologists and abduction researchers. There was even a former Congressional staffer in attendance, Scott Jones. Jones, who had just retired as a top aide to Rhode Island Senator Claiborne Pell – who with Jones had attended the MUFON Conference in Washington in 1987 – was rumoured to be part of the Aviary, a shadowy group of current or former government employees (with bird code-names – Jones was 'Chickadee') who took a keen interest in the UFO subject. Sceptics, and some of the Aviary themselves, said that Aviary members were merely UFO buffs who happened to have been government employees, although others insisted that Chickadee, Falcon, Penguin, Owl, and the other dark-suited fowl were actually agents of the government's UFO cover-up, their mission being to monitor UFO groups and to spread disinformation when necessary. Mina assigned Jones to the conference's 'Data Collection' working group, Jones's expertise in this area being listed, in the conference proceedings, under 'unconventional sources'.

A fellow named Hans-Adam Liechtenstein was also there at the conference. He was an even more remarkable character than Scott Jones, for he was a prince. He lived in a grand castle, Schloss Vaduz, in the little Alpine principality of Liechtenstein – the gingerbread and fairy-tale place parodied by novels such as *The Prisoner of Zenda*, and *The Mouse That Roared* – and once his ailing father passed away, would become the eponymous head of his state.

The Prince, like many royals and nobles and aristocrats throughout history, had long taken an interest in the paranormal and supernatural. Since the mid 1980s he had quietly been funding various ufological research projects, and the abduction phenomenon, when it exploded into public consciousness in 1987, had especially drawn his attention. It was rumoured, inevitably, that he himself was an abductee. In any case, he had put up most of the money for the conference.

The conference seemed to go off pretty well, although there was a certain amount of unease when Mina, in one of her several presentations, displayed a photograph of a young girl's genitalia. The story of the genitalia was that the girl's mother had come to David Jacobs with the claim that her daughter had been sexually mutilated by aliens. Mina, then in frequent touch with Jacobs, had suggested sending the girl to a gynaecologist; the girl's mother had complied, and the gynaecologist had advised her that the child's genitals were normal. Someone had taken the photograph during the gynaecologist's examination, and Hobart had somehow got hold of it. Hopkins was disturbed that the photograph, involving a further traumatization of the young girl, had been taken at all, and he was annoyed that Hobart had not simply reported that in the gynaecologist's opinion the girl's genitals were normal, rather than displaying the clinically graphic photograph to an audience of individuals who were in any case unqualified to judge the finer points of pre-pubescent female anatomy.

The business of the photograph wasn't the only source of tension between Mina and Budd Hopkins. Mina was beginning to insinuate that only trained clinical professionals should be allowed to investigate abduction cases using hypnosis: abduction researchers such as Hopkins and Jacobs had their uses, of course, and she was grateful to them for having blazed the trail and having brought the abduction phenomenon to the attention of the medical profession, but now it was time for the MDs and PhDs to take over. Only they had the training necessary to recognize the various disorders and psychopathologies with which the abduction phenomenon could become confused, and to deliver effective therapy, possibly including prescription medication, when it was needed. Investigators should concern themselves with investigation, but when it came time for therapy, they should take a back seat to the therapists.

There was, according to Mina, also the question of money. Investigators typically charged nothing for their hypnosis sessions, but then, being investigators – i.e. being less concerned with helping the abductee to cope than with digging information out of her – that was only proper. Unfortunately this had given abductees the impression that therapy should always be free. But while investigators such as Hopkins could be compensated later by lucrative book contracts, professional therapists had no such recourse, and were forced to charge money for their services, as any therapist did. Mina formalized this argument in a paper she circulated a few weeks after the TREAT conference, 'Therapist and Investigator: A Definition of Roles'. She planned to have it run in *International UFO Reporter*, the influential CUFOS journal. Her barbs were aimed particularly at the financial issues. The idea that abductees should be regressed for free, she wrote, 'represents a shocking, profound, and highly inappropriate devaluation of the skill and training offered to patients by members of the professional community . . . Indeed, too much eagerness to offer too many hours of cut-rate or free therapy may signal a novice or inadequate therapist and should provoke caution.' Inadequate post-abduction therapy was especially dangerous, she argued, because the abduction phenomenon was so large. Mental health professionals such as herself, as soon as they were allowed to take over, would have their hands full: '. . . we can predict that a significant portion of the hours available for the clinical services of a significant number of well trained and highly skilled practitioners may come to be required to deal with the abduction phenomenon.' But unless it was quickly established that these practitioners should be adequately compensated for their services, they would simply fail to take an interest in the abduction phenomenon, and abductees would languish under mediocre or non-existent therapy.

For Hopkins all of this was particularly painful, since it came from a woman who a year before had spent dozens of hours in hypnotic trances on *his* couch, and for free. He and Jacobs had also spent many hours, unpaid, training her in the use of hypnosis for abduction cases and in the special therapeutic requirements of abductees, and introducing her, as only they could, to the far-flung abduction research network.

Hopkins responded, firstly, that alien abductions represented a psychiatrically novel and unexplained phenomenon, which no amount of standard psychotherapeutic training could comprehend. In abduction research and therapy, a layman might be as good as – or, having fewer preconceptions, even better than – a trained therapist. In fact, an abduction researcher, having greater familiarity with the phenomenon and its psychological manifestations, would actually be better trained, in this sense, than a psychiatrist. Some professional therapists were so incompetent in the context of abduction research that abductees had begun to complain about them. In one case, a psychiatrist at one of Hopkins's support-group meetings had abruptly asked for a show of hands by 'anyone who feels he or she was sexually or physically abused as a child'. Several abductees complained about this attempted invasion of their privacy, and Hopkins was forced to apologize later for the psychiatrist's behaviour.

According to Hopkins, professional therapists who dealt with a variety of psychopathologies every day would tend, perhaps understandably, to lack empathy for and involvement with their patients. Investigators tended to develop a richer and therapeutically much more effective relationship with abductees, who time and time again had told Hopkins that they preferred ufologists such as himself to psychologists and psychiatrists. Hopkins could still remember his early days as an abduction researcher, when Aphrodite Clamar had merely acted as the hypnotic technician, even casually reading her mail during some of the sessions, while before and after the sessions, in long talks with abductees, Hopkins had acted as their real therapist.

Why, asked Hopkins, should therapy be left to medical professionals? Why should all forms of trauma be medicalized? Virtually everyone, in some sense, and at some time, acted as a therapist; the insistence that only expensive medical professionals be used for regressing abductees was unwarranted.

Hopkins sent a draft of a paper incorporating most of these points to Mina. She then forwarded copies of it to a few dozen TREAT members, with a covering letter which explained that, contrary to Hopkins's charges, she believed that investigators should play a major role in abduction research, albeit one separate from that played by medical professionals. She could not explain why Hopkins had reacted so unpleasantly. She hoped that the other members of TREAT could forget his regrettable personal attack on her.

Hopkins responded by sending the final draft of the letter to TREAT members with a covering letter of his own, making some additional points. One was that the existing abduction research network, which included ufologists and medical professionals in major US cities, and local abductee support groups, already offered sufficient therapeutic help to most abductees. Those who wanted paid professional help could always find it. None of the medical professionals who had volunteered their services on the network was complaining about not being paid; and all agreed that the network worked well. One who didn't had been dropped from the network after Hopkins had discovered that she had been charging what he considered to be exorbitant fees. 'This psychiatrist', wrote Hopkins, pointedly avoiding any reference to the doctor's gender, had charged an abductee over $1,000 for three hypnosis sessions, sessions which altogether had involved, he said, no more therapy or insight than the abductee normally received from him; the amount included a surprise $250 for what the psychiatrist had described to the abductee, allegedly without mention of fees, as 'a preliminary chat'. This despite the fact that Hopkins and Dave Jacobs had trained this particular psychiatrist, gratis, in the use of hypnotic regression and other forms of therapy for UFO abductees.

Hopkins circulated the paper with the covering letter from Cape Cod in late July. Mina, now planning TREAT-II, decided that on the whole it would be best not to invite Hopkins – or Jacobs, for he had been attacking her too.

Hopkins responded in late September by circulating a long paper entitled 'Mina Hobart, MD: Questions of Ethics and Competence'. In it, he revealed that the psychiatrist who had embarrassed abductees by requesting to know their childhood sexual abuse histories was one and the same as the psychiatrist who had charged an abductee an arm and a leg for three hypnosis sessions; this psychiatrist, of course, was Mina Hobart. Hopkins related in detail how he and Jacobs had generously spent time with Hobart, going over her possible abduction experiences, plugging her into the abduction research network, and setting her up with her own circle of abductees. He made further embarrassing allegations. In her third high-priced hypnosis session, given to a male abductee whom Hopkins referred to as 'H', Mina had seemed (to the abductee) to be dragging the session on and on for no obvious therapeutic purpose; she had later billed him $500 for the session, including a 'diagnosis charge' of $125.* Another abductee, 'J', had been billed $600 for two hypnosis sessions. According to the testimony of H and J, wrote Hopkins, Mina had exaggerated her experience in abduction research, and as a therapist had been relatively cold and distant, 'more interested in gathering data' – in J's words – 'than in helping me with my anxiety'. In support group meetings at Hopkins's and Jacobs's houses, said Hopkins, abductees had privately complained about Mina's behaviour, which they had described variously as 'arrogant', divisive', and 'authoritarian'. One abductee, seeing Mina in Hopkins's house for the first time, allegedly

---

* Her diagnosis was 'DSM-III: 309.28' – which means, in the parlance of the *Diagnostic and Statistical Manual of Mental Disorders* version III, that H was suffering from 'Adjustment Disorder with Mixed Emotional Features', i.e. depression and anxiety stemming from a traumatic experience.

recognized her as a therapist she had gone to years before, for problems apparently unrelated to UFOs. Before fleeing the house, the woman told Hopkins's wife April that Mina had been 'cold, unfeeling, and a terrible therapist. I never trusted her and I won't come back here again if she's going to be here.' Hopkins hardly needed to remind his audience of the apparent irony that it was this woman, Mina, who had insinuated that Hopkins and Jacobs were incompetent therapists.

Hopkins's letter went on and on, alleging Mina's incompetence in other areas, and painting the picture of an opportunistic monster running amok in abduction research: before the first TREAT conference, alleged Hopkins, Mina had screamed at Dave Jacobs over the phone about some minor disagreement over whether a particular person was or wasn't well enough qualified to deserve an invitation. After the conference, Mina had advised a possible abductee in the south-west US that aliens could get at her too easily down there, and that she should move to New York, so that Mina could hypnotize her. Mina also allegedly told the woman that she probably had a brain implant, and that she should contact 'my man in Indiana who does MRIs' – a reference to a clinical imaging specialist to whom Hopkins had introduced Mina a few months earlier. Mina had referred abductee H's mostly unpaid bill to a collection agency, which had sent notices to H care of Hopkins's address in New York, threatening legal action against H. Hopkins enclosed copies of these notices with his widely circulated letter.

The Prince of Liechtenstein read the letter with a certain amount of alarm. He had just sent Mina $15,000 to set up TREAT-II, and had also indicated that he would support a European-based conference – EUROTREAT – as well as a major abduction research project. He telephoned Mina and asked her what it was all about, and she explained that this was all just a personal spat between herself and Hopkins and Jacobs, and was irrelevant to her professional abilities, and that under the circumstances she had decided not to invite Hopkins or Jacobs to TREAT-II. The Prince, who was on good terms with both Hopkins and Jacobs, didn't like the idea of simply excluding them without an investigation of their charges against her, and made it clear that without a satisfactory solution to all this he would withdraw his $15,000 as well as his support for other Mina-organized events. Mina appeared to shrug the threat off, explaining that she had already received enough financing for TREAT-II from other sources. The Prince then suggested that the matter be settled independently, by the TREAT steering committee. A few days later, before the Prince had contacted the steering committee to explain his position, he was telephoned by Dick Hall, a Washington-based ufologist on the steering committee, who informed him that the steering committee had conferred by conference call and had decided that, given the vitriolic and privacy-invading nature of Hopkins's and Jacobs's attacks on Mina, the two researchers should be excluded from Mina's TREAT-II. The Prince then phoned Mina and asked her for his $15,000 back, plus his TREAT-II registration fee since he would no longer be attending. This was on or about 23 October. Mina said she would get back to him and responded on the 27th with a fax to the effect that her lawyer had advised that the request for the return of the $15,000 be made in writing. Three days later, a further fax arrived from Mina with the advice that: 'On 23rd October, 1989 your grant designated as support for TREAT-II of US-$ 15,000 was forwarded to VPI [Virginia Polytechnic Institute – the planned site of the conference].' Mina explained that she had asked the university official responsible for the holding of the grant whether it could be returned to the grantor, and that the university official had said that the laws of the United States prohibited it.

And that was that.

9

John and Ken

Of course, if one took the long view of things, the Mina Hobart affair wasn't so horrible or unusual. A new and interesting phenomenon would always stimulate the growth of organizations to study it, and people would always disagree over how to run those organizations, and over how to conduct research in general. Personal rivalries were sure to develop. It was all part of the process, like growing pains.

Down in Gulf Breeze, the pains were more serious. The problem was, a lot of people who were fairly enthusiastic about other very strange ufological tales, for example the one about the crashed saucer and the four embalmed aliens at Wright Patterson Air Force Base in Ohio, or the one about the MJ-12 government UFO cover-up, had become hard-nosed sceptics on the subject of Ed Walters's photographs. Something wasn't right with them. Why, of all the UFO abductees and blue-beam victims in the world, was Ed Walters the only one who had been able to take pictures? The only other people to come up with such good UFO pictures had been contactee sham-shamans such as George Adamski, whose alleged alien encounters had been decidedly friendly.

MUFON and CUFOS were split on the issue. MUFON's investigators had spent hundreds of hours running around Gulf Breeze trying to keep up with Walters and the blue beams, and although they never really shared any of his close-encounter experiences, they were satisfied that he couldn't have been making all of them up. On the other hand, CUFOS's man in the Florida panhandle, Bob Boyd, interviewed Walters and came away with the impression that, for a man who supposedly had been through so much blue-beam agony, he sounded remarkably calm and collected. The arguments raged. Some said that Walters's decision to publish

the photos anonymously, and then to submit to ufologists' investigations only pseudonymously, proved that he wasn't in it for money
or publicity. They also noted that he had passed two separate
polygraph tests – one of them on surprise short notice – and had
been evaluated normal on a battery of psychological tests. His
photographs had also been judged genuine by a number of photo
analysts.

Others suggested that the pseudonymous Mr Ed, in his initial
arm's-length dealings with the local papers, might simply have been
cautiously throwing out bait, waiting to see if a credulous world
would grab it. They noted that anyone, given proper instruction,
could beat a polygraph. They brought up the fact that Ed had had
a youthful scrape with the law, doing several weeks in jail. They
pointed to the stark distinctiveness of the case – it stuck out like a
sore thumb in the UFO abductee lore – and the fact that, whatever
their initial misgivings had been regarding fame and fortune, within
a year of the start of Ed's blue-beam visits he and his wife had
agreed to a reported $200,000 book deal and $450,000 TV mini-
series deal.

The book came out in February 1990, and despite an enthusiastic
introduction by Budd Hopkins, and a ringing blurb ('A devastat-
ingly powerful testament to the reality of this bizarre phenomenon')
from the supposedly anti-ufological Whitley Strieber, it didn't do
nearly as well as its publishers – William Morrow, who had been
Strieber's publishers – had hoped it would. Yet Ed and Frances
became very popular on the lecture circuit, so popular in fact,
within this mostly cosy milieu, that even Strieber, whose book sales
reportedly were lagging again, began to seem envious. According to
the story that later made the rounds, he phoned up Ed Walters and
suggested, ever so gently, that he and Ed and Frances might hit the
lecture circuit together, as a team . . .

Then in June of 1990, the occupants of the Walters's old house
(they had built a new one) were rummaging through the attic to
find a water shut-off valve, and found a very odd thing indeed: a
model of a flying saucer. The model had a remarkable similarity to
the blue-beam-spewing flying saucer depicted in Ed Walters's
photographs. Across its midsection it even bore the narrow
horizontal lines which Ed had claimed, in the book, to have seen on

the spacecraft during his close-encounters, even though they hadn't shown up on the photographs themselves.

Ed argued that the model had been constructed by debunkers to make him look like a hoaxer. MUFON backed up his claim, arguing that the characteristics of the model were different from those on the UFO in the photographs. The midsection of the model had been made from a section from an old building plan, which Ed claimed hadn't been drawn until the late summer of 1989, long after his UFO experiences had ended. But whereas Walters contended that the plan had been made for a Mr and Mrs Thomas, whose house was to have been built on Shoreline Drive, to others the section seemed to make a better match with a plan for a house to be built on speculation at 712 Jamestown Drive – a plan which had been drawn in early 1987, well before the blue-beam episodes began. The argument wore on, and UFO journals and newsletters across the country began to run lengthily detailed articles about the controversy, featuring copies of building plans with special attention to the denoted Living Areas and Slab Areas and whether they matched those written on the section from the UFO. Walters's claims would effectively have been debunked had the 1987 'spec' house plan been shown to have the same living area and slab area as the section from the UFO; unfortunately, investigators who tried to check those house plan records at Gulf Breeze City Hall found that someone had been there before them: the corner of the plan containing the living area and slab area indications had been torn off. Phil Klass, in his semi-monthly *Skeptics' UFO Newsletter*, asked in characteristically tongue-in-cheek bold type:

WHO WOULD HAVE ANY REASON TO VISIT THE GULF BREEZE CITY HALL AND TEAR OFF THE CORNER OF THE 'SPEC HOUSE' PLAN THAT SHOWED ITS LIVING/SLAB AREA FIGURES? Several potential suspects come to mind: The KGB, The Pope, Dolly Parton, Barbara Bush . . .

MUFON investigators claimed, meanwhile, that Mr and Mrs Thomas had found their own copy of the plans, which showed living area and slab area figures identical to those on the

UFO model. With Ed Walters, they suggested that the UFO model had been constructed, by persons unknown, from the plans which Walters had discarded in late 1989, long after his UFO encounters had ceased.

Before long, however, a friend of Walters's son, a teenager named Tommy Smith who was the son of a prominent Gulf Breeze lawyer, came forward with the claim that he had assisted Walters in faking some of his UFO photographs, using double-exposures and other techniques. Smith produced film which showed the same UFO Walters had apparently photographed. The arguments raged over whether or not Smith was telling the truth, but all sides seemed to agree that he had no obvious motive for lying.

Hopkins put a brave face on the Gulf Breeze affair, and continued to insist that the photographs as well as the Walters's abduction or near-abduction experiences were genuine. MUFON's director Walt Andrus took the same view, and although a number of prominent ufologists soon abandoned the case, it didn't seem to have a strong bearing upon the abduction phenomenon as a whole, research into which continued to move smoothly onward and upward. In the autumn of 1989, towards the close of the battle with Mina Hobart, Hopkins had founded the formal organization he had always sought – the Intruders Foundation, or IF – with funds from a Las Vegas businessman, Robert Bigelow, and also from the Prince of Liechtenstein; by 1990 the IF network of therapists and physicians and hypnotist-investigators had representatives in dozens of US and Canadian cities.

In 1990 the new star on the abduction research scene was another psychiatrist, John E. Mack. Mack had more than a medical degree. He was a professor at Harvard who had founded a psychiatric clinic. He had also won a Pulitzer Prize back in the 1970s with his psychoanalytic biography of the Arabist adventurer T. E. Lawrence. Here was a man, thought Hopkins and Jacobs and the other nuts-and-boltsers, who might finally be able to pull abduction research into the academic mainstream.

In fact, Mack had long ago slipped out of the mainstream, and was proud of it. His interest in UFO abductions wasn't so much psychiatric as it was cosmological. He wanted to explore every aspect of the wild, multifarious alternate reality which he believed to be out there . . . active and dynamic and world-influencing but for the most part hidden, by the blinders of modern technological culture, from our potentially wide-ranging consciousnesses.

Mack felt that he had had the blinders on himself for most of his life. His ancestry was German Jewish. His mother died when he was young, and his father raised him to be an atheistic rationalist, a scientist, a modern man. He grew up and went to college and to medical school and became a psychoanalyst, and learned about the unconscious, and motivations, and object relations and the id and the ego and the superego and so on. He wrote a lot of books, and became a Harvard professor.

Some time in the early 1980s Mack began to feel that modern psychoanalysis, as he had been taught it, wasn't the whole picture. Objects and egos and superegos and ids were all very interesting, but he couldn't help thinking that something else was out there . . . and was in here, too, in our minds. He developed an interest in the 'est' movement, and did some transformational large-group work, and made some other intra-psychic explorations, and as he waded deeper into it all he began increasingly to question the standard modern view of reality and rationality. In the summer of 1987 he ran into a man named Stanislav Grof, out at the Esalen Institute in California. Grof was a Czech psychoanalyst who had done some work with an experimental mind-altering technique back in the 1960s; this mind-altering technique, involving a certain chemical substance known as lysergic acid diethylamide (better known as LSD) had been pretty popular for a while – its better-known proponents had included Ken Kesey, the Grateful Dead, and one of Mack's predecessors in the Harvard psychiatry department, an ebullient MD named Timothy Leary – but then it had become illegal and Grof had developed another, more old-fashioned mind-altering technique which required only closed eyes, music, concentration, and deep breathing. Grof Holotropic Breathwork, it was called, and Mack tried it and found that the things, the emotions, he was used to discussing clinically and abstractly became very vivid, very real, as he regressed through bliss and grief back to infancy. And in that first session out at Esalen, he was encouraged to go further out into this new realm of expanded and transpersonal consciousness, to a past life, to a mnemonic identification with anyone out there on the broad tapestry of cosmic consciousness . . . Galileo, a Siamese slave-girl, a Corinthian courtier, an ancient artist and warrior . . . and suddenly, as his head grew light from all the deep breathing and the music swam in his ears he became . . . a sixteenth-century Russian whose four-year-old son had just been decapitated by the Mongol hordes. For Mack, it was a very real, very powerful experience, perhaps less than physical reality, but certainly much more than a dream. Precisely why he had locked consciousness with a sixteenth-century Russian wasn't clear, but Mack noticed that Escalen at the time was crawling with Russians who had come over to learn breathwork, too.

With breathwork-induced transpersonal travel the possibilities were almost endless. Mack particularly liked the idea that one could use it in psychoanalysis, to help people explore their pasts, to bring about catharsis and integration of their various traumas. Mack signed himself up for a three-year breathwork-training course in Boston, and he and the other students studied – and as far as possible experienced – a range of subjects which included Eastern religions, alternate realities, psychedelic drugs, shamanic journeys, Jung and the mythic unconscious, human physiology, and of course how to breathe and play music in the proper mind-freeing manner.

UFOs didn't enter into any of this directly, but one day Mack was reading a book by Grof about modern spiritual emergencies and it included a chapter on flying saucers. Grof seemed to take the view that flying saucers were a kind of visual rumour, derived from the mythic contents of the unconscious – in other words the view Jung had mooted in his own book on UFOs in 1952. But Mack wondered whether there might also be some genuine, intersubjective, experiential basis for UFO folklore – in other words, he wondered whether UFOs might be real. It turned out that one of the members of Mack's breathwork training group was a psychologist who had a patient who claimed that she had been abducted several times by aliens in flying saucers. The psychologist had heard someone lecture on the subject, a fellow named Hopkins or something, who worked exclusively with these UFO-abductees. Perhaps Mack should look him up.

He did, and hit it off with Hopkins right away. To overcome any scepticism Mack might have had, particularly over the fact that much of the abduction material came out of hypnosis administered by amateur hypnotists, Hopkins brought Mack over to one of the big boxes full of correspondence in his studio and pulled out a handful of twenty-odd letters he had recently received from apparent abductees who had heard about him and wanted to tell him about their experiences. 'John,' said Budd, 'you open them.' So Mack took them home and opened them and read them and, well, two or three seemed to be unbalanced, but the rest seemed to be ordinary, stable people who were having extraordinary experiences and couldn't make sense of them and honestly wanted help. Mack was hooked.

John Mack spent much of 1990 sitting in on abductee regression sessions at Hopkins's studio, learning how to put them into a trance and how to regress them properly, and becoming familiar with the bizarre scenarios that abductees regularly reported. Hopkins might have felt slightly queasy about training such a well-known psychiatrist, given his experience with Mina Hobart, but it quickly became clear that Mack was no Hobart. He was unamiguously nice, would sing Hopkins's praises wherever he went, and any discussion about how he had first become interested in the subject would inevitably be punctuated by a comment to the effect that 10 January 1990, the day he met Budd Hopkins, was a date he would never forget. He and Hopkins became fast friends, and even though Mack's academic and literary standing meant that he was likely to attract a larger and larger share of the limelight, Hopkins never said a dark word against him. Remarkably, their friendship also transcended an ideological divide – for although Hopkins was a true blue nuts-and-boltser, believing that the abduction experience was distinct from folklore and profoundly negative, Mack was convinced that abduction stories *did* have fundamental similarities to other fantastic-seeming tales, or transpersonal experiences as he called them. Furthermore, Mack believed that when it came to transpersonal experiences, whether they were psychedelic trips to dreamland or encounters with child-decapitating Mongol hordes or fairy princesses or foetus-snatching grey gynaecologists, every cloud had a silver lining. Alien encounters, like any other transpersonal encounter, contained an element of personal growth.

To understand all this one had to understand Mack's view of human consciousness and evolution: consciousness had to do with our total sense of being, our enmeshment with the world around us, our ability to take in certain sorts of information. Especially in primitive societies, but less so as culture evolved, people frequently had difficulty distinguishing the transpersonal, spiritual realm – the holotropic realm, as Stan Grof called it – from what we now consider to be the realm of ordinary physical reality. Our consciousnesses then were more porous; they let in too much information from the holotropic realm. Anyway, having this cognitive porosity was all right, as long as one didn't have to do anything more complex than hunt or fish or mate. But supposing one were sitting in one's grass hut and breathing and humming and smoking one's way into a shamanic trance, and suddenly the figure of a man with a spear burst into the hut. It would be nice to know whether he was an ancestor spirit, ready to teach shamanic wisdom, or a marauding member of the tribe in the next valley, ready to run one through with his very real and non-spiritual spear. People and cultures who knew how to sort out the real world from the holotropic world would have an obvious advantage, particularly as culture and technology became more complex. One wouldn't want to start shamanizing while one was driving a car through rush-hour traffic. In fact, as technological cultures tore through the remaining primitive ones, the holotropic realm had less and less use to men. By the age of the Enlightenment, it had been left to monks and theologians and opium-eating storytellers and poets and artists; and for the rest of us, our ability to access it atrophied, like a vestigial organ. Nowadays mystical, spiritual, holotropic experiences were considered odd, even by people who went to church regularly. They were more or less suppressed in the collective consciousness, mocked as 'fantasy' or 'hallucination' or 'folklore'. Which was why mainstream science would never take the UFO abduction experience seriously. Having lost the capacity to access the holotropic realm, they could no longer even *see* it. Those who *could* see it now had the advantage; they were more grown, more complete. They had begun to recover the ancient wisdom, however painful the process might be.

The accounts that Mack's abductees provided were a good

illustration of this idea, for no matter how many scoop-marks or slices or forebrain implants or excruciating gynaecological probes they had suffered at the hands of the aliens, no matter how many of their foetuses had been snatched, no matter how many pints of their blood had been spattered over spaceship floors and walls, the aliens still managed to give them a warm feeling of oneness with the universe, or healed their ailments, or conveyed to them valuable prophetic images of the rainforest burning, or the ozone layer melting, or somehow or other gave them reason to alter the direction of their life, towards the spiritual, holotropic realm. The aliens' mission seemed to involve hybridization, there was no doubt about that, but it seemed primarily to be a cultural hybridization, a re-insemination of the modern worldview with the seeds of the holotropic. Mack decided, as Leo Sprinkle and many others had long before decided, that the aliens were here to raise our consciousness.

The fact that abduction reports, taken together, were associated only weakly with independent UFO sightings, and often occurred in fairly crowded areas where one would expect a hovering space-ship to stick out, also suggested to Mack that the aliens were *not* flying around in nuts-and-bolts spaceships. They were not part of our physical reality at all, except in so far as they chose to be. They were from another dimension or plane of existence entirely. They could drop in on us without warning or detection in the same ineffable way that a three-dimensional object could drop in on a two-dimensional world. We might as well not even bother trying to catch them.

One rainy night back in the late 1980s, in the mountains of Wyoming, a limousine arrived at the gate of the United States Air Force's Deep Space Surveillance Center. The rear window rolled down a few inches, enough to make clear the identity of the passenger, a General Hanley. The gate officer saluted, and the limousine proceeded into the side of Cheyenne Mountain, where General Hanley – who looked remarkably like the shrimp-eating, Lincoln-quoting Army general who had sent Martin Sheen on his mission to Cambodia in *Apocalypse Now* – entered and descended by elevator to a room filled with radar screens and excited junior officers. The officers explained to him that a few hours previously an unknown object had penetrated US radar space and had performed impossible high-speed manoeuvres, disappearing from the screens somewhere in the midwest –

– in Logan County, Nebraska, to be exact, where a young woman, Mary, wandered zombie-like down a highway in her nightgown. Mary came to a roadside truck stop, and the police were called, and still in an amnesic daze she was returned to her home, some thirty miles away. She wasn't sure what had happened. As she returned to her bedroom her young son, standing at the door of his own bedroom, peered at her with poignant worry –

– at the same moment that a flashing yellow light awoke another young woman, Leslie, from her bed in Venice, California. Leslie looked at her clock – 3.20 a.m. – and groaned in sleepy exasperation. She went over to the window, and saw a telephone repair truck, or something very much like it, down on the street behind the house. She went back over to the bed and called the telephone company and complained, but they didn't know anything about it. She groaned again and then went over to the window. Just what were these phone company people up to? But now she wasn't so sure they were phone company people. The truck was just sort of grey, without markings, and the half-dozen men standing around outside it with uniforms and hats and telephone-repair kits didn't seem to have faces. She ran downstairs, then saw them coming towards the house from the yard. She panicked and fell to the floor crying and then they were coming through the walls – bloop bloop – just walking right through as if the walls didn't exist, and the next thing she knew she was lying on the couch downstairs in the morning, dishevelled and violated and more or less shattered –

– and determined to visit her psychiatrist, who then suggested that she see a colleague, Dr Neil Chase. Chase specialized in regression hypnosis, which could be useful in bringing out the childhood trauma that undoubtedly caused this kind of hallucination. Leslie went to see Chase that night, to talk about the possibility of regression, and explained to him about the telephone repairmen without faces, and how she had awakened on the couch in the morning three hours later. Afterwards Chase drove her home, and when she had gone inside he walked over to where two

Hispanic children, a boy and a girl, were sitting on a nearby doorstep. The boy was looking up at the sky. 'Whatcha looking at?' asked Chase. 'We're waiting for the moon,' explained his sister. She nodded towards her brother. 'He said the moon came down last night. He says he saw it touch the ground.'

Thus began *Intruders*, the four-hour mini-series which CBS aired in May 1992. The screenplay had been written by Hopkins's and Jacobs's old friend Tracy Tormé, in cooperation with both of them, although 'John E. Mack, MD, Harvard Medical School' was listed as the technical consultant. The Dr Chase character was, of course, based on Mack. Budd Hopkins and Dave Jacobs were combined into Addison Leach, an anthropology professor at Berkeley with a huge wart on his forehead and an abrasive, wild-eyed, Van Helsingesque style. The abductees were more or less telegenic blends from the lore. In fact, Tormé had thrown just about every sensational ufological motif into the story. There was a nasal implant, removed from Mary, which one of Neil Chase's colleagues analysed and found to be of advanced technology – so advanced that it disappeared as soon as he analysed it. Each abductee had been having abduction experiences since childhood, involving sexual and gynaecological operations, and – in one scene – broods of hybrid grey-human babies incubating in bubbling spaceship aquariums. Mary's boy Tim was also a frequent abductee, and whenever it happened his room would be filled with flashing blue lights, and his bedroom door would lock mysteriously, and afterwards he would have a terrific nosebleed. There was the standard UFO cover-up motif,* involving the spectral General Hanley and visits to Dr Chase by undercover intelligence operatives who urged him to cease his research. There was the repression-by-orthodoxy motif, represented by a villainous hospital chairman who forced Dr Chase out of his job because of his progressive ideas. There was a nod to the Roswell case; one of Dr Chase's patients, played by Ben Vereen, had once seen some strange squiggly symbols – the same seen by Mary and Leslie – inside a crashed saucer on a military base in New Mexico. There was even a

---

* The Cheyenne Mountain sequence was based on a passage from *Out There*, a book by a former *New York Times* reporter named Howard Blum.

quintuplet crop circle, of sorts, charred into a field by a spaceship outside Mary's house in Nebraska.

Mary's husband was a truck-driver named Joseph. Her sister, Leigh, was a gorgeous blonde television news presenter who lived in Malibu, California. The sexual tension that sometimes arose between abductees and abduction researchers was alluded to, delicately and harmlessly, when lovely Leigh fell for wifeless Dr Chase. Dr Chase was unlike happily married Mack in other ways, too; he was a sceptic at first, but then became a nuts-and-boltser. Dr Leach, unlike Hopkins or Jacobs, wasn't sure what plane of reality the aliens came from. He was also something of a gymnast, at one point vaulting abruptly from Dr Chase's rooftop patio. As for the aliens, they behaved like nightmare monsters in the beginning, but by the end they were flooding the abductees with pleasant emotions. In the final scene Dr Chase and Leigh hold hands atop some lover's leap in Nebraska, and muse upon the question of why the aliens were here. 'To start a new world?' wonders Leigh. 'Or to save an old one?' says Dr Chase.

Tracy Tormé did a fair job of satisfying his various constituencies within the ufological community, but on the whole, his portrayal of the aliens toed the Hopkins–Jacobs–*War of the Worlds* line. Mack, despite his billing as technical consultant, didn't like that one bit. He warned the people at CBS that the programme, when aired, might create needless mass hysteria, especially among those who had previously been abducted but might not know it yet.

There were many such unwitting abductees, as the Roper Poll seemed to show. The Roper Poll, whose results were announced in the spring of 1992, had been designed to indicate how many Americans had been abducted by aliens. The Roper Organization, which will conduct polls for just about anyone who pays them, had carried out the survey using funds provided by Robert Bigelow and the Prince of Liechtenstein, and using a questionnaire designed by Mack and Hopkins and Jacobs and Ron Westrum. The questions on the poll concerned unusual events or memories which, to the compilers, suggested a previous abduction, such as whether the respondent had ever awakened with paralysis and the sense of a nearby and unusual presence, or had seen a monster in her bedroom as a child, or had experienced missing time, or had seen a ghost, or had felt as if she were flying through the air, or had seen unusual lights in her bedroom, or had found unexplained scars on her body.

Armed with these questions, along with control questions designed to ensure the accuracy of the results, the Roper pollsters had begun their work in the latter half of 1991, and had managed to get complete answers over the telephone from about 6,000 adult Americans. Those answers, organized and analysed and tabulated in a booklet mysteriously entitled 'Unusual Personal Experiences', indicated that one adult in five had awakened with paralysis and a strange presence; one in eight had experienced missing time; one in ten had experienced the feeling of flying through the air without knowing why or how; one in twelve had seen unusual lights in his or her bedroom; one in twelve had discovered puzzling scars on his or her body. If one took only the lowest figure, it indicated that 10 to 15 million American adults had been abducted at one time or another. Which was remarkably high. If one counted only those people who had had at least four of those five types of experience – which Mack and Hopkins and Jacobs and Westrum retrospectively decided to do – the number dropped to a more plausible level: 2 per cent of the American adult population, or about 4 million people. Even that sounded a bit much, and when Mack and Hopkins and the others spoke to reporters about the poll, they would often talk in terms of 'hundreds of thousands', adding 'millions' only as a possibility.

At any rate, there were very many abductees out there. And when they were exposed to the *Intruders* mini-series, they might panic, and if so all hell would break loose.

Fortunately, that didn't happen, at least not as far as the media were concerned. There were a couple of newspaper articles and end-of-the-evening-news shorts, but most of the media coverage concentrated instead on the abduction research conference being held at MIT at about that time. David Pritchard, an MIT physics professor who had become interested in studying abductee implants a few years back, was hosting it, and Mack was there, with Hopkins and Jacobs and Tracy Tormé and the Prince of Liechtenstein – who with Bob Bigelow was putting up a lot of the money – and Eddie Bullard and Hilary Evans and Jenny Randles and Leo Sprinkle and about 150 others, plus abductees and a few carefully chosen members of the press.

One of the papers presented at the MIT conference was by a psychology professor at the University of Connecticut, Kenneth Ring. Ring had made his name a few years back with his researches into near-death experiences, which had been a hot topic ever since Raymond Moody's *Life After Life* in 1975. Ring's first book on the subject, *Life at Death*, had been released in 1980 by a Putnam imprint, Coward, McCann, and Geoghegan, and it had done sufficiently well to earn him the backing of William Morrow & Co., who published his second book, *Heading Towards Omega*, in 1984. Its thesis was that NDEs were transformative experiences designed to push humanity towards the Omega Point – that ineffable singularity, named by the French Jesuit, anthropologist and proto-Aquarian Pierre Teilhard de Chardin, at which the consciousness of human beings will not only be united into one collective mind, but be reunited with the nirvanic over-consciousness of the cosmos.

Of course, William Morrow was also Whitley Strieber's publisher, and as soon as the first copies of *Communion* had rolled off the presses in January 1987, Ring had received one in the mail from his editor. Read this at once, advised Ring's editor, because it's relevant to your work. Ring thought so, too, when he saw in the narrative that Strieber, despite all of the brain-zapping blue-meanie trauma of his experiences, was concerned about the ozone layer and nuclear winter and his own spiritual transformation. Concern over the ozone layer and nuclear winter and spiritual transformations were right up Ring's alley, since they were the kind of thing that tended to happen to NDEers, too.

Ring read *Communion* and decided to perform a psychological study of both NDEers and UFO abductees, to see how deep the similarities between them might be. He developed a series of questionnaires designed to elicit the psychological background of NDEers and abductees, as well as the various life-changes associated with their experiences. He sent the questionnaires to a hundred or so NDEers who had corresponded with him over the years, and to another 100 abductees referred to him by Whitley Strieber, Leo Sprinkle, Budd Hopkins, the Boston researcher Joe Nyman, and the literary agent and researcher John White. Ring also sent questionnaires to control groups of people who hadn't had NDEs but were interested in them, and to people who hadn't been abducted but were interested in UFOs.

The results were striking. Near-death experiencers and UFO abductees appeared to be distinct from other people – even other New Agers and ufologists – in several remarkable respects: they were relatively likely to have claimed rough childhoods, involving physical, sexual, and psychological abuse, neglect, and a negative household atmosphere overall. During childhood they were also likely to have had encounters with 'nonphysical beings' – imaginary playmates or fairies – and were likely to consider themselves as having been psychically sensitive. They were easily hypnotizable, and often 'blanked out' spontaneously during routine tasks.

According to the respondents, their respective experiences wrought remarkable physical and mental changes. Typically, or anyway to a significantly greater extent than controls, they became more sensitive to light, noise, and humidity. Their metabolic rates, body temperatures, and blood pressures decreased. They needed less sleep at night. They experienced occasional ecstatic surges of energy through their bodies, as well as mood swings. They sensed structural changes in their brains. Their mental awareness expanded and their paranormal abilities increased. They developed the gift of healing. Electrical equipment tended to malfunction when they were nearby. They developed allergies and migraines. They became altruistic and spiritual, appreciating all forms of life, and developed passionate concerns for the fate of the planet. They believed – with the possible exception of Budd Hopkins's abductees – that mankind was being nudged by some higher intelligence towards a glorious New Age.

Now this was clearly music to the ears of the abduction psychosocialists. Claims of childhood trauma were practically a prerequisite for the dissociative personality. The theory was that dissociative experiences, such as chatting with little men who were invisible to everyone else, often represented a psychological defence against the threats of the outer world. Such experiences meant a turning inward, a creation of a separate reality. Paranormal experiences, including everything from clairvoyance to strange electrical phenomena, were somehow a concomitant of this separate reality, for they also had long been linked with dissociative disorders. Ring's data made perfect sense: UFO abductions were the product of minds which in childhood – or perhaps genetically and unavoidably – had been over-stressed and made permanently, though not necessarily sociopathically, prone to experience fantasy as reality. These people were temporal lobe labile. How could it be otherwise, when NDEs, to which abductions now seemed closely related, clearly were not actual physical experiences, and their contents seemed for the most part to have been culturally derived? Ring even noted a case in which a woman who had apparently just discovered a tumour in her breast suddenly blanked out, and, while her concerned husband watched her collapse unconscious on the living-room couch, experienced several abduction-type themes:

The next thing I remember was looking out of a round window and seeing the blackest blackness with tiny white sparkles (I later realized I was experiencing deep space). I felt cold – colder than I have ever experienced. I was unconcerned about my predicament and I turned my gaze from the window (to my left). There was a bright white light directly above me with four [to] seven thin, tall figures around me (I later realized I was on some kind of operating table). I was given two messages (telepathically):
1. Look and see – it is gone.
2. Follow your husband (we had been experiencing marital difficulties at the time).

All of a sudden, I was tumbling head over heels (figuratively, as I was out of my body) and saw the earth as geometric green and [was] shown land masses, changing, getting closer and closer, not unlike an airplane crashing, [travelling at] unbelievable speed, and finally falling from the couch to the floor; vomiting relentlessly.

Two hours passed, and when I washed the vomit off, the lump was gone – totally ... In the ten years since this experience my health has been excellent and I have (with my husband) found a close personal relationship with God.*

However, Ring was not a psychosocialist, and instead was inclined to interpret his data in terms of Teilhard's Omega Point theory. If NDEs were pushing us towards Omega, and NDEers were similar to abductees, then UFO abductions might be pushing us towards Omega, too. NDEs and abductions and OBEs and shamanic journeys and fairy encounters and Mothman encounters and Men-in-Black encounters and Grof holotropic breathing and TM and earthlight-electromagnetic fugues and astral projections and acid trips and hypnopompic visions formed a related collection of experiences featuring an altered state of consciousness. This altered state might enable access not to an idiosyncratic dreamland, as the psychosocialists argued, but to an actual alternate reality, something which you and I and anyone else, under the right conditions, could experience simultaneously. It was similar to Grof's holotropic realm, except that it was somehow even more closely connected to human consciousness, or unconsciousness. In fact, it was something like the old idea of the collective unconscious, God's dreamworld, where Jungian symbols disported, in translucent fountains of spiritual energy, with blue meanies and Tin Woodmen and Lemurian blondes, and time ran backwards and forwards and sideways. Another writer, Michael Grosso, had called this über-dreamland 'Mind at Large', for it was just sort of ... out there – a benevolent, transcendent force which consisted of mind and could react with matter. At times of extreme planetary crisis – such as 'our own singularly dangerous ecocidal era', in Ring's words – Mind at Large could intervene, forcing the changes in consciousness necessary for survival. How? By broadcasting, on the hidden frequencies of intellect and will, its worldview-shattering, eco-apocalyptic, consciousness-raising scenarios to whoever had ears to hear. The ears to hear were, of course, in a manner of speaking, the psychic and dissociative gifts arising from genetic abnormality or childhood trauma, gifts which made their bearers

* Researchers will find this case discussed in Ring's *The Omega Project*, New York, Morrow, 1992, p. 109.

both the mediators and the embodiments of the next, and glorious, and last stage of psychological and cultural and spiritual evolution. Ring called these people the Omega Prototypes. Each of their transformative experiences was a microcosm of the planet's crisis-induced transformation. The imagery they reported represented nightmare views of the world of the future. Thus, perhaps, we could evolve into large-headed putty-faced aliens if we refused to change our ways. The hybrid breeding experiments, as Mack and others also argued, were another coded message, a gory allegory, to the effect that we needed to infuse some radically new ideas into our consciousness. Those radical ideas could best be incorporated if one's encrusted terracentric nine-to-five worldview were first knocked to pieces. Vivid confrontations with speculum-wielding monsters tended to be good at knocking crusty terracentric nine-to-five worldviews to pieces.

And when the pieces were reassembled, into a new and improved whole, human consciousness would find its true home, its promised land, in the realm of myth and imagination, and no clocks . . .

William Morrow published Ring's *The Omega Project: Near-Death Experiences, UFO Encounters, and Mind at Large* in early 1992, and it set the abduction research community buzzing. Some of the buzzing had to do with the fact that the foreword had been written by Whitley Strieber. It was evident from this foreword that Strieber, despite his own vivid experiences, and despite his quite recent enthusiasm over the Gulf Breeze blue beams, had now become a sober student of transpersonal psychology, a gentleman scientist. He had never been abducted by aliens. He had never even claimed to have been abducted by aliens. Those 'dreary' grey creatures, they were so 'tedious' . . . even fair-haired angels were tedious. They had all been in his mind, most of them generated by his own well-schooled imagination, with perhaps one or two doomsday channels picked up on the wavelength of Mind at Large. The message to Whitley from Mind at Large was that the market economy would soon fail, 'deeply, profoundly, and utterly', while the environment heaved about in wounded agony, and the old world, 'so tremendously poisonous, so bankrupt of ideas, and so strained by its own rigidities', collapsed in a bruised tangle of metaphor and hyperbole.

Whitley wished to emphasize, however, that he was being sober and rational. 'I am not a millennialist, and I do not anticipate the extinction of mankind. I am impatient with talk of "earth changes", some mysterious force upwelling to right the wrongs that man has done.'

But through all his impatience at tedious alien beings and upwelling energies, his impatience with the ufological and New Age flakiness in which he had deliberately and publicly and quite lucratively immersed himself years before, the essential Whitley shone through: 'I struggled both with the experience and with a great deal of worldwide media attention.' 'I have been more or less ostracized as a heretic from both the intellectual and literary communities.' 'I went through five years of sheer hell . . .'

*Oh that my grief were thoroughly weighed, and my calamity weighed in the balances together! For now it would be heavier than the sand of the sea . . .**

* Job 6: 2–3.

10

The Porcelain Angel

All of this might as well have been going on in another world, as far as Budd Hopkins was concerned. He was working on a case that would blow every psychosocial, imaginal-realm, and Mind-at-Large theory right out of the water, establishing the objective, physical, nuts-and-bolts, sperm-and-speculum reality of the abduction phenomenon once and for all.

The case centred on a woman named Linda. She was a slim brunette, sloe-eyed, Italian-American, fortysomething. With her husband and two young sons she lived in a crowded high-rise on the lower East Side of Manhattan. She had contacted Hopkins back in April 1989 after reading *Intruders*. Certain things in the book had led her to believe that she might have been abducted before. For example, in 1976 she had felt a lump in her nose; a physician had examined it and had insisted that she must have undergone some kind of prior nasal surgery. She was quite sure she had not, at least not at the hands of a human doctor. Hopkins brought her in, and performed a few hypnotic regressions. It appeared that she had indeed been abducted and had been given nasal implants several times in her life, beginning in early childhood and ending when she was in her twenties. She and her family had also long been plagued by ghosts and poltergeists, or at least they had *seemed* like ghosts and poltergeists. However, unlike most of the younger abductees, Linda's abduction experiences by 1989 had largely ceased. Yet she soon joined Hopkins's regular circle of abductees, coming in for regression sessions and support group meetings.

On 30 November 1989, she telephoned Hopkins in a state of excitement to say that she had just been abducted again. She had been staying up late doing the family laundry, and at 3 a.m. had gone to bed beside her sleeping husband. Almost immediately she had felt a creeping paralysis – the usual precursor to bedroom abductions – beginning in her feet and moving towards her head. Her husband would not awaken. A putty-faced grey approached the bed. She threw a pillow at it. Then her arms became paralysed too, and everything went blank. Later she consciously recalled having seen white fabric moving up towards her eyes and then down again, and also recalled the sensation of someone, or something, palpating her spine. Under hypnosis a few days later it emerged that three or four greys had come into the room and had floated her through a closed window out into a blue beam, and thence upwards, into a circular craft where the greys did the usual things before returning her, with a thump, to her bed beside her husband. Her husband was as still as death. So were her two sons. She put a mirror under the nose of one of her sons, to see if he was still breathing. He was. Then the other son began to breathe, and her husband began his familiar snore. God be praised, her ordeal was over.

To Hopkins it was just another bizarre abduction case, and he filed away the tapes of the regression session with the hundreds of others in his studio. Linda continued to attend support group meetings and regression sessions.

Then about fifteen months later, in early February 1991, Hopkins received a letter which began:

Dear Mr Hopkins:
My partner and I are police officers . . . we have been in a serious dilemma because of our strict profession. One early morning, about 3.00 to 3.30 a.m. in late November 1989, we sat in our patrol car underneath the underpass of the FDR Drive . . . observing the surroundings ahead. Sitting on the passenger side of our vehicle, I reached into my shirt pocket for a stick of gum. As I opened it, I looked down at the silver wrapping that was left in my hand and saw it reflecting a firelight type of reddish glow. I looked up through the windshield to see where it was coming from, and there it was – a strange oval hovering over the top of an apartment building two or three blocks up from where we were sitting. We don't know where it came from.

Its lights turned from a bright reddish-orange to a very bright whitish blue, coming out from the bottom of it. It moved out away from the building and lowered itself to an apartment window just below. I yelled for my partner who was sitting beside me, behind the wheel of the patrol car, and he was just as excited as I was. I had to be sure of what I was seeing so I went into the glove compartment to get a pair of binoculars. We grabbed hold of each other and were going to get out of the car, but what could we do for that poor little girl or woman wearing a full white nightgown? She was floating in midair in a bright beam of whitish blue light, looking like an angel. She was then brought up into the bottom of that very large oval (about three-quarters the size of the building across).

The letter went on to explain that the oval rose up and flew over the FDR Drive, then plunged into the East River, not far from Pier 17, behind the Brooklyn Bridge. The two officers waited for forty-five minutes, ignoring radio calls from their dispatcher, but never saw the UFO re-emerge. They agonized over whether to tell anyone what they had seen, but finally, fifteen months later, they decided to go ahead and do so, and they wrote to Hopkins. They felt guilty that they hadn't been able to prevent the abduction. They wanted to know if the abducted woman were alive and well. They signed themselves: 'Police Officers Richard and Dan'.

Hopkins broke the news to Linda, and she broke down in tears. She had hoped that her experience had only been imaginary, but now . . .

A few weeks later, according to Linda, Richard and Dan came by to see her. They were very emotional. 'My God, it's really her,' said Dan, putting his head in his hands. Richard hugged her and there were tears in his eyes. They told her what they had seen. Linda urged them to speak to Hopkins in person, but they would agree only to write out a statement and read it into a tape recorder. They didn't want to get too close to Hopkins, since public exposure would probably ruin their careers as policemen. They were getting close to retirement age, and wanted to protect their pensions.

Actually, by this time it was beginning to seem doubtful that

Richard and Dan had ever had police pensions waiting for them. Hopkins had spoken to officials at the relevant police precinct headquarters, and they had assured him that none of their officers named Richard or Dan had been in the vicinity on that date at that time.

Shortly thereafter Hopkins received the dictated letter from Richard, plus another letter from Dan reporting that Richard had taken leave of absence because of the emotional trauma the case had caused him. Among other things, Dan mentioned that Richard had become obsessed with Linda and had begun secretly to follow her around. A few weeks later Hopkins received another letter from Dan, who explained that he and Richard were, after all, not police officers. They had only claimed as much in order to further disguise their identities. In fact, they were security agents who on that fateful night in November 1989 had been driving a very important world political figure to a lower Manhattan heliport. Their limousine engine had died suddenly and inexplicably, and they had pushed it to a more easily defended position beneath the FDR Drive overpass. From that vantage point they had seen the light show over Linda's apartment building. The VIP in the back seat had seen everything, too, and had become hysterical.

Some time in April 1991, Linda told Hopkins that she had been abducted again – this time by Richard and Dan. She had been walking around in lower Manhattan one afternoon when a car driven by Dan had appeared. Richard, in the front passenger seat, asked her to get in. She refused. Richard then forcibly brought her into the car, where she remained for several hours as their captive. They asked her if she were, in fact, an alien. Aliens, they said, had no toes; they made her remove her shoes to prove that she was human. Another car followed them during the kidnapping, and under regression Linda was able to remember the licence numbers of both cars, which Hopkins soon traced to the UN missions of two countries, Britain and Venezuela.

In May, they accosted her again on the street, but this time she escaped, running out into traffic and briefly being knocked down by a car, before fleeing into the safety of a store.

Later that year, on 15 October, Linda was out walking again in Manhattan when Dan pushed her into a red Jaguar and took her to Long Island. Linda had with her a tape recorder and was able to record some of her interrogation by Dan before he discovered the recorder and confiscated it. Dan drove her to a beach house, inside which he ordered her to remove her clothes and put on a white nightgown he had purchased for her. He explained that he wanted to see her just as she had been on that fateful night in 1989. Eventually, she agreed to put on the nightgown over her clothes. When she had done so, Dan fell to his knees and ramblingly began to speak of her as his 'Lady of the Sands'. She fled the house, running out on to the beach. Dan caught her and ducked her repeatedly into the surf. Then he smeared sand in her face, removed her wedding ring, and threw it into the surf. At one point a mysterious force knocked Dan backwards. Linda escaped from Dan and ran back towards the beach house. Then Richard arrived, and persuaded Linda to return with him to the beach house. He made Dan a drink, spiking it with a knock-out pill, and while Richard put the increasingly comatose Dan under the shower to wash off the accumulated mud and sand, Linda recovered her cassette tape and noticed, on a desk somewhere in the house, stationery which bore the crest of the Central Intelligence Agency. Richard drove Linda back to Manhattan, and she immediately went over to Budd's studio where, dishevelled and still covered with sand and seaweed, she related to him the story of this second abduction by the mysterious security agents. Photographs which Richard had taken of her on the beach arrived in Hopkins's mailbox a few weeks later, along with a note from Richard explaining that he and Dan had hoped to interrogate her about the time she had been hit by the car in May.

A little over a month later, on 21 November, Linda saw Richard outside a bank in Manhattan. He told her that Dan was becoming increasingly unstable, and had been committed to a mental institution. Three weeks later she received a Christmas card and letter from Dan which made clear that this was the case. The card depicted a little boy looking up a fireplace chimney, with the caption 'How does he do it?' Inside there was a quote from Charles Dickens: 'For it is good to be Children sometimes, and never better than at Christmas . . .' The letter read in part:

Dear Pretty Linda – MERRY XMAS!

The Porcelain Angel

By the time this Xmas greeting reaches you, I will have managed to get out of this place successfully. If you don't see me, then you'll know that I'm still in here thinking my way out. Did you believe that I would let you go so easy?

The staff here usually keep me pretty sedated. You see, they like me and give me special favors. This is how I was able to get this letter started . . .

It seems like yesterday when I wanted you to go back from where you came. I hated you because I needed to live a normal and stress-free life again, but the thought of you wouldn't let me. Sometimes the hate still creeps out of me, until I think about looking into those big, deep, brown eyes of yours. Then the hate goes away. In fact, I can't wait to watch you move, as you walk by. I'm going to kiss that pretty nose and inscribe our names with my lips, on that full, heart shaped mouth that looks unhappy only when it's with me.

I will control the strong unnatural mind you possess. And I will, because I have learned much about what has to be done here in this place, in order to do this. I enjoy the helplessness you show, when you're not in control. You're fragile and very lovely, like a blown glass figurine.

But, my little Lady of the Sands, when you are in control – your tears become the swells of the sea. Your breath has the strength of high winds, and your eyes become the storm that so faithfully protects you. Yes, you've inherited the unnaturalness of your ancestor [Linda had claimed to be descended from Joan of Arc] through your mother's bloodline. St Joan of Arc was a powerful woman when she needed to be. Her strength came from above, just as yours has. But, Joan's came from God. Yours comes from them. You are half of them, but very similar to her. You are not a saint, but you are an angel.

The letter went on to describe a number of charitable acts Dan had seen Linda perform, such as carrying groceries for the elderly, buying a hot dog for a poor soul on the street, giving a shivering child her hat on a cold day.

Linda, you don't belong here, but I'll find a place for you.

When I do, you'll teach me your ways and your special language . . .

We'll be covering a lot of miles, Linda. Prepare yourself for a happy and comfortable life abroad. Pack your toothbrush, in order to travel lightly at any time. You'll make a beautiful bride, dressed all in white, just like the morning of November 1989.

If you see Richard, tell him I said 'Go to Hell.'

If I don't get out of here, I'll be thinking of you. If I do, I'll be looking at you.

Happy Holiday, pretty!

Danny

At about this time – on 15 and 16 December to be exact – Linda was followed by Richard near the South Street Seaport shopping district. Richard had been driving a black sedan with Saudi Arabian UN mission licence plates.

By now, Hopkins had received corroborating evidence for the story from other sources. First, a retired telephone operator from Putnam County, New York had written to him to explain that she, too, had witnessed the abduction in November 1989. She had been driving across the Brooklyn Bridge at about 3.15 a.m., returning home from a friend's retirement party, when her car had stalled suddenly, its lights going out. Along with other drivers on the bridge, she had seen a bright reddish light, turning white as several small figures tumbled out of an apartment building beneath it. One of the figures, she wrote to Hopkins, had worn a nightgown:

She was taller than the others. Perhaps she was a little bit older. Maybe she was a porcelain mannequin?

She had witnessed the aliens and the porcelain-like white figure in foetal positions floating up inside the blue beam to the spacecraft. She had been frightened, and other motorists on the bridge had actually run from their cars in terror. The woman, a widow in her sixties, had since then been too traumatized to return to New York City, even in daylight.

The woman from Putnam County told Hopkins that the abduction spectacle had been so garishly bright that thousands of others must have witnessed it. The fact that no one else had come forward therefore seemed odd. However, Hopkins soon unearthed a case, originally investigated by a group out on Long Island, in which a woman living on the upper East Side had been abducted from her apartment by aliens on the same night, at the same time, that Linda had been abducted. She also remembered seeing a bright reddish object flying down the river.

There also seemed to be hard evidence that Linda had been abducted. At around the time that Hopkins found out about the woman in Putnam County, Linda produced an X-ray photograph, taken by a relative of hers who was a surgeon, which seemed to indicate the presence of a metallic implant in her nasal cavity. After having seen the photograph, Linda had decided to go to her own doctor for a second X-ray, but the night before her appointment she had had a nosebleed, and subsequent X-rays showed no more implant. Anyway, Hopkins showed the first X-ray negative to a neurosurgeon friend of his, who expressed the opinion that the quarter-inch long object with coiled wire at each end was clearly not a natural part of Linda's nose.

More impressive evidence, as far as Hopkins was concerned, had come that year in the form of a letter from the VIP whom Richard and Dan had been guarding on the night in November 1989. The Third Man, as he signed himself, thanked Hopkins for his interest in the case, but explained to Hopkins that if asked publicly he would deny having had his experience. Hopkins already knew who the Third Man was, of course, for Linda, Dan, and Richard had already told him: the Third Man was Javier Perez de Cuellar, who in November 1989 had been the United Nations Secretary-General.

Hopkins never mentioned this in public, of course; he would only refer cagily to an 'important world political figure'. Nor would he mention the fact that Perez de Cuellar hadn't merely been a spectator on that fateful night in lower Manhattan. Along with Linda and Dan and Richard, and one or two other foreign dignitaries* in the motorcade that had been headed to the heliport that night, Perez de Cuellar had been abducted, too.

*

* The Canadian prime minister Brian Mulroney was rumoured to be one of these dignitaries.

The Prince of Liechtenstein soon found out about the case from Hopkins, and decided to write a VIP-to-VIP letter to Perez de Cuellar in New York. Perez de Cuellar, who was then about to hand over the reins of the UN to Dr Boutros Boutros-Ghali, was a good friend of the Prince, and had recently been his guest at Schloss Vaduz, admiring the Schloss's extensive art collection. The Prince figured that if anyone could convince Perez de Cuellar to open up, he could.

The Prince began his letter by making some boilerplate diplomatic comments about nationalism and the break-up of the old world order and so on, referring to a speech Perez de Cuellar had recently given on the subject. He then went on to remark casually that he had recently been at a party where he had met a friend of de Cuellar's, a woman named Linda, 'who had been dressed as the Lady of the Sands'. Her friends Dan and Richard had been with her.

The Prince sent the letter off and waited. A week went by. Then two weeks. The Prince was unused to such delays, even when corresponding with the world's most important political officials. What was keeping de Cuellar from responding? Finally, a letter came back from Perez de Cuellar. The Secretary General thanked the Prince for his comments on nationalism and the break-up of the old world order; the Prince's opinions had been very much appreciated, and Perez de Cuellar wished him all the best, etc. As for the business about Dan and Richard and Linda and the Lady of the Sands ... well, Perez de Cuellar ignored it as if it had never been written.

To the Prince, as to Hopkins, this was strong evidence that Perez de Cuellar was hiding something. Why hadn't he simply denied any knowledge of Linda and Richard and Dan and so forth? Why had he simply ignored it?

Despite such tantalizing leads, however, Hopkins's thoughts were increasingly preoccupied by Richard and Dan, and by their treatment of Linda. Hopkins had been talking about the case at abductee support group meetings since the summer of 1991, and his abductees were also becoming concerned by the fact that these two men Dan and Richard were out there abducting and harassing people.

Early that autumn, one of the abductees, a fellow named Rich Butler who did hypnotic regressions on other abductees down in southern New Jersey, invited a friend named Joe Stefula along to one of the support group meetings. Stefula was about to be named the New Jersey state director for MUFON, and was also a former Army CID officer – a military detective – who had investigated serious criminal cases including rape and murder. Linda showed Stefula a photograph of two men, one of whom, she said, was Dan. Stefula thought that Dan looked fairly young for someone nearing retirement age, but anyway he suggested that if she needed any protection, he might be able to arrange it for her through his contacts with state and federal police and security agencies.

A few days thereafter Linda was kidnapped by Dan and taken to Long Island for the battle on the beach, and the harassment continued. Rich Butler remained in contact with her as the months dragged by, and found himself sinking deeper into the story. In January 1992 he spoke to Linda on the phone. Linda complained that Hopkins, despite demanding her silence, was talking freely about the case to his friends. People in England had even heard about it. She also worried about Richard and Dan – especially Dan. Dan had somehow found her medical records, for his Christmas letter alluded to her unusual physiology, which only she and her doctor knew about. Dan believed that she was a hybrid alien-human. The Third Man did, too. The Third Man had seen how she had dealt with the aliens back in November 1989, as well as on subsequent occasions. She had seemed able to hold her own against the speculum-wielders, somehow. There was something very unusual and remarkable about her. Nevertheless, she was very worried about Dan. She did not mention to Butler that Dan was in a mental institution. She only mentioned that Dan had expressed in his letter the desire to take her away, forcibly, to a foreign country. She had been having nightmares in which Dan and she were walking through an airport terminal, and she was too drugged to protest. Butler sounded sympathetic, and suggested that he and Stefula and Stefula's friends, if necessary, might be able to teach Dan a lesson – maybe track him down and rough him up and dump him on Hopkins's doorstep. Linda sounded encouraged, and suggested that she and Butler might meet to discuss it all further.

Linda and Butler met four days later, with Stefula, in Manhattan. Linda emphasized that they were not to tell Hopkins about the meeting. Hopkins wanted her to keep silent about the case. He wanted to investigate it for himself. He had paid private detectives to track down Dan and Richard. He had shown nasal X-rays to a well-known neurosurgeon. But after all, Hopkins was only an abstract artist, and what could he do against people who could abduct others at will off the streets and take them to CIA safe houses on Long Island?

Linda told Butler and Stefula that her apartment was under surveillance by people in a silver-grey van. The Third Man would sometimes watch her, too. The Third Man was fascinated by her unusual physiology, which, she now admitted, had to do with her red blood cells, which were immortal. This may have been the result of her frequent alien liaisons, or it may have been because she was the product of the alien-human breeding programme.* But where, Butler and Stefula wanted to know, was the doctor who had discovered the unusual properties of her red cells? Well, said Linda, she had tried to track him down recently but unfortunately had been unable to do so.

According to Butler and Stefula, Linda told them that the November 1989 abduction had begun while she had been sitting on the couch in her living-room, waiting for her husband to come home – not, as she apparently told Hopkins, while she had been in bed beside her husband. Butler and Stefula told her that they thought the Third Man was Perez de Cuellar, and that the only way the case made sense – the only reasonable explanation for the fact that Dan and Richard and Perez de Cuellar had waited so long to contact her – was if they had been abducted with her. She admitted that they had, and asked Butler and Stefula not to tell Hopkins that she had told them.

* The Tungus shaman Semyonov Semyon, interviewed in 1925, spoke of how the spirits of his ancestors, before initiating him into the shamanic mysteries, had been delighted to learn of his physiological abnormalities: 'They cut up my flesh, separated my bones, counted them, and ate my flesh raw. When they counted the bones they found one too many; had there been too few, I could not have become a shaman.' In Celtic folklore, apparently odd physiological attributes were commonly considered as evidence that a person was a fairy 'changeling'.

The Porcelain Angel

She also told them that in the early 1960s she had been a professional singer. In fact, she said, the voice of the lead singer for the all-girl group the Angels, on the recording of the 1963 hit, 'My Boyfriend's Back', was hers.

> My boyfriend's back, and you're gonna be in trou-u-ble.
> [chorus] Hey la, hey la, my boyfriend's back.
> When you see him comin better cut out on the dou-u-ble.
> [chorus] Hey la, hey la, my boyfriend's back.
> You've been tellin lies that I was un-true-ue-ue.
> [chorus] Hey la, hey la, my boyfriend's back.
> But look out, now, cause he's comin after you-ou-ou.
> [chorus] Hey la, hey la, my boyfriend's back.

According to Linda, the lead singer listed on the album cover had stepped down for some reason, and she, Linda, had taken her place.* Linda later had lost her own voice suddenly one morning, sometime in the late 1960s; she had gone into the shower, and when she had come out again she had barely been able to hold a tune.†

According to Stefula and Butler, Linda told them that Hopkins planned a book about her case; she and Budd, she said, had agreed to split the royalties 50–50.

Butler and Stefula did not betray their emotions directly to Linda. They played the role of anxious protectors. But by this time they had serious doubts about her credibility. Stefula, in particular,

---

* *The All Music Guide*, San Francisco, Miller Freeman, 1992, edited by Michael Erlewine and Scott Bultman, notes of the Angels that: 'With Linda Jansen as lead and sisters Jiggs and Barbara Allbut providing harmony, the Orange, NJ trio signed with Caprice Records in 1961 and hit with "Til". Jansen was replaced by Peggy Santiglia (b. May 4, 1944) and the trio signed with Mercury's Smash subsidiary in 1963, cutting the bouncy "My Boyfriend's Back" at the height of the girl-group craze. "I Adore Him" proved mildly successful later that year.' Incidentally, a TV-movie about a problematical reunion of the group – pseudonymized as 'The Bouffants' – was broadcast in the US in 1989.

† In conversations with Linda's relatives, Hopkins apparently confirmed that Linda had undergone a sudden shift in personality while a teenager; her interest in singing had been replaced by a fascination with meteorology. Linda's mother had been alarmed enough to send her daughter to a neurologist.

had dealt with cases in his old job at Fort Dix in which women had told stories about being raped and otherwise brutalized, going into incredible detail about the things which supposedly had been done to them, and all of it demonstrably untrue – a ploy, he believed, just to get attention. Moreover, according to Stefula, after one of Hopkins's support group meetings that winter, when the abductees walked over to a pizza place on Eighth Avenue, Stefula had come along and had overheard the other abductees saying some very heretical things . . . to the effect that Linda was going too far, was drawing too much limelight, had caught poor Budd, their Budd, in her manicured clutches. Who did she think she was, anyway? They had referred sarcastically to Linda as the 'Queen Bee abductee'.

Winter turned to spring, and the MIT conference came, and Hopkins talked about Linda; when reporters called him saying they wanted to do a story about abductions, he told them about Linda, and when the Prince of Liechtenstein came to town, he introduced him to Linda. Then in July, when the annual MUFON conference was held in Albuquerque, Hopkins devoted the entirety of his talk to Linda, at one point stepping aside for her to give a brief, heartfelt account of the case herself. Someone from the audience asked why she hadn't gone to the police. She said it was because the case involved national security, and she didn't want to end up in . . . little pieces . . . at the bottom of the East River.

Joe Stefula was sitting in the audience listening to this. Next to him was a friend, George Filer, the MUFON Deputy State Director for New Jersey, who also knew about the case. Hearing Hopkins and Linda talk about the case from the stage, Stefula and Filer snorted with derision. Not only was the case absurd on its face, they believed, but there were numerous inconsistencies – her story about being on the couch at the start of the first abduction, for instance – plus the fact that Hopkins was downplaying the role of the Third Man, and was soft-pedalling the antics of Richard and Dan, to make the whole thing sound more plausible.

Stefula and Filer were sitting there in the audience, making uncomplimentary noises about what Hopkins and Linda were saying, when a grey-haired gentleman in the row in front of them turned around to face them. Evidently he had been listening to their discussion, for he had a curious, slightly leering grin on his face. He wanted to know more.

He was, of course, Philip Klass.

In the months that followed, encouraged by Klass, Filer, and others, Stefula and Butler looked further into the Linda case. They were joined by one of Stefula's friends, George Hansen, a civil engineer turned parapsychologist who had a side-interest in UFOs and had made a hobby of exposing fraudulent paranormal claims. Don Johnson also joined the group; he was a practising psychologist and enthusiastic ufologist who managed an enormous UFO-report database, called UFOCAT.

Stefula, for his part, felt that the evidence for a hoax was already overwhelming, and would have preferred to go no further in researching the case. He had promised Linda that he wouldn't publish anything until after she had gone public, and now she had gone public. After the Albuquerque conference, he had rung MUFON director Walt Andrus to suggest that he and Butler write a piece in *MUFON UFO Journal*, giving their own side of the story. Andrus, however, was a friend of Hopkins; he told Stefula that any criticism of the Linda case would be premature. Hopkins also, according to Stefula, refused to debate the case, and demanded that Stefula and his friends abandon their investigation.

Angered by what they considered to be a circle-the-wagons reaction by Hopkins and his network of influential friends, Stefula and the others set out to expose the Linda case as a hoax as soon as possible, lest it be mocked by the popular press to the detriment of ufology as a whole.

They began by checking the basic facts of the case. Stefula and Butler drove to lower Manhattan and videotaped the view from beneath the FDR Drive and from the Brooklyn Bridge looking towards Linda's apartment. From those distances, it seemed to them, a witness would have been unlikely to see the kind of details – such as Linda's nightgown and the fact that she was in a foetal position – which Richard and Dan and the woman from Putnam County claimed to have seen. Linda's high-rise apartment also turned out to be only two blocks away from the loading dock of the *New York Post*. Stefula tracked down the man who had been the *Post*'s loading dock manager in 1989; he told Stefula that the loading dock was normally in use until 5 a.m. every morning, and that he hadn't seen or heard anything about a UFO down the street in November 1989.

Butler called the UN Security Investigation Unit, which was responsible for looking into suspicious or unusual activities reported by UN personnel. Butler wanted to know whether there had been any unusual incidents, perhaps UFO-related incidents, involving Secretary-General Perez de Cuellar in late November 1989. The UN Security people responded that there had been no such incidents to their knowledge. Butler also spoke to the Secret Service – the evidence by this time suggested that Dan and Richard might be Secret Service agents – and they also denied that any of their personnel were involved in any UFO incident in late November 1989. The CIA public affairs office explained, as they explained to numerous such queries, that even if there had been such an incident involving its employees, it could not reveal any information about it.

The Downtown Heliport, at Pier Six on the East River, was also contacted by the group. The Downtown Heliport was the only heliport located in the direction in which Perez de Cuellar's motorcade had allegedly been travelling. The Senior Airport Operations Agent went back through the log and could find no record of any helicopter departures outside of normal hours on the night of 29 November 1989. The normal heliport hours were 7 a.m. to 7 p.m. The heliport official remembered that some months earlier he and his colleagues had been approached with a similar request by a slim, silver-haired man, apparently in his fifties. The man had mentioned something about an unidentified flying object that had crashed into the East River.

Don Johnson obtained copies of personality and IQ tests that had been administered to Linda by a prominent Manhattan psychologist, Gibbs Williams. The profile, according to Johnson's analysis, suggested an individual with external passivity, internal activity, spontaneous curiosity, and a high degree of creativity. Fantasy was easily provoked, and easily maintained. She probably suffered from worse than average nightmares, talked in her sleep, and occasionally somnambulated. According to Johnson, she would be socially adept, alert to subtleties in her interpersonal environment, but at the same time having a degree of detachment; outwardly she would be sensitive and empathic, while inwardly narcissistic. A lot of artists and intellectuals and writers were like that. One psychologist had looked at her profile and had noticed a similarity to the profiles of people with multiple personality disorder; he had suggested that Linda might have had some kind of trauma in her childhood. Another psychologist had matched Linda's profile with those of two young women who had scored high on ESP tests at Stanford Research Institute. Johnson had interviewed her for a few hours and had noticed that she had a tendency to exaggerate. Even the other psychologists, the ones on Hopkins's side, had agreed that some of Linda's stories, such as the one about being descended from Joan of Arc, were difficult to accept at face value . . .

One of the odder pieces of evidence turned up in the form of a science fiction novel that had been published in April 1989, at just about the same time Linda had first contacted Budd Hopkins. The novel, called *Nighteyes*, had been written by a man named Garfield Reeves-Stevens, and had to do with UFO abductions and international intrigue: one of the heroines, Sarah, is abducted from her Manhattan high-rise into a hovering spaceship. Two government agents, Derek and Merrill, involved in a stakeout early one morning, have their work interrupted by another UFO abduction. Derek, during his abduction, meets Wendy, another abductee. Wendy then goes to see Charles Edward Starr, a prominent UFO abduction researcher and writer based in New York City. Subsequently, Wendy is kidnapped by Derek and Merrill. Derek takes Wendy to an FBI safe house on a beach. Derek and Wendy become romantically involved. Derek becomes so emotionally unstable, owing to the trauma of the case, that he has to be hospitalized.

Because the novel also mentioned Budd Hopkins, it had been referred to at one or two support group meetings shortly after its publication.

During this period, from midsummer to the early autumn of 1992, Stefula and Butler and Hansen kept up a steady barrage of correspondence with Hopkins, challenging him to address the apparent problems they had uncovered in the case, and circulating a proposed article they had written about it. Hopkins responded with his own circulated articles and private correspondences, attacking their arguments point by point: the *New York Post*'s loading dock, for example, was enclosed within a garage, and faced south; a UFO two blocks away to the east might easily have gone unnoticed. Four people other than Linda had told Hopkins that they had met Richard. Perez de Cuellar's identity as the VIP abducted by aliens on that fateful night in November 1989 had been verified by two independent sources. *Nighteyes*, read as a whole, bore only the slightest resemblance to the Linda case. John Mack had evaluated the letters to Linda from Dan, and agreed that they represented the disordered thinking characteristic of someone in a progressively paranoid and delusional state. Mack had also evaluated Linda in a face-to-face meeting, and believed her to be telling the truth.

In general, Hopkins asserted that he had much more information about the case than was available to Butler and Stefula and their colleagues. For instance, he said he had in his possession more than eighty pages of correspondence from Richard and Dan, only a fraction of which had so far been released. He noted that if the case were a hoax it would be the most complex in ufological history, requiring numerous participants including Linda's husband and sons. Hopkins also referred to the souring of his relations with Butler and Stefula, after Stefula, he said, had rather roughly interrogated some other abductees at a support group meeting, and after Butler had proposed that some of Hopkins's abductees weren't really abductees because, according to Butler's theory, only peoples of Native American and Celtic extraction were ever abducted. He suggested that Butler and Stefula, having fallen out of favour, were motivated by revenge. He condemned them for having leaked Linda's name, as well as details of the case, not only to the diabolical Klass, but to James Moseley, the almost equally diabolical editor of a Key West based ufological gossip newsletter, *Saucer Smear*.

By the second week in September the controversy still raged, as memoranda pro and anti Linda reverberated through fax machines and the national postal system. Hopkins decided to resolve the dispute once and for all. Butler and Stefula and Hansen had been pestering him to meet them to discuss the case, and now he assented, proposing that they should meet at his place, in early October. It would be an opportunity for them to present their charges to Linda and her family, who would in turn be able to respond.

The meeting was held on 3 October. Butler, Stefula, Hansen, and Don Johnson were there for the anti-Linda side, with one of Stefula's friends, a security consultant, present as an expert witness. Hopkins, Jerome Clark, Walt Andrus, Dave Jacobs, Penelope Franklin, the psychologist Gibbs Williams, plus Linda and her husband and two sons, represented the defence. The meeting started out with Linda's husband explaining briefly, in halting, Italian-accented English, that Linda had introduced him to Richard outside church one Sunday. Linda's son Steve then explained how Richard, disguised as a vagrant, had approached him on a bus, questioning him about the family. Linda's youngest son, Johnny, then allowed that he had had several contacts with Richard.

Gibbs Williams presented the results of standard IQ and personality tests administered to Linda. From these tests, Dr Williams indicated delicately, it appeared improbable that Linda could have organized and perpetrated such an elaborate hoax. Indeed, he said, to pull something like this off would have taken the mind of a Bobby Fischer.

Butler and Stefula discussed their version of the case, among other things reciting a transcript of a telephone conversation between Butler and Linda; according to the transcript, Linda exhorted Butler not to tell Budd she had been confiding in him. Then Stefula's security consultant friend, who for a time had served as US Defense Secretary Dick Cheney's personal security officer, explained that UN Secretary-Generals, when they wanted to go somewhere, didn't simply get into the back of a limousine and tell the driver where to go. Perez de Cuellar's journey would have involved advance planning and extensive communication with other security elements; any problem such as a car's stalling, or a delay in passing a checkpoint, or an abduction by little grey men, would have prompted an instant and massive reaction from UN security. Stefula's friend also went through some of the VIP-security vernacular with Hopkins, suggesting that if Richard and Dan were unfamiliar with this vernacular, then they probably were not who they claimed to be.

Throughout the meeting there was a sort of cross-examination of Linda and her husband by Stefula and Hansen. Hansen asked Linda's husband where he had been born. In Italy, said Linda's husband. But Linda had earlier claimed to Hansen that her husband had been born in the US; now she acknowledged that she had deliberately misled Hansen (according to Hopkins, so that Linda could trip up Hansen should he later accuse her barely Anglophonic husband of being the voice of Dan and Richard). Stefula asked if it were true that, as Linda had told him, she had an agreement with Hopkins to split the royalties from any book about the case. Hopkins said that this was not true. Linda explained that she had said this to Stefula in order to plant 'disinformation'. Linda's husband, despite his wife's entreaties to stay a bit longer, shortly excused himself and left, in order to drive young Steve to a date with his girlfriend.

Stefula noted that Linda refused to report Dan and Richard, who had kidnapped her – and, in Dan's case, had apparently attempted to murder her – to the FBI or other law enforcement agencies. Linda said she would testify against them, but didn't want to press charges. Hopkins, Andrus, and Clark backed her up. Involving the government in such a sensitive case, they argued, would only complicate things unnecessarily. Stefula and Butler were persuaded to agree to wait six months before notifying federal authorities – but Hansen agreed to nothing.

Tempers occasionally flared. Hansen harped on the FBI business, which had been a sore point with Hopkins ever since the talk show debate with Klass in 1987. Hansen also kept coming back to the fact that Linda had been caught out in two fibs. Penny Franklin said that under the circumstances Linda was justified in lying to people about such matters. Hansen, Butler, and Stefula attacked Hopkins as a sloppy investigator for not even having found out what the weather had been like in New York on the night of the big abduction. Then Stefula said something that Jacobs found particularly objectionable, and Jacobs, according to Stefula, jumped out of his chair, eyes blazing, teeth bared, fists clenched. Stefula, who was younger, taller, and built like a linebacker, glared back with mocking defiance.

The meeting ended on a mostly cordial note, but the controversy over the Linda case wouldn't go away easily, or quietly. In an article in the September issue of *MUFON UFO Journal*, summarizing the case, Hopkins had suggested that government intelligence agents within ufology might be mobilized to subvert the case. Butler and Stefula's investigation had already made them suspicious in his eyes, and a few weeks after the October meeting, word went around that Hansen, too, was now thought by Hopkins to be a possible government agent. Meanwhile, Stefula informally notified friends in the Secret Service about the case; and although Hopkins had decided by now that Richard and Dan worked for a US agency other than the Secret Service, Hansen sent the Treasury Department (which oversees the Secret Service) a formal request for an investigation of the kidnappings of Linda by the alleged federal agents Richard and Dan, summarizing the details of Linda's allegations and naming Hopkins, Jacobs, Clark, Andrus, and even John Mack as potential witnesses, helpfully providing their telephone numbers and home addresses.

11

The Man in the Blue Striped
Pyjamas

Throughout that autumn, Budd Hopkins continued to devote a great deal of his time and attention to the Linda case. While attempting to turn the bare facts of the case into a marketable book proposal, he lobbied prominent ufologists to raise support for Linda and her story, and wrote articles about the case for ufological journals, and lectured about the case around the country – indeed, internationally – seemingly wherever abduction conferences of sufficient seriousness were being held. And every so often he would interview Linda or another witness about new developments in the ever-unfolding mystery – the government surveillance van that lurked outside Linda's apartment, a new high-rise abduction, the schemes and bedevilments of Richard and Dan, and of course the thorny interferences of Hansen and Stefula and their gang.

It was more than enough work, and enough stress, for anyone, and yet this was merely Hopkins's surface preoccupation, his public ufological pursuit. The Hopkins of day-to-day life attended to numerous other abductees, whether they had been in his circle for years or were distraught first-timers. Daily he listened to myriad tales, epic tragedies, of invasion and violation by men and monsters. Daily he answered piles of mail, from every corner of the globe. Dear Mr Hopkins, I recently purchased your *Intruders* book and after reading it I suddenly remembered a strange incident which occurred to me many years ago . . . Daily he watched over IF, the ever-growing Intruders Foundation, raising funds for it, recruiting psychologists and psychiatrists and other professionals to its ranks, and flying around the continent to train them, sometimes dozens at a time, in the techniques of abductee hypnosis. There were letters and phone calls to answer, from ufologists, abductees, therapists, philanthropists. There were newspapermen to speak to, radio chat show audiences to entertain, television documentaries to sit for, would-be authors to cooperate with . . .

The door of Budd Hopkins's house was barred and battleship-grey, the buzzer button marked, somewhat confusingly, Kingsley Hopkins – Kingsley being April, Budd's wife. Inside, away from the gloomy urban tableau of 16th Street, a stairway led left, up to the main living quarters, while a level passageway led into the structure, then left, right, past a bathroom, a bedroom, walls covered with family photographs and price-tagged boxes of painted porcelain – April's – and down a narrow wooden stairway to the bright lower studio.

Budd Hopkins was dressed in dark trousers, a blue artist's workshirt, and a grandfatherly shawl-collar cardigan. His salt-and-pepper hair, as his first wife Joan once described it to me, was now almost entirely salt, but showed no signs of thinning. He wore clear-rimmed – and again, somewhat grandfatherly – glasses, although his grin was youthful and benevolent, with perhaps a touch of good-old-boy mischievousness, his mouth sculpted close to the nose and curving gently beneath it in placid amiability. He favoured his bad leg as he negotiated the stairway, but spoke animatedly to his visitor about his work, his art. 'Are you interested in art?'

'Budd,' I explained, 'I am a complete philistine.'

Near the lower terminus of the staircase another set began, reaching up to the upper studio. From there a young man peered down at us – Peter Robbins, he of the 1987 MUFON abductee panel and the youthful blue-beam incident with his sister on Long Island. Greetings and handshakes. Robbins was one of Budd's part-time assistants, helping with all the mail and phone calls. Budd and I went down to the lower studio.

In the lower studio the wooden floorboards were painted grey, and the brick walls were painted white, and on the walls hung a row of Guardians in red, blue, gold, green, purple . . . gorgeous canaries in a monochrome jungle. On the floor beside the Guardians lay a few pieces of dark wooden sculpture, the Altars, which looked vaguely like those puritan-era stocks where town miscreants, their heads and hands locked in, could be cuffed and mocked by their neighbours. Over at one end of the studio, beneath the stairway, was one of Budd's earlier works, a large triptych with a Sun-Black style hypnotic circle in the centre and a series of rays and bars hurtling outwards from it in bursts of colour. This was *Mahler's Castle*, the small collage-like study which, when purchased by Ira Wender, had played a cameo role in Hopkins's first book contract. Incidentally, there was no great significance in the name *Mahler's Castle*; Hopkins had chosen that name merely because he had often listened to Mahler while painting it.

Within another wall of this lower studio, facing the Guardians, were deep shelves full of canvas boards and smaller one-eighth scale studies for the Guardians. Somewhere in there were also the studies for the Ixions – the round-headed creations which, the reader will recall, had been inspired by a mortal's mythopoeic attempt to seduce the Queen of the gods.

On a sill beneath the shelves with the Guardians and the Ixions lay a small framed pencil drawing, *Les Lutteurs* (*The Wrestlers*), by the cubist Fernand Léger. Beneath the Léger was a black leather couch, where abductees would lie during hypnosis. Facing the couch was a small, paint-flecked wooden chair, where Hopkins would sit during these sessions. This chair, this couch, this art-cluttered studio comprised the world's most active, and arguably most important laboratory for UFO abduction research.

This was a more or less typical day in the life of Budd Hopkins, and I was only one of many aspects of that day. But for a while we were uninterrupted and Budd spoke of paradigm conflicts and the ramparts of orthodoxy, and his early days as a ufologist and an abduction researcher, and the great cases he had seen, and the great abductees – Charley Hickson from Pascagoula, for example, whose elephant-skinned, lobster-clawed, cone-eared abductors had been transmogrified, on the same black couch where I was sitting, into the usual big-eyed greys. Most people were unaware of it, but Hopkins had established that Hickson had a long history of abductions, going back to his childhood in the 1930s.

Budd spoke of his investigative techniques, and his development of an inner sense of when people were telling the truth or not, and how he had hypnotized about 400 abductees since 1976, and how with *Intruders* in print in America, Britain, Germany, Holland, Sweden, Japan, Italy, Spain, Poland, Hungary, and God knew where else, he was getting letters from all over the world, a polyphonous blizzard – and every few minutes the phone would ring in the upstairs studio, and Peter Robbins would pick it up and try to deal with it, but occasionally the call was so important that Robbins would instead yell down to the lower studio something such as, 'Hey Budd! Dan Flemiel on the phone; he's trying to get in touch with Charley Hickson!' or 'Hey Budd! It's Barbara from LA. Can you give her a minute?' or 'Hey Budd, it's Davey-boy!' – Davey-boy being David Jacobs – and Hopkins would yell something back or excuse himself and make his way up to the upper studio and take the call before coming back to resume the interview.

At one point the door buzzer rang and a minute later a young woman walked shyly to the top of the stairs above the studio. She had strawberry blonde hair and a pout. 'Hi there, Lucy, come on down!' said Budd with a deliberate enthusiasm that suggested to me that she was an abductee who had been through hell and required careful treatment. However, for the past couple of hours she had merely been out with a German TV crew doing an interview about her experiences. 'How did your interview go?' asked Budd. 'Longer than I thought it was going to be,' said Lucy. 'But they're nice people,' said Budd. 'They're nice,' agreed Lucy, laughing shyly. 'I had them all crying at one point. Not crying but – ' she made a sniffling sound – 'you know, tears and . . . you know . . .'

Budd invited Lucy to sit with us, but she elected instead to go to Budd's daughter Grace's bedroom and rest. Grace was away at university. Lucy was staying here at Budd's house for a few days, for the interview and to undergo regression for some of her recent abduction episodes. She had indeed been through a lot, Budd told me. Quite a few of the abductees found his house a sanctuary during difficult times.

We spoke about Whitley Strieber, and several of the more bizarre incidents which he said had eroded their friendship, and *Communion* – 'a new genre,' said Budd: 'Involuntary Fiction' – and the

Linda case, and the Third Man, and pestilential Stefula and Butler and Hansen, and eventually, after lunch and more interviewing, Lucy appeared at the top of the stairs – 'Hi, Budd' – with another abductee, a mirthful brunette named Nicole. They had bought Budd a gift: a plastic Cyrano de Bergerac nose. With a certain amount of embarrassment Budd dutifully put on the nose and modelled it for us, and thanked them for it.

After a while one of the German crew came down and said that they wanted to film an introductory shot of Budd outside, walking on 16th Street. While he went outside I listened to a tape Budd had given me, a recording from one of Linda's early regression sessions in 1989, having to do with an abduction episode outside a cabin up in the Catskills in the late 1970s, when she had been five months pregnant with one of her boys. The aliens had lured Linda from her bed beside her sleeping husband and outside into the parking area and had just brought her into their ship and had placed her, sobbing fearfully, on the examination table when Budd returned with one of the Germans.

The German apologized for taking so much of Budd's time. Budd said that he didn't mind, because he knew that the Germans planned a high-quality production. 'You know, the *Unsolved Mysteries* thing was really good,' he said, referring to the Robert Stack-narrated series on NBC which had recently aired a special about UFO abductions. 'And they spent a lot of time. 20/20 came in, and they took less time . . . it was still pretty good. David Cherniak, when he did that special for his talk show, was very good, but there've been a lot of really slipshod . . .' His voice trailed off. 'I think it's always better to try to do less in variety and more in depth.' He turned to me. 'I don't know if you saw Linda Howe's last film.' Linda Howe was a television producer who had made a widely praised documentary about UFO-related cattle mutilations back in the early eighties. Recently she had developed a weekly half-hour show called *Sightings* for the Fox network. *Sightings* dealt with just about everything that was paranormal or supernatural or strange, and in a recent broadcast they had concentrated on UFOs. 'It covered every aspect of the whole thing,' said Budd, disgusted at its implicit superficiality. 'Cattle mutilations, saucer crashes and retrievals, crop circles, underground bases, abductions, sightings, poltergeists, blah, blah, blah – and everything had about a minute and a half. You know, it was like reading the headlines on the *National Enquirer* or something.'

We went to the upper studio where the Germans were doing some short takes of Budd's Altars and Temples and Guardians, and then were setting up their lights and cameras for a long interview with Budd. One of them, the producer, mentioned something about Lucy, how it was incredible that she was abducted so often, and Budd agreed that it was astonishing. He had done thirty or forty regression sessions with her already. He pulled out a photograph taken of one of Lucy's ankles, during the MIT conference. She had been abducted in the middle of the conference and the aliens had undressed her and had put her into some kind of stirrup arrangement and the stirrups had had little metal clamps on them, and you could see in the photograph where the clamps had made little impressions on her flesh. But why? the German producer wanted to know. *Why do zey use clamps when zey have mind control?* Budd responded to the effect that their mind control was never perfect, otherwise how would we know about abductions at all. And perhaps, in a gradual way, they wanted us to know . . .

Budd sat down at his desk amid the TV crew's lights and opened his mail while we spoke. The first envelope was from his bank. He began to shake his head in disgust. It was a notice informing him that payment on a $1,000 cheque he had deposited had been stopped. He had been given the cheque for a lecture fee somewhere, but apparently whoever had given it to him was broke or was just reneging. He shook his head in exasperation.

'You could attribute that bounced cheque to the aliens, Budd,' said a member of the German crew. 'I prefer to attribute it to the CIA,' joked Budd.

Next envelope. 'Little Rock, Arkansas.' From an abductee, apparently. A good-old-boy grin stole over Budd's face, and he mimicked a female letter-writer's voice: 'When Bill Clinton and I were parked in this car, late at night . . .' We all laughed.

Budd traded more jokes with the crew while they set everything up, and then he showed us some sketches that Richard and the woman on the Brooklyn Bridge had made. The sketches depicted little figures floating up a beam into a flying saucer. One of the little figures was dressed in white. The others were big-headed greys. Linda had made some sketches, too, and so had her younger boy, Johnny, who had also been abducted on one or two occasions. Budd noted the artistic differences between the sketches, which suggested that they had indeed been made by different people, and not all by a lone hoaxer. Budd complained again about the attacks that debunkers had made on the case. If this thing were a hoax, he said, the woman on the bridge would have to have been a cold-blooded liar. A lot of other people would have to be lying, too. 'There is,' said Budd, 'no such thing as a hoax with a thousand and one moving parts.'

'Budd,' said the German producer after a moment, 'could you please sit down for a second so we can see what it looks like?' They wanted to adjust the lights and the cameras with him in front of them.

'We've got this big shadow over there,' said one of the cameramen.

'That's the shadow of the future hanging over me,' said Budd.

While the Germans did the interview with Budd, I sat in his daughter Grace's bedroom talking to Lucy and Nicole and Peter Robbins and Gretchen Kelly, an assistant producer who specialized in UFOs and the paranormal and was helping the Germans with their research. Gretchen had spent a lot of time in the last few days hand-holding the Germans. All of this business of UFO abductions had frightened them, she said. They couldn't sleep at night. One of them, in a moment of despair, had asked her, 'What if we're all going to be –?' 'Relax,' she had said, 'you can worry about that when it happens.' Gretchen said it was often like that for journalists dealing with the subject for the first time. You had to know how to deal with it. Especially because the UFO subject was becoming so big.

Someone handed me a deck of trading cards; each card depicted some famous person from ufological history, from Ray Palmer to George Adamski to Philip Klass. The card for Klass said that under the pen name of William Tenn he had written over fifty science fiction stories.

Peter and Lucy and Nicole were playing around with a doll that

Nicole had made. It was about four feet tall, and looked like a somewhat slender version of Mickey Mouse, but it was only a screen-memory Mickey; his nose and ears were part of a mask that slipped off easily, revealing a no-nosed no-eared big-eyed grey. Over on Grace's night-table lay a little grey plastic-figurine tableau, featuring an alien hypnotist and alien patient, and a little sketch that the hypnotized patient had made of the horrifying otherworldly entity he had encountered: a human baby. I was impressed by the fact that these young women could laugh at their misfortune in this way, and Peter emphasized that it was all cathartic. He noted that the human sense of humour seemed to be something that the aliens couldn't figure out. The aliens seemed to have lost their own sense of humour somewhere.

Peter was in his early forties and was an artist by training. He lived with his sister, who was now a moderately successful rock singer, in a nice apartment on the upper East Side overlooking Central Park. He had been an artist for some years and had taught here and there, and then one day in the mid 1980s, when he had been living down in Chinatown and the Chinese New Year celebrations had been going on, with strings of firecrackers cracking and sparklers sparkling and dancing in the streets and so forth, he had suddenly remembered the blue-beam episode from his childhood. It had been buried deep in his memory, but on that Chinese New Year's day it had begun to flash vividly in his mind, like a movie. The sunny blue 1960s sky was there, and the smell of the grass, and the metallic sheen of the saucers as they hovered watchfully over the Greenbergs' house across the street . . . After remembering this, and recovering somewhat from his shock, he had called his sister. He hadn't wanted to tell her the whole story; he had wanted to see if she remembered it herself. So he called her up and said, 'Do you remember the time when we were kids sitting out on the lawn that day and –?' She had finished the thought for him. She had remembered everything. He had turned to run inside and tell their mother, but then a blue beam had come down and paralysed him, and he had been just frozen there, and meanwhile she had been abducted.

After that, Peter's life had changed. He had lost his interest in art and had developed an interest in UFOs and other esoterica. He had travelled in England, fascinated by ley-lines and tumuli and stone circles. He had met Budd – 'the Budd-Man', he called him cheerfully – on the ufology lecture circuit and when Robert Bigelow had put up some money to support Hopkins's research, Peter had become the Budd-Man's first employee. Now he was working on a book about the Rendlesham Forest mystery, which centred around an apparent UFO landing and abduction at a US Air Force base in Britain in 1980, and the subsequent government cover-up. His co-author was Larry Warren, one of the USAF officers involved in the encounter; it was fun working with Warren but it was also a hassle because the National Security Agency had tapped his phone. A retired general with an interest in ufology had confirmed the telephone tapping to them after making inquiries. Peter and his co-author had also drawn the interest of a fairly prominent New York agent.

Peter's position as Hopkins's sidekick, and as a ufologist in his own right, had led people to approach him with their own abduction experiences. One such individual, a student at NYU who came from a famous old family, had approached him because his family had been plagued by aliens for years. It had begun when the father had been a Naval officer in the early 1950s. His ship had been towing a destroyer for bombardment practice – the tow-cable was a few miles long – when a saucer-shaped object had suddenly appeared overhead, causing all sorts of electrical problems on the ship. The captain had refused to report the incident in the ship's log, but the young officer whose son would one day confide in Peter Robbins wrote it all down and saved it after he left the service; he still periodically got together with his old Navy buddies, despite their class differences, to discuss the incident and the effect it had had on their lives. Apparently the father was abducted fairly often, and so was the son. The aliens had more or less the free run of the house. When the mother had seen a copy of the Gulf Breeze book, with a drawing of an alien, she had recognized it right away.

'How did you get interested in abductions?' Nicole asked me. 'Have you had any . . . experiences?'

I said that I didn't think I had, but that I guessed I had always had a soft spot for strange phenomena.

Nicole and Lucy and Peter looked at each other and nodded.

'What kind of dreams have you had?' asked Nicole. 'What kind of nightmares?'

'Pretty ordinary ones, I guess.'

'Like what?'

'Like the one where I'm walking home from elementary school and the street goes quiet and the sidewalk turns to a railroad track and my shoelaces are caught in the trestle and I can hear the freight train hurtling down the hill behind me –'

'Have you ever awakened in the middle of the night with paralysis?' asked Nicole. 'With the sense that someone else was in the room?'

I said that I hadn't, but that there had been times when I had been very tired or recovering from a severe case of the flu and had had the sudden sense that although paralysed I was floating or levitating.

'Levitating?' asked Nicole and Peter and Lucy together. They exchanged more meaningful glances.

I hastened to say that I had always attributed these experiences to ordinary physiological causes, such as an insufficient blood-flow to the brain, or stress resulting from illness. But I could see that I had set Nicole and Lucy and Peter to wondering just how deep my interest in the subject might be. Peter told me the story of a young reporter who had ended up writing a tongue-in-cheek story about alien abductions for the *Wall Street Journal* back in May 1992. Peter and Budd had spent a lot of time with him, going over the history of the subject and the extent of the phenomenon, and had told him about the Linda case and had allowed him to sit in on a regression session with a male abductee. At one point, Peter quietly had asked the reporter why he had decided to do a story about UFO abductions. Had his editor simply assigned him to it, or had he, the reporter, proposed it himself? The reporter replied disarmingly that he had heard that his editor wanted a story about abductions and he had volunteered for it – because he thought that, yes, it was possible that something UFO-related had happened to him when he was younger. Peter had believed him at the time, but now he wondered if the guy had only been telling him what he wanted to hear . . .

*

A few weeks later I was up at Budd's house again to sit in on a hypnotic regression session with Nicole. She had had a strange dream recently; it was especially strange because Linda had reported a similar dream on the same night.

Before starting, Budd and Nicole and I went to a restaurant around the corner on Seventh Avenue for a quick lunch. We ordered sandwiches and Budd started up about Stefula and Butler and Hansen – 'the meter maids', he called them derisively. The meter maids had been circulating short essays criticizing not only the Linda case but Budd and Dave Jacobs and Walt Andrus and Jerome Clark and the others who had defended it. The meter maids seemed to have inserted themselves pretty deeply under Budd's skin. 'It's stupid,' said Budd. 'I threw Stefula out of the support group meetings, and then they decided to get me.'

Nicole and I noticed that Budd looked tired. There were dark pouches under his eyes.

'You should get away from here, Budd,' said Nicole. 'Go to a cabin somewhere and don't answer the phone.'

'I just went to Australia,' said Budd, referring to a recent lecture tour there. 'I didn't do too many regressions. Only a couple.' Each regression session was enormously draining, and recently Budd had been doing four or five a week.

Back at the studio Budd showed me some pictures that Nicole had drawn from her dream, after a previous regression session. In one picture, an attractive brunette – human-looking except for her large, black, slightly slanted eyes – stood at the head of an examination table. Linda stood next to her, in peach-coloured pyjamas, and Nicole stood slightly behind Linda, also in her nightgown. Linda was looking at a Coca-Cola can, holding it out in front of her. Along the far side of the table lay a row of strange hand-like shapes, as if four Nosferatus had folded their hands on the table edge and one could see only the parts of their hands and their long waxy fingers that actually lay on the table, everything beyond the table edge being in some other invisible dimension. On the table lay Linda's boy Johnny. Nicole was a good artist and the picture was very clear. She had dreamed this a few months ago. Actually, she had dreamed that two black men had broken into her apartment; she had told Linda about it and Linda had mentioned that she had had a similar dream. Under hypnosis, the dreams had become more elaborate, and more frankly abduction-related, but the similarities remained. We discussed some of the details of the dream which had already been revealed to Nicole in a previous hypnosis session, and Budd made Nicole promise not to tell any of the details to Linda. Nicole, rolling her eyes with exasperation because Budd asked her this so often – Budd was worried because Nicole and Linda had become close friends, and usually spoke to each other by telephone every day or so – duly promised that she wouldn't breathe a word of it to Linda.

The hypnosis would take an hour to an hour and a half. It was as if one were going on a long trip where one couldn't get out of the car, so Nicole first went upstairs to the bathroom. When she returned, she removed her shoes and lay down on the black couch; Budd put a blue blanket over her. Nicole, like many other abductees, tended to become cold during hypnosis, and today she was wearing an extra pair of socks and a heavy sweater. Budd clipped a tape-recorder microphone to the blanket near her head and we turned down all the lights. Budd sat on the wooden chair by the couch. He leaned over the couch, his forehead resting on his right fist; I couldn't help thinking that he looked like that sculpture by Rodin.

'All right,' Budd said soothingly to Nicole. 'I want you to get that feeling of going down into yourself . . . down into yourself . . . feel the way the bed curves to match the contours of your body . . . all along the underside of your body . . . feel the perfect support all along the underside of your body . . . the room is cool . . . you can feel the coolness on your face . . . the blanket is keeping your own body warmth inside . . . you're feeling comfortable and relaxed . . . and as before I want you also to take notice of your feet and the very familiar sensation . . . that delicate restlessness of the nerves, that tightly stretched skin, spreading upwards into the hollow soles of your feet . . . soft, vulnerable skin . . . a tingling sensation . . . feel each one of your toes separately . . . you can feel each one of your toes separately . . . feel the way toe touches toe, touches toe . . . feel the muscles relaxing . . . feel it spreading slowly like a warm soothing liquid into your legs . . . flowing higher now, into your legs, into your torso, into your upper body . . . flowing up across your shoulders . . . your muscles are becoming unclenched

. . . you're feeling comfortable, relaxed, peaceful . . . you're feeling peaceful and relaxed . . .'

Budd coaxed the tingling sensation up into her head and then he put her on a lovely beach which she had visited once in San Diego, to relax for a while and to enjoy the sunshine and the ocean; it was a kind of staging ground for the mnemonic descent to follow.

After Nicole had been on the beach for a half-minute or so, Budd said, 'I want us to go back to the time we've been talking about this fall, when you had something very strange happen in your apartment, involving going up to the skylight in the bathroom, the sense of moving to some odd place. I want you to go with me to that odd place where you're up high, looking down, looking down into a room, and you see a person down there, a dark person, somebody with dark skin – it's unclear, but you can bring yourself into focus . . . bring into focus that room where you're going to see your father in a moment. I want you to look down, and if you look down from this slightly elevated place where you are, I want you to describe very clearly what you see when you look down. Speak whenever you like. Tell me what you see when you look down.'

'I'm in a curved room,' said Nicole. 'I go out the door. Then I see my father.'

'OK, let's see where you see him. Where's he standing? Is he in the same curved room or is he outside?'

'No, he's in the hallway.'

'Mmm hmm. OK. Look at your father closely, get a sense of – First, what's he wearing?'

'He's wearing a white T-shirt. Jeans. He has white hair.'

'Is he wearing blue jeans?'

'No, he's wearing beige pants.'

'Beige pants. And he has white hair.'

'My father doesn't have white hair. He has black and white hair.'

'And it looks like it's white hair?'

'White hair.'

'Do you think this is really your father? Does this look like your father? Or can you tell?'

'He has a slender face. He has a bald head. A big head, forehead. Thin nose.'

'Let's look at his white hair again. Is it thin, is it thick? How does it look? How is it combed?'

'He has an egg-shaped head.'

'Does your father have an egg-shaped head?'

'No.'

'This might not be your father, then?'

'I feel he is my father. His hair is combed back.'

'The way your father combs his hair?'

'No, my father doesn't have this head of hair.'

'OK. We won't worry about this point exactly . . .'

'He's my height. My father's not my height, my father's taller.'

'Let's look at the paint-spattered pants,' said Budd, apparently referring to an image from a previous session. 'Do they look like your father's pants? They seem like an artist's pants.'

'No. He's a thin man. My father's not thin. He's narrow. He's got a thin waist. My father doesn't have a thin waist.'

'Doesn't seem to be your father, in fact.'

'No. But I feel he's my father.'

'Well, let's look at the pants again, that will be our identification. Can you see colours on them, like paints?'

'Mm mmm.'

'OK. You can't see the paint. OK, now let's just see what happens. So you're there, and your father's with you. We'll just call him your father – we don't know what that means exactly, but we'll just use that term. You feel comfortable using that term, or would you rather –?'

Nicole indicated that the term was all right.

'OK. So it's your father, so what's going to happen? Let's just see what happens next.'

'I'm dragging him. I have to pull to push him. And there are greys around us, one on either side. We turn a corner. And we go up a ramp. There's a banister on the ramp – one side, to the right.'

'Like a railing?'

'Mmm hmm. A railing. A pipe. A pole?'

'A pipe, right side. What's on the other side?'

'Emptiness. No, just one banister. There's a wall, but there's a cut-out doorway. I'm standing with my father on top of the ramp. There's a black man approaching us. He's wearing baggy clothes.'

He's wearing a cap on his head. I'm scared because I feel he's going to kill us, or something bad's going to happen. He turns a corner, and he just looks at us and he walks away. He just goes inside that doorway.'

'Mmm hmm. He opens the door and closes it behind him?'

'There's no door, just a cut-out. No door. I go up some steps, and then I'm on another level.'

'Are you still with your father?'

'My father's not with me. My father's – He's taken away. He's not with me now. I sit by. I'm at a table. I see Linda. She's not paying attention to me. Her head is turned. She's talking to a woman. We're crammed in there; it's very tight. We're in conference. I don't feel like I should be there. I don't know what's going on. I'm just there. Linda's been there for some time. There are objects on the table. She picks up an object, and she's looking at it. It looks like a can, a Coca-Cola can.'

Around them are human beings, milling and bustling, as if in a busy hospital. But it is not a hospital, it is a spaceship and Nicole is standing over the examination table with Linda as in her previous drawing.

Budd began to question Nicole about Johnny, who lay naked on the table, but Nicole seemed to be uncomfortable with the subject and instead described some of the people around the table. Linda was wearing peach-coloured silk pyjamas. Her hair was tied back. The woman with big eyes was next to Linda. Her eyes were black but not as harsh as the greys' eyes. On the whole, in fact, she was beautiful, and vaguely reminded Nicole of Marlo Thomas from the old *That Girl* TV series. She had a long neck, and slender wrists, and a flat chest. It was clear that she was at least part alien because she had four fingers – three long, one short – on each hand. She was wearing a snugly fitting robe without buttons. She looked, said Nicole, like 'a porcelain doll'. She expressed herself with her hands and by telepathy, primarily. She was trying to explain something to Linda: something about the fact that her meeting Nicole, her friendship with Nicole, was premature. She was even slightly scolding in her tone. Nicole was trying to make out exactly what she was saying telepathically but Linda's own mind was so jumbled and loud and gabby that she could only hear bits and pieces of what the Marlo Thomas woman was saying, about how things should have happened in their natural course, and not the way they actually had happened.

There were the four pairs of hands on the other side of the table, belonging to the greys. The greys apparently didn't want to show themselves, and all that Nicole could see beyond the hands were four shadows.

Next to the shadows, at the opposite end of the table from the Marlo Thomas woman, was a man. He was clearly the same man whom she had originally mistaken for her father, except that now she didn't seem to feel that he was her father, and he had changed from a T-shirt and beige pants into blue striped pyjamas. He seemed to be shocked by what he was seeing – his head was tilted and his arms dangled – but otherwise he was a handsome man in his sixties. He had brown eyes and a big shiny forehead. He looked wealthy; he wore a gold signet-type ring on his right hand, and was very well-groomed, with his white hair combed back, and nice teeth. He just had that glossy, smooth-jowled look to him that men with money have. He also seemed grandfatherly in a way, as if he were related to Linda. He seemed concerned about her and about Johnny. But he didn't look at all like Linda's father. The man in the blue striped pyjamas didn't really remind Nicole of anybody in particular.

Did this man have any distinguishing features? asked Budd. Any scars, nicks, a moustache –

Yes, he had a moustache, thought Nicole. A small one. And now he seemed to be accepting what was happening to him. All of this was confirming something that he had doubted. He was happy, although he seemed to be worried about Johnny. Linda, meanwhile, was panicking. She wanted to get the hell out of there.

What did the man look like? persisted Budd. Was he Waspish, Jewish, Negro, Arabic? He didn't look American, said Nicole. He looked like a cross between an Italian old man and someone from Spain. He had that Latin skin. Did he remind Nicole of some famous person, perhaps George Bush or – or Senator Lloyd Bentsen, whose picture had been in the *New York Times* that day?

No, said Nicole. He looked like one of those men in spaghetti westerns – those handsome older men that are always sitting in

saloons playing poker or just smoking and drinking quietly when
the hero or the villain walks in.

Budd suggested that she start moving her recollections forward a
bit, and Nicole described how there was a commotion around the
table and she and Linda were dragged back to the ramp and
through a door and into a park somewhere. There were trees and it
was bright and sunny. It seemed as though they had just walked
out of a house. A green brick house with a green lawn. Did it look
real? asked Budd. No, it didn't look real. The house looked like a
façade. So did the other houses. And the windows weren't right.
They didn't have shades on them. Everything was quiet. There
were no bird sounds or other noises, and the air was dead. Johnny
and the man in the pyjamas were still back in the room with Marlo
Thomas and the Nosferatus, but now some greys had come along
with Nicole and Linda and they had very strong grips and Nicole's
arm hurt where they were gripping her. With the greys were some
taller aliens, also grey and big-headed but as tall as humans. They
were marching Nicole and Linda down the street through all of this
fake greenery to a bright light. They had to wait there and then
suddenly they were in another room, standing by a wall, and a dry-
ice fog seemed to be flowing everywhere. Then Johnny, now
wearing his own pyjamas, entered the room with the grandfatherly
man. Linda acknowledged neither of them. She was acting very
oddly. Nicole didn't like the way Linda was acting; in fact she
didn't like the whole business. She felt that her job was probably to
be there to take care of Linda but it was beginning to seem that
Linda and Johnny were related to the man in the blue striped
pyjamas, and Nicole felt as if she were intruding on a family
situation. She felt embarrassed.

Finally it was time to go. Johnny and Linda left the room. Then
Nicole was led out and into a hallway where the air was cold and
damp and a clutter of humans sat around on benches, as if they
were in an overcrowded hospital somewhere. On a bench nearby
sat a blonde woman and a man with brown hair; both were
naked and expressionless. After a few moments the greys came for
Nicole again and, grabbing her arms, took her into another room
that had a hole in the floor. Above the hole there was something
like glass, and in any case she couldn't see through the hole. Then

she was in the hole and she was floating down ... through the skylight above the bathroom in her apartment, and she was concerned because she was re-entering at an odd angle and she thought that she might hit the lamp and the bowl of pot-pourri which stood on the back of the toilet. She caused no damage, however, for one of the greys was already there in the bathroom to guide her down, and with the other greys he escorted her into her bedroom and lifted her up and put her down on the bed, legs first, and then let her head fall back with a slight thump. Then the greys walked casually into the corner of the room and disappeared, and Nicole fell asleep and in the morning she remembered that she had had a strange dream.

Now it was time for Nicole to exit not only the dream but the hypnotic state as well. 'Just feel that nice sense of relaxation,' instructed Budd. 'All this is over, now, it's behind you ... you're just feeling the relaxation ... all the tension you've been feeling, the confusion and so forth is all gone now, it's just a memory ... it's still there as a memory, but you're now feeling relaxed ... I'm going to wake you up, counting from five back to one ... and when you awake, you'll feel again a sense that you're gaining parts of your life, memory pieces that you haven't been able to remember before, and now they're coming together, so you're feeling again that sense of wholeness, gaining a sense of wholeness about your life ... you're going to have a new and deeper sense of your connection, friendship, warmth that you feel with Linda, and also with her son, Johnny, you're going to feel the importance of that and you're going to feel the pride that you should feel, the sense that you were there to help protect her, and to help reassure her, and how important it was considering how upset she was, that you were actually there, being of use to her, of help to her ... that's going to give you a very very good feeling ... you're going to feel again a sense that life has a rich dimension and meaning that you've hardly been aware of before . . .'

Then Budd counted down from five and Nicole awoke. She had been crying during the hypnosis session and she joked with Budd about the first time, when afterwards her eyes had been surrounded by big black circles of smeared mascara.

Nicole excused herself to go to the bathroom again, and when she had left the studio Budd said quietly to me that he was going to try an experiment and that I shouldn't give the game away. All right, I said, and Budd went up to the upper studio and returned with a set of a dozen or so xeroxed photographs of various public figures. Some of them I recognized, such as Michael Caine, and Lloyd Bentsen, and Senator Phil Gramm, and former Arizona governor Bruce Babbitt, and the Hong Kong governor and former British politician Chris Patten, and someone who looked like Jimmy Hoffa standing in front of a KCBS microphone. There was also, of course, the former UN Secretary-General, Javier Perez de Cuellar.

Nicole came back and Budd suggested that she go through these pictures of various people and tell him which ones looked more like the man in the blue striped pyjamas and which ones looked less like him. That way we would have a better idea of what he really did look like. It was the same sort of thing the police did when they were trying to sketch a suspect. Nicole apparently didn't recognize any of the men – not Perez de Cuellar, not even Michael Caine – and Budd didn't tell her who they were. She went through the pile, and for most of them she said no, he didn't look like that, but for three of them – Phil Gramm, Lloyd Bentsen, and Jimmy Hoffa – she said yes, he did look sort of like that. Perez de Cuellar languished in the No pile.

Budd wasn't going to give up so easily, however. He took the best six photos, in which group Perez de Cuellar was included, and ran them by her again, for each one covering up this or that part, or asking her to suggest changes to make him more like the man in the blue striped pyjamas. Nicole looked at the six photos again, but she still liked Bentsen and Gramm and Hoffa. Perez de Cuellar was too chubby, too florid-faced. However, Nicole did like Perez de Cuellar's hair, and his eyebrows. In fact, the more she looked at Perez de Cuellar's photograph, the more she liked it. Eventually, after several more rounds of evaluation and re-evaluation, it came down to Perez de Cuellar and Lloyd Bentsen. Budd asked Nicole to score each one's resemblance to the man in the blue striped pyjamas on a scale of 0 to 10. She gave Perez de Cuellar an 8, and Bentsen only a 7. Then Budd took out a colour photograph of Perez de Cuellar which had appeared in *Vanity Fair*. It was a frontal shot which reduced his apparent girth. Now Perez de Cuellar rated a 10.

Budd had won. He told Nicole whom she had identified, and then he went upstairs and brought back some glasses and a bottle of scotch, and we all sat in the studio drinking and talking. Budd told us that Johnny, Linda's boy, who during his own abduction episodes had also seen a grandfatherly man with white hair and smooth jowls, had also picked Perez de Cuellar out of the same line-up. He hadn't expected to find Perez de Cuellar in Nicole's abduction experiences, but the fact that he had done so only strengthened the Linda case. The business of Perez de Cuellar's signet ring also seemed to strengthen the case. Budd went upstairs again and brought down a gold ring which Richard had sent to Linda. It was shaped like a signet ring, with three diamonds in a diagonal across the top. Inside was inscribed '11.30.89 14 kt'.

'That's a three, four hundred dollar ring,' said Budd. Nicole looked at it fearfully, as if it removed any possibility that the dream about the man in the blue striped pyjamas had merely been a dream.

Another abductee, Carlotta, came by – she and Nicole were going out later for drinks – and the four of us talked some more. Budd told us about some other wild cases in which people had met other humans during their abductions and had learned their personal histories and so on and then years later had met them in real life. In fact, abductees seemed generally to gravitate together; it seemed as though they could pick each other out of a crowd. Carlotta wondered if this might all be part of the aliens' plan; but I suggested that even as ordinary humans we all might be more sensitive to character cues than one would expect. Budd agreed, and he told us a story a psychologist friend had told him some years ago, about a fellow who had come in for counselling because he had the unfortunate habit of wetting the bed at night. He had felt that he couldn't have normal relationships with women, and so he had more or less shut himself off from the world. One day, however, he had met this woman and they had fallen utterly in love. After a few preliminaries, they had made plans to spend a weekend together. The bed-wetter became anxious about what would happen should he fall asleep beside his new girlfriend. He was in an anguish of worry. But eventually he decided he would stay awake at night so he would never lose control of his bladder.

He went away for the weekend with her, and the following Monday morning, he walked into his therapist's office. He was beaming with pride and joy. 'You made it,' said his therapist. 'You managed to keep from wetting the bed.' 'No, no,' said the guy, 'I found out that she's a bed-wetter too!'

Not long afterwards, I went up to see Budd and Nicole again. By this time Budd had regressed Linda through the same dream that Nicole had had, and despite minor differences, as he put it, in their hypnotic recollections, it had become clear to him not only that Linda, Johnny, Nicole, and Javier Perez de Cuellar had been abducted on that same night in August 1992, but that the aliens were trying to create the impression that Linda and Johnny were somehow related to Javier. That, said Budd, was the sort of thing that the aliens did; they would implant certain emotions that made an abductee think that she was related to another abductee, and then they would sit back and watch how the abductees behaved. To them it was all a grand behavioural psychology experiment.

In Linda's case, the experiment had seemed to work quite well. She seemed to be convinced that Javier Perez de Cuellar was her real father. And according to Linda and Johnny, Javier Perez de Cuellar was also convinced of the relationship. Budd sat me down and showed me a videotaped interview he had recently done with Johnny. In the video, Johnny, who was about thirteen years old, sat on the couch in his mother's apartment and explained that he had been walking along the street one day when a big limousine had pulled up alongside him. From the back seat of the limousine, a man who looked like Javier Perez de Cuellar had beckoned for him to get in. Johnny had refused. This had made the man very sad. He had wanted to give Johnny a present – a great bronze helmet from an old-fashioned diving suit. The man said that he would deliver it to Johnny's house if he preferred. Johnny said OK, and suggested that it be delivered in the morning at a certain precise time, when his mother was in the shower and his father was at work. The delivery was duly accomplished, and when Linda had found the diving helmet she had thought she was going crazy, because she couldn't remember buying it. Then Johnny had told her the story about the man in the limousine, and she had grounded him for a week and had warned him never again to accept gifts from strangers. Johnny somewhat ruefully displayed the diving helmet for Budd's video camera.

Budd showed me another video interview, done with Linda and Nicole in the lower studio, with *Mahler's Castle* as a dramatic backdrop. The interview had occurred after Linda's most recent regression, when the congruency between her August abduction and Nicole's had become clear. In the video, Linda examined the sketches Nicole had made and indicated that they were an accurate representation of what she had seen during her abduction. Looking at the camera, her voice half-choked by sobs, Linda pleaded with her eventual audience to take the phenomenon of alien abductions seriously. They were kidnapping her boy. They were kidnapping her. She and her boy had no one to turn to, except Budd of course. The implication seemed to be that the government authorities should become involved. Nicole looked on quietly, with an expression of sympathetic pain.

I heard later that Budd passed Nicole's sketches around at an abductee support group meeting. Just about everyone had recognized the porcelain Marlo Thomas woman with the slanted black eyes. One young man had stared at it for fifteen minutes, murmuring about the Lady in the Moon, whom he had met many times and had sketched, compulsively, in the margins of his notebooks when he had been a teenager in high school.

12

The Underworld

A kindergarten teacher asked the children in her class to paint whatever they wished. Later, she inquired of each child what subject he or she was painting. 'A picture of Mommy', or 'my cat' were typical answers. One child, however, said, 'I'm painting a picture of God.' 'How can you paint God?' the teacher asked. 'No one knows what God looks like.'

'Wait till I finish my painting,' the child replied.

– Budd Hopkins, *Sacred Spaces*, a photo-art essay, 1983

Through the next several months, in telephone calls, over drinks and dinners, and in visits to Budd Hopkins's studio in New York, I tried to become better acquainted with Nicole and Lucy. This was not merely because they were very charming and enjoyable to be with, which they certainly were, but because I wanted, if I may bend a phrase from Nabokov, to fix once and for all the perilous magic of abductees.

I say perilous because of the invisibility of their uniqueness to the incidental observer, or to the enchanted researcher. As Budd Hopkins and Dave Jacobs and their colleagues had long been arguing with regard to abductees in general, Nicole and Lucy in ordinary social interactions were more or less unremarkable; or perhaps I should say that they were remarkable by their unremarkableness, considering their claimed trauma.

However, beneath this level of public composure lay a surprising sub-terrain, over which, I believe, folklorists and sociologists and social workers and anthropologists and psychologists and neurologists and theologists and ufologists and ordinary souls have been drifting and stumbling for centuries. This terrain only begins to be visible when one considers the full range of experiences with which the abductee has been confronted, or claims to have been confronted, throughout her life. It is the terrain already pointed to by the work of such diverse scholars as Hilary Evans, John Keel, John Mack, Michael Persinger, and Ken Ring, and which is touched by such terms as dissociation and temporal lobe lability and Omega-prototype and holotropic. However, I think that none of these terms can express adequately the strangeness conveyed by an abductee's personal history, a history not as God or a fly on the wall has seen it but as the abductee has seen it, as she has told it, as she has crafted – and I say this somewhat agnostically – her own mythology.

First, Nicole. She was born and raised in a large Atlantic coast city. Her parents did not seem particularly religious, but like her father and grandfather before her, she had a special, often painful sensitivity to the spiritual realm. She heard people breathing around her bed at night. Monsters rushed vividly at her from the corners of her bedroom. Sometimes she awoke with the tingling beginnings of paralysis in her feet, moving slowly, like liquid, up to her head, and she often dreamed – were they only dreams? – that she was rolled by someone or something off her bed and through the window or through a wall and then into a bright light, after which she met strange beings with whom she interacted, sometimes innocuously, but more often traumatically. Nicole often had high fevers as a child, and suffered convulsions; both her convulsions and her supernatural experiences tended to coincide with the fevers, while a reduction in fever often followed the experiences.

Quite naturally, Nicole developed a fear of the dark. She would check beneath her bed and inside her bedroom closet before attempting to sleep at night. She would frequently change her bed's position, to confound the nocturnal visitors. She made necklaces of charms and hung them from her door, to ward off evil. Nothing worked, and as she grew older, things began to happen to her during daylight hours. She would experience strange fugues of missing time. She would set out for a given destination but arrive hours later than she should have, with no memory of a detour. Her internal sense of time was constantly being contradicted by the events of the outside world; without a wristwatch she was lost.

Nicole was very creative, and developed an early interest in art.

However, the underworld intruded even into this aspect of her life; she would sometimes return from school carrying skilfully rendered art-class sculptures of ordinary animals – horses and pigs and so on – with large, oddly shaped black eyes. On ceramic bowls, she would sculpt pointed faces with large eyes, slit mouths, and horns. She once sculpted a foot-tall version of what years later would be instantly recognizable as a grey. Greys would also stare out from the doodle-filled margins of her schoolgirl notebooks.

Yet the night attacks were the most terrifying, and when she reached university they intensified. One night in her senior year, the night after Hallowe'en in fact, Nicole was asleep in a dormitory bunk-bed with another student, Eva, in the bunk beneath, and a third girl, Fumiko, in a bed across the room. In the early hours she was awakened by a shuffling sound on the floor, as if a mouse were loose. Then she noticed that it had become very cold. She looked up and saw that the window was still closed. She wondered where the draught might be coming from. Then, in the grey half-light of the darkened room, she noticed that between the bunk-bed and Fumiko's bed a black wall had formed. It had no shape or texture; it was simply impervious to light. The other side of the room had become invisible. Nicole screamed, and Eva awoke and shouted, 'Nicole, I see it!' Eva rose from her bunk and went towards the black wall, but upon approaching it she was thrown back violently. At the same moment Nicole lapsed into unconsciousness. In the morning, Eva no longer remembered the wall, but Fumiko did; she had seen it rippling strangely, and she had been paralysed, unable to cry out. Nicole was so shaken by the experience that she returned home for two weeks.

After college, Nicole spent a year at a design school in London. The strange nocturnal events followed her there. One night she left her bed to go to the bathroom, and as she did, a strong gust of wind blew across her. Yet the windows and doors were closed. The creeping paralysis and rolling levitations also continued. Once she awakened in the morning with the dream-like memory of having been rolled out of bed and through the wall and through a bright light and into a room where there had been a tall pale being dressed in black and working at a computer. This prompted her to approach the British Society for Psychical Research, where she was introduced to a grandmotherly woman to whom she explained the kinds of experiences she was having.

'Do you use drugs?' asked the SPR woman.

'I don't *need* drugs!' protested Nicole.

The SPR woman suggested that Nicole was probably psychic, and she suggested that Nicole attend the SPR's advanced psychic class. Nicole went in for her first class, and saw a room with twelve or thirteen young women sitting around meditating. She didn't like the look of it, and walked out. Aside from the fact that a room full of thirteen meditating psychics was slightly unnerving, she didn't believe she was a psychic herself. If she had been a psychic, she reasoned, she would long ago have won the state lottery. Yet despite numerous attempts, she had never won so much as a penny.

She returned from England in the summer of 1989, and moved to an apartment in the city. She stayed there for a few months and then moved to another one, and then to another one. It seemed that wherever she went, the strange things would happen, often when she was feverish, or had injured herself, or was stressed in some way. She would hear people breathing around the bed. Things would touch her on her hand. She would feel dark presences in the room. She would see white owls at the window, white cats on the carpet, white gorillas in the corner. She would wake up with the sense that the building was on fire, and then would strangely fall asleep again. And of course there was the paralysis and the room with the pale beings. The things the pale beings were doing to her became steadily worse, and often, absurdly, she would find herself waiting in line, with other humans in pyjamas and nightgowns, before submitting to her own ordeal. The frequency of her experiences also varied frighteningly, from once every few months to several times per week.

She began to frequent the New Age/occult sections of bookstores, reading about ghosts and hauntings. A few years before she had seen *Communion*, but the alien face on the cover hadn't triggered any sense of recognition. It was only in the summer of 1990, when she picked up a paperback reissue of a book entitled *Missing Time*, by an artist named Budd Hopkins, that she began to suspect that her experiences had to do with the alien abduction phenomenon. She telephoned Hopkins's house and left a message; he never returned it. For a while nothing happened, and she decided that her experiences were simply the result of an overactive imagination. Then the experiences increased in frequency around December 1990, and she telephoned Hopkins a second time. The woman who was then acting as Hopkins's assistant took her call, and within a few days Nicole was at the house on West 16th Street. She said she wasn't sure whether her experiences really represented abductions by extraterrestrial beings, but Hopkins explained that her experiences fitted the abduction pattern, and soon Nicole was being hypnotized on the black leather couch in Hopkins's lower studio, beneath the drawing by Léger, and the brightly coloured Guardians.

Nicole joined Hopkins's regular circle of abductees, and soon met people whose experiences made her own seem humdrum. There were the sisters, for instance, who had been chased home from school in the 1950s, in broad Brooklyn daylight, by greys who hovered in the trees. There was the woman from Connecticut who had been abducted along with her car; the car's finish had bubbled and burned in the intense heat.

As the years went on, Nicole began to meet, during her abductions, other women from Hopkins's abductee circle. One night, while she was queuing up for the inevitable ordeal, in a cave, apparently, and a strange glowing globe hovered in the air above the line of waiting abductees, she heard a bold voice from behind her which she knew could only belong to –

'Carlotta!' Carlotta was naked, like everyone else in the queue, and as Carlotta and Nicole communicated, Nicole saw an appendectomy-type scar on Carlotta's abdomen, and a scar around one shoulder, and a scratch across her upper chest. The next morning, Nicole telephoned Carlotta and asked her if anything had happened and if she had scars in those places. No, nothing happened, said Carlotta, but she did have scars in those places. Nicole then asked Carlotta's brother, with whom Carlotta lived, if anything had happened that night, and Carlotta's brother said, yes, something had happened. His bedroom was beside the stairs leading to Carlotta's bedroom, and he had awakened in the night with paralysis and had seen the greys going up the stairs. Nicole told Budd Hopkins, and Budd brought Carlotta in for hypnosis, and sure enough . . .

*

That was Nicole's story. Lucy's story began with the claim that when her mother had been pregnant with her she had come down with measles, and she, Lucy, had been born with a heart murmur, a cleft palate, and ear problems. From her earliest years, she seemed to have a difficult relationship with her mother. And her life was undeniably coloured by tragedy. When she was eight years old, she had witnessed her father's death in a gun accident. Her mother, she said, hastened her from the accident scene, and for weeks did not tell her that her father was dead.

Shortly after it became clear to Lucy that her father had died, she was summoned by her mother. It was time to go camping. Lucy's mother took her out to the backyard of the family home, and there was a great light, and a young man of about sixteen standing beside the light. 'Let's go, child,' said the young man. Lucy clung to her mother, screaming, 'Please don't let me go with him,' but the young man took her to a remote cabin in the woods which, Lucy notes, had a tunnel beneath it, part of the same system of storm drainage tunnels which underlay her neighbourhood and provided a natural sanctuary for childhood games. In any case the man who took her to the cabin raped her intermittently there for three days. The young man, who had blue eyes, dark blond hair, and a coarse face, was named Steven. He told Lucy that her father's death had not been by his own hand, but by hers, and that if she ever became close to anyone again, she would kill him, too. Steven was the only one she could ever truly care about. He was the only one who would ever understand her. However, his existence was to remain a secret. If she told anyone else about him, he would hurt her younger sister and brother. When Lucy returned from 'camp', her mother said, 'Oh, look at you, you've been sitting on some poison ivy! What were you doing sitting on poison ivy without your underpants on?'

When Lucy was nine or ten, a policeman came to her school one day to teach the children how to be good observers, in case they ever witnessed a crime or an accident. Two children, Lucy and another girl, were selected to describe a friend or relative to a police artist. Lucy described a blond man with blue eyes and a coarse face, and brought the resulting sketch home for her mother to admire. She told her mother that it was a picture of Steven, the man who had taken her to the cabin. Her mother took out her cigarette lighter, ignited the sketch, and as it burned to ashes in the kitchen sink said coolly, 'Don't you ever mention that name in this house again.'

Many years later, when Lucy was in her late teens, she noticed that her first sexual experience hadn't been at all painful. She mentioned it casually to her mother and her mother responded that Lucy, when only a year old, had broken her hymen by sitting on a funnel. She had bled for a day or two and then she had been brought to the hospital.

Lucy's mother eventually remarried, and Lucy grew up amid relative prosperity. Steven continued to visit her, however, frequently raping her. Lucy knew that she had an active imagination, and sometimes fantasized, and even had had 'imaginary friends' such as children often have, but she knew the difference between fantasy and reality, and was convinced that Steven belonged to the latter category. Although eerily ageless, he was flesh and blood. She once bade him remove his shirt, and plucked blond hairs from his chest. He had some connection with her family – her mother certainly knew who he was – but the details were a mystery to her. Before raping her, he would often say something such as, 'You will enjoy this,' and afterwards, 'Tell me you've enjoyed this.'

Lucy was also visited now and again by a Hispanic-looking man named Ricardo. Ricardo seldom molested her sexually, preferring to molest her psychologically instead. For example, he would arrive on her doorstep in the middle of the night and pound on her door, merely for the pleasure of making her panic. With Steven, at least, Lucy knew where she stood, but with Ricardo almost any kind of random mischief was possible. Ricardo also wasn't entirely human. His fingers began at his wrist, and there were only four on each hand.

Years later, in hypnotic retrospect, it would become clear to Lucy that in her childhood other, more obviously unearthly entities had visited her and subjected her to various sexual and gynaecological and psychological tortures. And as was the case with so many other abductees, machinery had malfunctioned around her. Electric wristwatches even with new batteries frequently ran slow or stopped altogether; lightbulbs blew; unplugged radios blared when she passed; the telephone would ring but no one would be there. She was also, like Nicole, prone to sleepwalk, and was subject to strange amnesic fugues; in one incident which particularly shocked her family, she went snowmobiling one cold winter's night and disappeared; she was found several hours later, collapsed in the snow, with her scarf folded neatly beside her, but with no ill effects from the sub-freezing temperatures. Another time, vacationing in Argentina in the summer before she entered university, she was waiting at a bus stop late one night with two other American girls and suddenly everything went blank and they were all inside a room with cushions everywhere, and she and her friends were talking to a man who described himself oddly as a yo-yo salesman working with the Nestlé company in Chile, and then everything went blank again and Lucy and her friends found themselves in a field outside the town where they had been staying, and five or six hours had passed.

Perhaps even more remarkably, the odd events which plagued Lucy seemed to run in the family. She suspected that her mother had had such experiences, and one night at the family dinner table, shortly after one of Lucy's grandmothers had died, a strange thing happened to her brother. He had been away for some reason, and hadn't known of the death of the grandmother. When told, he had suddenly seemed to change his personality, speaking to the family in an odd, mostly unintelligible voice as if he had been possessed by a spirit or demon. After a few moments he had returned to normal, remembering only that he had had an out-of-body experience; his astral self had floated to the other side of the dinner table and, from that vantage point, had observed his corporeal self speaking.

Lucy's own paranormal experiences were seldom so benign. One night, her college roommate Sarah awoke with a strange paralysis, and a sense – had she heard a man laughing? – that things were going on elsewhere in the house. In the morning, Lucy awoke tired and visibly bruised;* they had come for her again.

---

* Sarah confirmed to me that she had seen Lucy on several occasions in the morning with severe bruising. Although I have disconfirmed nothing about this account, I have also confirmed almost nothing, and reiterate that the reader should interpret all of it – not only the abduction stories but the stories about real people such as her mother – with agnosticism, or at least extreme caution.

Another night, Sarah and Lucy were returning home from a party downtown, and suddenly happened upon the scene of a traffic accident involving five or six separate cars. The odd thing was, the scene was deserted – except for some men dressed in black whom Lucy (though not Sarah) saw in her rear view mirror. Her car engine began to run rough, as if it were about to stall. The men drew nearer. Then the engine came to life again and Lucy and Sarah continued homewards; aware only when they arrived that they had apparently experienced at least a half-hour or so of missing time.

On yet another occasion, a girl down the hallway who was into witchcraft developed a fixation upon Lucy, rearranging her furniture and possessions when Lucy was away, and writing threatening letters when Lucy decided to move elsewhere. The electrical problems continued. Her strange experiences, and in particular her tendency to disappear suddenly when no one was looking, made relationships with men difficult; one time she was housesitting for someone and she invited a young man over and things went well between them, and before going to bed she left the bedroom for a moment to turn out the hall light . . . and the young man waited for her, and waited, and waited, and then searched the house from top to bottom, and waited some more, and finally fell asleep alone. In the morning, Lucy awoke in a closet in a strange corner of the house, and went back to bed. She told the young man that she had no knowledge of the missing time. He called her a liar and stormed out of the house and out of her life.

One day in 1987, at a bookstore on her college campus, Lucy saw a copy of *Communion*, with the face of the gaunt grey on the cover; the shock was so great that she sank to her knees and began sobbing uncontrollably. Later, she read more about aliens and abductions, and about Budd Hopkins, and within a few weeks she wrote to him, outlining some of her recent experiences. To her surprise, Hopkins telephoned her, and soon she was on her way to New York. Some of her friends had warned her about hypnosis, that she would be helpless, that this Budd Hopkins fellow might try to take advantage of her. When Hopkins offered her coffee or tea, she refused, worrying that it might be drugged. Her friends telephoned every half-hour or so, to make sure she was all right.

Lucy was all right. She liked Budd Hopkins. For a time, fearing that Budd might not accept her stories about Steven and Ricardo, she kept their existence a secret from him. But she eventually told him, and Budd seemed to believe her. Ricardo soon stopped visiting her, but Steven continued his harassment, and so did the greys. In fact, her experiences on the whole seemed to increase once she joined Hopkins's circle of abductees. She would awaken to green mists and greys flowing through her bedroom window. Steven would visit her at will, with his trademark taunt – 'You will enjoy this' – and his redneck sexual violence. She would experience sudden episodes of missing time, lasting hours, on the street, in the subway, in her apartment, anywhere. Under hypnosis, it became clear that the night-time incidents generally involved greys and gynaecological manipulations, while the daytime incidents involved human gang-rapists in dark suits and government limousines. After one such incident emerged under hypnosis, and was discussed at an abductee support group meeting, Joe Stefula approached her and pressured her for a description of the car which her assailants had driven. His intense questioning led to Lucy's complaint, Hopkins's ban on Stefula, and, according to Hopkins, Stefula's attacks upon the Linda case.

The MIT conference had been something of a nightmare for Lucy. For one thing, Hopkins's abductees there – only she and Carlotta had attended – were vastly outnumbered by John Mack's and Leo Sprinkle's and Joe Nyman's abductees, who as far as she was concerned took a mawkishly optimistic view of the phenomenon, and seemed primarily concerned with the ozone layer and the rainforests and their own spiritual growth and so forth. One of the other abductees had even changed her name to Skye something, because the aliens had told her to. Lucy did not disbelieve such stories, since the aliens often ordered abductees to do strange things; but she believed that what the aliens told her, or what they told anyone, should be taken with a grain of salt.

Late in the conference, Lucy took Budd Hopkins aside and told him she thought something was going to happen. That was the oblique way she usually phrased her premonitory concern: 'I think something's going to happen.' She had a bump over her ear that would become inflamed just before an abduction, and besides that she had a familiarly eerie internal feeling, a vague tingling sensation throughout her body. Unfortunately, Hopkins was just about to deliver a paper, and it seemed that the last thing he wanted was an anxious abductee worrying about being taken forcibly by aliens or government agents from a crowded conference room. Hang on, he told her. Just hang on for a few hours until the day's lectures are over. Lucy went outside for a stroll and then everything went blank and she regained consciousness standing on a busy pavement in the middle of Boston, miles away from MIT, with those odd clamp-marks on her ankles.

This drew Hopkins's attention. It drew a lot of conference-goers' attention. Hopkins and Dave Jacobs questioned her about it, and John Mack questioned her about it, too; in fact, as far as she was concerned, Mack was almost as bad as Stefula had been, pestering her about where exactly she had been in Boston, what neighbour-hoods and so on, when she didn't know Boston from Bratsk. Anyway, word got around generally that Lucy had been abducted, and people began to hover around her ... *yeah, she's one of Hopkins's abductees; she got abducted yesterday* ... and the tele-vision producer Linda Howe heard about it, and Linda Howe wanted to know what the hell had happened, and she asked Hopkins and Jacobs to tell her what had happened, invoking scientific collegiality and so on, and Lucy began to feel that Linda Howe and half of ufology were following her everywhere.

After the MIT conference, things seemed to become worse for Lucy. Normally, after a major abduction, she would suffer insomnia for a week or two, but this time the insomnia went on and on. Through June, and into July, she was unable to get more than a few hours' sleep per night. Her therapist prescribed Valium, but even when she took only half a Valium pill, she began to hallucinate. Something like this had happened earlier in the year, when she had had surgery on her wrist, for something to do with the ulnar nerve. They had given her a high dose of Valium beforehand, and she had suddenly become extremely depressed. She had begun to sob uncontrollably.

In any case, in the summer of 1992 Lucy's therapist checked her into a neurology clinic for a temporal lobe epilepsy test. They placed EEG probes deep into her nasal cavities, with little gadgets on the end that felt as if they were hooking on to the bottoms of her eyeballs, and they flashed strobe-lights in her eyes to see if they could set off anything on the EEG, and she closed her eyes, and the strobe lights felt as if they were somehow inside her head, and the EEG . . . Christ! Suddenly the technicians were scurrying around. Something was wrong, here! She wasn't having a seizure. She was going into a deep trance . . . Lucy felt the examination table fall away beneath her, and she was floating in space . . . The technicians were shaking her, yelling at her, trying to bring her out of it, but she enjoyed being in the trance . . . She had had so little sleep lately, and it felt so relaxing . . . Finally they shook her out of it, and the neurologist, who looked a bit disturbed by it all, explained to Lucy that she had a very rare tendency to slip reflexively into a trance – a reflexive trance, they called it – and her therapist, after reading the neurologist's report, said that Steven and the greys were most likely the hallucinatory product of her trances, which her mind used to avoid or to distract her from stressful situations. Lucy patiently explained to the therapist that the greys, when they abducted her, often did the same thing that the neurologist had done, putting her on a table and flashing lights in her eyes and forcing her into a trance, and they had been doing this all her life, which was why she slipped into trances so easily. The same, she said, was true of other abductees. But the therapist didn't seem to believe her, and no longer seemed interested in her stories about Steven and the greys, and only wanted to prescribe Valium, and so she flushed the Valium down the toilet and started seeing a different therapist – one who believed in the reality of abductions.

By this time Lucy had moved to a house in the Washington suburbs. Steven still visited her, as did the greys, and her wristwatches never worked, and the phone would ring and no one would be there, and one night the doorbell rang and she opened it and stepped out to see who was there and she saw her father, her dead father, standing in the bushes. On other nights she would awaken in the early hours and the green mist would be flowing through her window and there would be a roaring sound in her ears, and in the morning she would awaken with horrible bruises. She would leave for work at seven in the morning, and would awaken, hours later, on the subway in the wrong section of the city. Her boss and co-workers began to complain about her frequent absences. One day she had to take some documents over to a government building, and drawing $10 from petty cash for a taxicab she left the office. She came to on the street several hours later; she still had the $10, but her panty hose were nowhere to be found. Under hypnosis it emerged that she had been abducted by the government dark suits, who had driven their limousine to a back alley and had raped her. Hopkins considered calling Lucy's boss and explaining the situation to him. John Mack argued that it wasn't fair that Lucy should be discriminated against because she was an abductee.

Lucy began to spend long weekends at Hopkins's place, in search of sanctuary as much as anything else, but even there she wasn't safe; Steven visited her one night in Grace Hopkins's bedroom, and gave her a tour of the house, and another night she experienced a full-blown abduction by the greys, whose pitter-pattering little feet another abductee-boarder heard from the couch in the lower studio. One night, a Friday night, she turned to Budd and said, 'I think something's going to happen.' Hopkins wasn't about to let her get away this time. She had been destined to sleep alone on the couch in the lower studio but now Hopkins took a cot down so he could sleep on it nearby, or at any rate between her and the door. Not long after that, she got out of bed and made a run for the door. Hopkins went after her and stopped her, but she fought him. Her personality seemed to have changed. She was yelling something about a man she had to see outside. Eventually, Hopkins splashed a glassful of water in her face to wake her, and finally she settled down and went back to bed. In the morning she rose and had a forty-minute conversation with Hopkins about the man she had to meet. Again, she did not appear to be her normal self, and afterwards she only remembered the conversation as a kind of vague dream.

One of the things she had said, however, had to do with a car. The man she had to meet was in a car. So Budd and his wife April took her outside to look for the car. She spotted it soon enough. A man was getting out of it. April, carrying her camera, stepped forward to take a picture of the man and his car, but then it became clear to her from the licence plate that the car was an unmarked police car and that the man was a plain-clothes policeman, and that she might get into trouble for taking his picture. Budd and April took Lucy to lunch to talk the whole thing over. At one point Lucy excused herself to go to the ladies' room. The ladies' room was down a narrow stairway. Lucy went down the stairway and a strange man grabbed her and pushed her into a storage room and pinched her arm in such a way that she was paralysed, and told her to be careful, and that he would hurt Budd and April if she told them anything. He showed her his gun and his badge and then fled out of the restaurant through the kitchen.

After that, Lucy had a strange tingling sensation in her neck. She had been scheduled to leave on the train for Washington the next morning, but as she was packing her bag that morning, she suddenly collapsed. She couldn't move or speak for five minutes. Budd and April found her, and almost called an ambulance – April poked pins in her arm to check her nerves, and Lucy couldn't feel them – but she talked them out of calling an ambulance, and eventually, by the end of the day, she was well enough for Hopkins to take her to Penn station and put her on the train, waiting until the train began to move before he let her out of his sight.

It was at about this time that the greys began to make very peculiar dietary demands of Lucy, such as that she should no longer eat anything but eggs and vegetables – and whenever she tried to eat anything substantially beyond the prescribed diet, she would vomit and break out in hives. Lucy's traumatic experiences came so thick and fast, requiring so much commiseration and attention from Budd Hopkins, that April Kingsley began to be annoyed. In the autumn of 1992, Hopkins referred Lucy to a psychiatrist down in Winston-Salem, North Carolina, who was said to have a novel technique for making abductees immune to abductions. As Lucy understood it, the psychiatrist, using some kind of custom-made hypnosis machine, would put her into a deep trance for eight hours, repeating this over three days, and the deep trance would somehow remove whatever mental pattern the aliens used to identify and target her, and she would be free at last. Lucy telephoned the psychiatrist to set up an appointment, and one of the psychiatrist's female assistants answered, and started out by warning Lucy that if she, the assistant, said anything strange over the telephone, then Lucy was not to mind it because the aliens occasionally made her say strange things. Lucy thereafter became sceptical of the assistant's sanity, and of the psychiatrist's competence, and when the assistant later claimed that Budd Hopkins had told the psychiatrist that the aliens had killed Lucy's father – which Budd denied having done – Lucy declined to deal any further with the woman or her employer.

An attempt at solace soon came from another direction, however, when a young ufologist gave Lucy several hundred dollars' worth of electronic equipment – tape recorders and motion-detectors and so on – to enable her to keep the aliens at bay, or at least to record their visits. Lucy accepted it all very sweetly, humouring the young man's ufological bravado, but didn't have time to bother with it all and so stowed the equipment away under her bed, and her abductions continued.

I listened to such stories with fascination and some sympathy, but also with frustration, for I suspected that participation in the underworldly experiences of Lucy and Nicole and their scarred sisters and brothers was off-limits to mortals like me. No sloe-eyed alien, no sulphur-breathing rapist, would allow me to watch him at work or at play, or would even sit for an interview. I could experience only the presence of morosely cheerful storytellers, and their stories, and their stories of stories.

Lucy must have sensed my frustration, for she soon told me a story that suggested I might have some consolation after all. One night in mid October 1992, she said, not long before I was to meet her, a fire engine drove noisily along her street, parking outside and shining a light at her house. It had no markings, and eventually departed. Lucy wondered about the fire engine but then went to bed. In the morning she awoke and noticed that her nightgown was torn and dirty, and that she had the familiar exhausted feeling of having been somewhere else during the night, on her feet. She travelled to New York and Budd Hopkins hypnotically regressed her, and it became clear that she had got up from bed in the middle of the night and had driven in her car to Front Royal, Virginia, on the edge of the Blue Ridge mountains, an hour or so west of Washington. Under hypnosis she could remember certain places where she had been. She had stopped at an all-night 7-Eleven in Front Royal and had driven past a K-Mart department store, and then at the top of a hill on the left she had seen a Mexican restaurant, and then after turning left she had travelled along a road for a few minutes and there had followed a turn-off into the hills, with signs indicating that she was entering some kind of national park. Along that road after a few miles she had stopped and on her left there had been a flat rock and on her right there had been a steep drop of a few hundred feet to a field full of people in their pyjamas and nightgowns. She had somehow walked or floated down to the field and the aliens had come and had shepherded them all into the side of the hill where there was an opening. It led steeply down through the limestone under the hill to a large room, with a high ceiling, where the abductees congregated and the aliens inscrutably watched them. Lucy's sister was there, and their dead father, and a bearded man in a suit who looked uncomfortable in the suit and said that his name was Tom McKinney, and that he was a former ship's cook who had jumped ship and had settled on the island of St Bartholomew in the Caribbean ... and then somehow Lucy was back in her car and she drove back to Washington and returned to bed.

I heard the story from Lucy in early December. She told me about it in her usual matter-of-fact, even jaded manner, but there was enough that was tangible about the story – the 7-Eleven, the K-Mart, the Mexican restaurant, the national park sign – that she thought perhaps she should retrace her route, to see if she could find the cave where she had been abducted. She invited me to come along, and of course I said I would. Nicole wanted to come, too. She was coming to Washington to stay with Lucy over the New Year, and so we planned to go then.

Nicole took the train down to Washington, and on New Year's Eve, the night before setting out for the cave, we all went to a party. Lucy and Nicole told me that someone else at the party was an abductee, and that I should guess who. But it didn't seem likely that I would be able to guess who. Everyone seemed perfectly normal, engaging in normal discussions about the recession and the soon-to-be-inaugurated new President. One woman was a psychologist. One fellow was even the son of an important Bush Administration official. He seemed like a very nice guy. We were talking about this and that, the recent presidential election and the budget deficit, and then somehow he began to speak about UFOs, and he seemed knowledgeable about the subject. He told me about the UFOs and about the greys and Nordic blonds (another, more benign species of alien) who piloted them, and how the aliens were in league not only with the US government – the secret US government rather than the overt government of elected officials and appointees – but also with the KGB, too, and some years ago he had been somewhere and a man had walked past him with an umbrella and on the pin-sharp end of the umbrella had been a tiny pellet doused with ricin, a potent toxin, and at the moment that the ricin pellet had made its intradermal plunge, the KGB man had tipped his hat – what sangfroid the Russians had in those days! – and of course it had been the same weapon they had used against Georgi Markov, the Bulgarian dissident, in 1976 on a bridge in London, and the ricin had killed Markov, but fortunately my interlocutor, my unexpected usher into the abductee underworld, had only spent six days in the hospital. The aliens had picked up with him where the KGB had left off, however, and he explained to me that he had since lost his house and his job and – given that he was now being treated for a psychiatric disorder – a certain amount of his mental clarity.

The following morning I picked up Lucy and Nicole, and we steered west for Front Royal. It was a pleasant enough drive, and we listened to the Doors and spoke of the caves and the underground bases and the conspiracy theories that were circulating concerning the government's cooperation with the aliens, and people who had disappeared out in New Mexico or wherever it was that the aliens had their main underground base.

We stopped at a petrol station in Front Royal and asked directions to the K-Mart, and then we found the K-Mart and from there, following the directions that Lucy remembered from her hypnosis session with Budd, we found the 7-Eleven and the Mexican restaurant. We stopped at the Mexican restaurant and had a long lunch, and discussed UFOs with the proprietor's wife, who improbably told us that there was, hanging over Front Royal, a 'negative vortex' of Christian fundamentalism and redneck disbelief which deterred the local reporting and even the appearance of UFOs.

After lunch, we drove down the road a few miles and Lucy directed us to take the turn-off to Skyline Drive. Skyline Drive was a stretch of highway running along the tops of the hills for forty or fifty miles; it was a beautiful stretch of road and in general people drove along it for pleasure rather than to arrive anywhere. Skyline Drive was administered by the National Park Service and we drove through the Park Service gates and past the big Park Service signs and on up into the hills. Lucy told us to look out for a place where there was a big flat rock on the left and on the right a steep drop-off to the valley and then in the valley the field where she and the others had congregated before being herded by the aliens into the cave. If we could find the flat rock and the field, said Lucy, then she had a pretty good idea where we could find the cave. We had our flashlights and hiking boots ready for the cave.

We went up along Skyline Drive and passed a scenic viewpoint, and there was no flat rock and the view into the valley was not quite right, and we went on to the next viewpoint. It went like this for an hour or so, and we stopped and looked for flat rocks over the road and suitable fields down below in the valley. The views were lovely and Nicole and Lucy were good company and we listened to Motown music on the car stereo and it was a fine day, but eventually we decided that we would never find the flat rock or the field or the cave.

We had the rest of the day to kill, and Lucy and Nicole cheerfully agreed to an alternative adventure which I proposed in the spirit of energetic, if quixotic, investigative journalism – namely, that we three drive out somewhere into the countryside after dark and park the car, and wait for UFOs to come down after us. Of course I was well aware that Lucy and Nicole's reported experiences were for the most part considered by them to be traumatic; but Nicole and Lucy joked so often about aliens and abductions that they did not consider my suggestion supercilious at all, and even seemed to look forward to the adventure – although they warned me that my abduction might not turn out to be a journalist's pleasant fantasy. In any case, Lucy was sure we would all be abducted no matter where we were or what we attempted to do. 'Something is going to happen,' she would say, and had been saying since the previous evening when the bump over her ear had begun to throb.

Before nightfall we diverted ourselves with a trip through a nearby tourist cave, full of coloured lights and stalagmites and ghosts but no greys, and then we dropped in to chat with two very nice women in a neighbouring town who lived together and were regularly taken to other, hidden caves by the greys and were there reproductively abused, and were otherwise plagued by poltergeists and by government helicopters, and by the oracular conviction that the world would shortly dissolve in a grey apocalypse.*

Later, over dinner in Front Royal, Nicole proposed that we await our ufological rendezvous in a nearby town where, she had discovered during a brief inquiry at the local police headquarters, two state highway patrol cars had chased a flock of UFOs several years before. Neither Lucy nor I were very enthusiastic about that proposal, since the town in question had no obvious hilltop on which to wait. Lucy proposed alternatively that we park along Skyline Drive – but Skyline Drive was closed at night, and had been since early November, to keep out deer-poachers. I suggested that we drive a few miles west to West Virginia, up into the hills, until we found a remote Forestry Service road, down which we would drive and park and turn out the lights and wait. Lucy and Nicole appreciated the poetic significance of waiting for a UFO in West Virginia, the state where Budd Hopkins had been born and raised, but I also remembered that West Virginia was the state of the Mothman and the un-men, the state that had nearly driven John Keel crazy. At about eleven o'clock we left Front Royal and headed west.

We found the small road that wound up through the hills to West Virginia and in about a half-hour we had passed the state line and were coming down the other side of the hills. A quarter moon was setting and the stars were bright and the air was cold. We found a dirt road, a forestry road as it turned out, and drove along it for about a half-mile, and then I turned off the engine and the lights. Lucy reminded us that she felt that something was going to

---

* I have not noted it before, but female twosomes feature with inordinate frequency in the abductee lore. One of the most famous such cases is recounted in Scott Rogo and Ann Druffel's book, *The Tujunga Canyon Contacts*.

happen, and Nicole said she had the feeling that it would involve a triangular ship, but we had all had a few beers, and our lightheadedness was compounded by tiredness after the travels and travails of a long day, and I suspect that they found it difficult to take seriously the prospect of a joint abduction with a tape-recorder-wielding journalist. We waited for a few minutes and nothing happened. 'Hey guys . . .' said Lucy jovially, addressing the aliens and waving up at the sky. 'Come here, come here!' Then Lucy entertained us with some jokes. I had thought that Budd Hopkins knew some good jokes, but it turned out he had heard them all from Lucy. Nicole saw something move outside. Lucy and I couldn't see it. Finally, Lucy and Nicole suggested that to pass the time, as people do when marooned in automobiles with nothing better to do, we should invent an amusing story. One of them would start the story and the next one would carry on from there and then the first one would add her own bit, and I would insert a strange twist here and there, and so on, purely as an amusing diversion. Lucy and Nicole began the story and it involved two lovely earthgirls and a handsome earthman named Blake, and an alien spaceship and greys, and a nine-foot-tall blonde female alien (my addition) who descended from the spaceship in a blue beam, and an eight-foot-tall blond male alien (their addition), and there was whipped cream and chocolate sauce and a strawberry, and by the time we got to the strawberry, and Blake, still dripping chocolate, had flown off to the stars with the nine-foot-tall blonde, an hour or so had passed, and Lucy and Nicole and I decided that we had given whatever aliens were out there ample time to abduct us, and so we made our way uneventfully home, Lucy and Nicole sleeping soundly as I drove.

I met Lucy and Nicole the following day, and fully conscious of the irony, we toured the Air and Space Museum in Washington. Afterwards we went to dinner and stayed late at Lucy's house, drinking and talking. Lucy still felt that something would happen, but whatever it was had not happened yet. The day after that was a Sunday and Nicole was not leaving until Monday morning, but I had other plans, and so we said our goodbyes. A few days later I spoke to Lucy and she told me that on the Sunday night something had happened. She didn't remember much, but was going to be regressed by Budd about it later. All she remembered so far was that she and Nicole had watched a video, *Die Hard*, until late and then had fallen asleep on her bed. She had awakened at about four in the morning with the phone ringing – it rang once and stopped – and the feeling that something had happened. Nicole also had been awake. 'Lucy,' she had said, 'something happened.' 'I know,' said Lucy testily. 'Don't talk to me now.' Exhausted and angry, Lucy had been grateful at least that she had another hour or so to sleep before getting up for work.

I spoke to Nicole and she told me that she had been shivering all Sunday evening with the onset of the flu, and had been drifting feverishly in and out of sleep all night, and had been awakened by Lucy saying loudly, 'The power's out,' and after that had felt the paralysis and had seen the room illuminated with hundreds of tiny lights, with the haziness of fly-zapper lights but green rather than blue, and over-lit with a green strobe light, and there had been shadowy figures in the bedroom and then she had been somewhere else, in a square windowless room, on a metal examination table, and Lucy had been beside her and several tall greys had been standing in the room and outside in the hallway had been standing a woman and two young children, and then a young redneck type with blue eyes and dirty blond hair and a coarse face had come in and had grabbed Nicole's wrists and had said, 'You will enjoy this,' and Nicole had turned to Lucy and had asked, 'Is this Steven?' And in the morning her fever had subsided.

A girl who was a co-tenant in Lucy's house, and had been there that night, remembered nothing unusual, but as the week wore on Lucy experienced more flashbacks about what had happened. She remembered Steven and the greys and that something horrible had occurred, and that the room had had a carpet and a lovely picture-window view of a city with a river flowing through it. Also, on one wall of the room had hung a painting. It had been an abstract expressionist painting.

When she remembered the painting she told Budd about it, and he seemed interested. He asked her to describe it. She told him that it had been an arrangement of various rectilinear, two-dimensional shapes, in different shades of blue, with an orange line running diagonally through them all.

She told him she didn't think it was one of his.

Epilogue

There are dense little black bruises at the corners of his eyes and beneath his nose, as if there has recently been an explosion inside his head. He wears an expression of dull post-traumatic shock, staring straight ahead, unseeing. But it is going to be all right now. His girlfriend is taking him home from the hospital, here on a sunny autumn day in Snowflake, Arizona. It is going to be all –

'Hey! Travis!'

His girlfriend opens the door to the house and there are people everywhere. 'Heyyyyy Travis!' 'Travis!' 'All right, Travis!' They are shouting at him happily, clapping him on the back, hugging him. They break into applause. 'Travis!' 'Yeahhhh, Travis!' A friend flourishes a tabloid newspaper. 'Hey Travis, look at this.' It is the *National Inquisitor*, and on its cover there is the headline: ARIZONA MAN KIDNAPPED BY ALIENS.

Travis is still staring dully straight ahead. The rest of them see it and sympathize. 'You all right, Trav?' Poor Travis. He has been to hell and back. Still, he's back now, and it's time to party. 'Come on, Travis . . .'

Travis begins to have flashbacks of a dark, dirty room, with horrific dentist-drill-type instruments hanging from the high ceiling. Music starts up from an orchestra somewhere, harsh blares from the horn section, signalling that the tension is rising and that something is going to happen. Travis has a flashback of being inside some kind of suit or shrink-wrap fabric, with strange instruments fastened to his head, and everything is vibrating as in that scene in *2001: A Space Odyssey*, when the astronaut has passed through the Jovian monolith into the time warp. Travis's girlfriend begins to serve food to everyone, and after a few minutes she notices . . . 'Where'd Trav go?' Travis has disappeared. Eventually she finds him in the kitchen, under a table in the corner, trembling and crying, tucked into a foetal position. 'Travis? Honey?'

Travis starts to thrash and kick. He's not sure where he is. He's not sure who this person is, this woman calling his name. He kicks one of the legs of the table and a bottle of maple syrup falls over and the syrup runs in a smooth stream along the surface of the table as the music rises and he kicks harder and his girlfriend is hysterical now, too, and the river of syrup goes over the edge and ... right into his mouth! ... that taste! ... that syrupy taste! ... his hand is in his mouth now and his hand is covered with –

– thick green gelatinous goo ... *Auugghhh!* Oh yes! He is in the spaceship now! The flashbacks have taken over! He is in the spaceship, in some kind of glaucous pod, a pod with walls of bulging glistening goo that quiver and squish wetly when he tries to move. *Augghhh!* But one side of the pod is sheer and semi-transparent. He puts his hand through it. He breaks his way out. He – Whoa! He splashes out of the pod and now he's floating in zero-gravity, in the middle of a great dark sepulchral cylinder, whose sides are covered with little rectangular coffin-pods like his, little man-sized modular units, as if the place has been designed by some otherworldly Modernist, some sadistic grey Le Corbusier ...

He's holding on to the end of some kind of tether that connects to his pod, trying to take this all in, this weird mausoleum, and he pulls the tether too hard ... whooop! ... he's not used to zero-gravity ... and he's headed now for the side of the chamber and –

Ooooff! He's through the glaucous wall of someone else's pod. His hands are in the goo again. But it's not quite the same goo. It's – the gelatinized red-brown innards of some poor dead human who's been rotting here for God knows how long ... 'Aggghhhh! Agghhhhh!' Oh Christ, the horror ...

But now he's out in the middle of the chamber again, and the keys to his motorcycle, on a key-ring with a giant plastic snowflake, somehow float out of his pocket, and he tries to chase them through zero-g. There is a light at the top of the chamber and the keys head for that, and he follows, and finally he ends up in a room where some spacesuits are hanging, with big black eye-like visors on the helmets, and he is looking at one of the suits when another of the suits comes alive and inside it is a wrinkled grey-green alien, with no nose and a slit mouth and small wrinkly eyes and tremendous deltoid and latissimus dorsi muscles, and overall a tough, weatherbeaten appearance. He is ET's bad-boy cousin, and he is taking no nonsense from this earth kid with a plastic snowflake key-ring. Another alien turns up – with their giant lat muscles, these fellows look like steroid-crazy wrestlers – and they drag Travis by his feet down a dark, dirty, dystopian, metal-ribbed, head-banging corridor, through the detritus of past struggles with earthlings (tennis shoes, papers, a pair of broken eyeglasses) into the high-ceilinged room with the dentist drills. They put Travis on a table and rip off his clothes in a business-like fashion and put some kind of fabric over him and then a gas comes down and Travis screams bloody murder and the fabric is some kind of gas-sensitive shrink-wrap, and for a few moments he's frozen in the shrink-wrap like Han Solo in the carbonite in *The Empire Strikes Back* but then one of the aliens scalpels open holes for his mouth and one eye and they put some horrible red jelly-like gunk in his mouth and follow it with a metal contraption which has some kind of metal cable in the centre, and the cable runs down his oesophagus with a sickening metallic roto-rooter noise and he gags and then they put some kind of bizarre metal contraption over his right eye and they put some drops of a whitish, caustic-looking fluid into the eye and a metal electrode stabs into the side of his neck and by now he's moaning and squirming and trying like hell to get out of the way of the dentist-drill arrangement which is dropping down towards him and unfolding its various sharp appendages one of which appears to be a giant needle which telescopes out into smaller and smaller needles but the smallest one still looks huge and is headed for his eye and it's so close he can't focus on anything else and the music rises –

– And watching all of this in a movie theatre in Manhattan, Nicole and Linda cluck their tongues and shake their heads because to them this is nothing like the real thing. It is so far off, it isn't even funny. Spaceships aren't like that inside. They aren't messy and metallic and dirty. People don't lie around rotting in gooey, gelatinous Le Corbusier coffin-pods. And the aliens are not wiry and tough-looking and built like wrestlers. They are thin and weak-looking and grey – except for the Nordics, but that is another story – and they have big dark glistening eyes, and their spaceships are neat and white and dry and clinical, and they don't bounce people around like that; their methods of coercion are more subtle . . .

The movie was called *Fire in the Sky*, and it was 'Based on the True Story' – the Travis Walton story. Produced by Paramount and written by Tracy Tormé,* and more than five years in the works, it opened in American theatres on 12 March 1993. For many of the opening night viewings, in various cities around the country, a panel of MUFON officials was on hand to answer questions afterwards, from members of the audience anxious to know more about UFO abductions. Some of the better-known abductees were also invited to the opening night screenings, and Nicole and Linda were among them. They and the other critics around the country panned the film, although some of the criticisms were not what one might have expected. A *Washington Post* reviewer was disappointed not because the UFO abduction phenomenon was a silly subject, but because it was a serious subject that deserved better treatment. For whatever reason, moviegoers tended to stay away from *Fire in the Sky*; when I saw it one night in a suburban Washington, DC theatre, less than two weeks after it had opened, the audience numbered about half a dozen.

Lucy quit her job in Washington and moved back home to the midwest. Before she left, the well-meaning ufologist who had previously given her all kinds of electronic and video gear that she had stowed beneath her bed now gave her one of those electronic Illumistorm devices one sees in toy-shops, the kind that has a

---

* Tormé told ufologists apologetically that he had originally scripted an abduction scenario as typically described by abductees, but that Paramount executives, wishing to distinguish the film from CBS's *Intruders* mini-series, had insisted on a more violent and unusual spectacle.

charged ball of metal in the centre surrounded by low-pressure air inside a plastic bubble, with little blue streamers of plasma wafting out from the ball to the inside edge of the bubble. If one places one's finger on the outside of the bubble it alters the electric field and the little plasma streams concentrate into a single intense river and head for one's finger. The well-meaning ufologist told Lucy that the aliens didn't like that kind of thing and that if she kept it on by her bed at night, she would be safe. One of David Jacobs's most frequently abducted abductees had used it successfully for several months before feeling a strange compulsion to turn it off – and then being abducted. Debbie Tomey had been safe for as long as nine months with one of the things, too, but eventually had also felt the compulsion to turn it off and had had a major abduction. Lucy tried it for a few nights but she didn't much like it. When it was on she could hear an annoying buzzing noise in her head, and before long she began to have vivid dreams in which she would smash the thing against a wall or a tree; eventually she just turned it off and it joined the pile of gear beneath her bed.

Lucy's abductions and other strange encounters remained frequent and complex. One night while she was staying at Hopkins's place in New York, she went out for a walk and two un-men in black approached her and gave her a bottle of wine, with instructions to give it to Budd with their compliments. Another night, she was visited by Steven and the greys, who left stains all over her sheets. She folded up the sheets and mailed them in a parcel to Hopkins in New York, so that he could analyse them, but mysteriously, the parcel never arrived. Yet another night, during an abduction research conference in Maryland, Lucy was staying with Budd Hopkins in someone's house. Hopkins slept in a bed nearby, to make sure she didn't get abducted, but his efforts were in vain. In the middle of the night she awoke and got out of bed. Hopkins heard her stir and got up, too. She saw him in the hallway and explained that she was only going to the bathroom. He went back to bed and fell asleep, and in the morning Lucy awoke with her clothes on and with the familiar exhausted feeling. Under hypnosis, it emerged that she had been taken by six human-looking men to a room somewhere. In the room there had been a screen and on the screen a video. The men wanted her to watch the video. One of the men was Steven and another was a black man who wore what appeared to be an Air Force uniform. The Air Force man was talking about the things that needed to be done to make things more efficient. Lucy didn't know what that meant. Lucy became agitated and didn't want to listen to the Air Force man and didn't want to watch the video but Steven put his hand on her shoulder and told her to calm down and to watch it. Later Steven told her that he, Steven, was a member of her family, and that she had to accept this. She wasn't sure that Steven was telling the truth.

Steven didn't bother her for a while after that, but apparently he was very busy with other abductees. By this time Nicole had drawn a picture of Steven based on her experience at Lucy's house, and Hopkins brought the picture with him when he went to abduction conferences. A lot of people said they had seen Steven before, and almost always, when they looked at the picture, they shuddered with revulsion. To those who had met him, he was almost worse than the greys.

According to Lucy, Hopkins wasn't sure what to make of it all, but the fact that so many UFO abductees had seen this human-looking fellow, Steven, convinced him that there was something new and interesting here. Perhaps Steven was somehow in league with the greys? Lucy certainly thought so. Hopkins mentioned the Steven business to one of the producers for the *Sightings* show, and the *Sightings* producer sounded interested, and wanted to arrange an interview with Lucy, and Hopkins asked Lucy if she wanted to go public, and Lucy thought about it and decided that, yes, she did want to go public, as a kind of catharsis, and also to alert people to the fact that someone like Steven was on the loose. She tried to bring up the subject with her mother, to explain that she was going to go public with her Steven experiences, but apparently the subject of Steven was a sore spot with her mother, and she wouldn't hear anything about it. Lucy decided to go ahead with it anyway. However, the *Sightings* producer, perhaps distracted by other paranormal pursuits, never called her.

At about this time, Lucy began to suffer from increasingly severe abdominal pains, apparently related to her alien-enforced diet of eggs and vegetables, and she saw a gastroenterologist and the gastroenterologist asked for a stool sample and it turned out to have blood in it. A diagnosis of a bleeding ulcer was suggested, and she went in for a gastroscope test. Just before the doctor put in the gastroscope, he gave her some Valium. Then suddenly Steven was in the doctor's office. However, the doctor, and Lucy's stepfather who had accompanied her, couldn't see Steven, and Lucy concluded that in this case Steven was only a hallucination, caused by the Valium. The doctor who performed the gastroscope test could find no active, bleeding stomach ulcer. Lucy then predicted, to Budd Hopkins and to others including myself, that the doctors would find no direct evidence for a bleeding ulcer, and in fact, after ultrasound tests and a colonoscopy and radiodiagnostic evaluations, no evidence for a bleeding ulcer could be found – other than her stool samples which continued to have blood in them. The source of the blood was never determined, but Lucy did appear to be anaemic, and it also was found that her gall bladder was not processing fat properly. Plans were made to remove the gall bladder, but these were postponed when it was determined that she suffered from hypoparathyroidism, a rare dysfunction of the parathyroid gland which can lead to abnormal bloodstream levels of certain minerals. She was referred to an endocrinologist for further tests.*

It was at about this time that Ricardo made a reappearance, bumping into Lucy one day while she was jogging; that night, at midnight, he terrorized her by pounding on the door to her house, and she was forced to call her mother and stepfather for help. Soon afterwards, Lucy visited Budd Hopkins for more regressions, and while dining alone one night before going to stay with Nicole, she was given drugged wine – it tasted suspiciously salty, but the waiter insisted that she drink it – and came to her senses several hours later, having apparently been driven to a Hasidic neighbourhood in Brooklyn by strange men, several of them military officers, who

---

* Hypoparathyroidism, which can cause calcium deposits to form in the brain, has been associated in some cases with neurological and psychological problems such as anxiety, dementia, hallucinations, and paranoid delusions. However, I learned later that doctors had apparently detected no calcium deposits in Lucy's brain.

showed her family pictures of Budd Hopkins, and other documents which she could not understand. One of the officers, she remembered, was named 'Colonel Jack Laranax'. She noted the odd similarity of the name to 'larynx'. When she arrived back at Nicole's apartment, she was extremely thirsty and drank half a gallon of water, and her body temperature seemed to fluctuate wildly. Later, when Hopkins showed her his own family photographs, it became clear that these were the ones she had been shown by the strange men. Lucy told other abductees about her Brooklyn adventure, but some of them declined to believe her, suggesting obliquely that her experience might have been related to her gastrointestinal problems. However, according to Lucy, David Jacobs reassured her: 'A lot of people are saying that Linda's case is the case of the century, but your thing in Brooklyn overshadows it. If Budd doesn't write a book about you, or you don't write a book, I'd be surprised.'

Notwithstanding this encouragement, Lucy became increasingly despondent. After one particularly violent encounter with Ricardo, who had threatened her life and the lives of her parents if she continued to tell Hopkins about her experiences, Lucy told me: 'My life is over.' While she waited for Ricardo's return, she decided to take some Valium again to help her sleep, but it only gave her intense nightmares from which she found it difficult to escape. Resigned to sleeplessness, she took a gun from her step-father's house, loaded it, and placed it beside her bed every night, ready for use on Ricardo or Steven or the inexorable greys.

Nicole also continued to be abducted, and although her abductions occurred relatively infrequently, she became increasingly distracted by telephone calls, at all hours, from other abductees seeking solace or passing on the latest gossip. The gossip was becoming ugly, especially as the Linda case wore on and absorbed a greater proportion of Budd Hopkins's attention. Some of the abductees seemed to be accusing Linda of being a hoaxer, and were attacking Nicole, too, because she was a friend of Linda's. Nicole vowed to me that she would soon break out of the abductee underworld, into the world of ordinary life.

At Laurentian University in Ontario, Michael Persinger maintained his usual pace of work, putting out a new paper every few months or so, and concentrating much of his efforts on understanding the geophysical basis for UFOs and the neurophysiological basis for anomalous experiences such as UFO abductions.

On the geophysical side, his tectonic strain theory became a bit more specific and elaborate. Almost fifteen years of trying to connect seismic activity with UFO reports around the world, and even with a spate of appearances of the Virgin Mary over a Coptic church in Egypt, had left him with a pile of correlations, but since mere correlations, to most empirical scientists, didn't constitute strong evidence for causation (because, for example, two correlated events could have been caused by a separate event), Persinger found himself in a bit of a dead end. To show causation, he needed to perform an experiment; ideally, he needed somehow to produce tectonic strain, then to wait to see how many UFOs were reported. That, of course, was impossible.

Or was it? John Derr, a geophysicist friend of Persinger at the US Geological Survey in Colorado, dug up an interesting old case that came close to being a tectonic-strain-creation experiment. Between 1962 and 1967, hundreds of millions of gallons of industrial waste fluid had been injected into the bedrock beneath the Rocky Mountain Arsenal Well, near the town of Derby, Colorado. During that period over 1,500 earthquakes had been recorded in the area, and at the time had been attributed by geologists to the injection of the waste fluid – which appeared effectively to have lubricated whatever faults they had flowed across, allowing them to slip more easily and, by a kind of domino effect, causing faults further out from the epicentre to slip, in what amounted to the propagation of a slow wave of tectonic strain. Derr and Persinger found that the UFO reports not only increased with the injections of fluid, but slowly propagated outwards from the injection site, at between thirty and eighty miles per month, presumably accompanying the slow wave of tectonic strain. Having already noticed that heavy rainfall and higher-than-average river volume seemed to precede earthquakes and UFO reports in certain areas, Derr and Persinger now proposed that some hydraulic triggering mechanism, in combination with tectonic strain, lay behind earthquakes and their associated luminous phenomena. Interestingly, in some cases, Derr and Persinger had observed that UFO reports, within about a six-month period before a significant earthquake, tended not to propagate from but to *converge upon* the epicentre of the eventual quake – suggesting that UFO reports might some day be used as an earthquake early warning system.

On the neurological side, Persinger by early 1993 had put forward experimental evidence for a broad range of hypotheses concerning the mechanisms of anomalous experiences and the workings of the temporal lobe. According to Persinger, people with greater than average temporal lobe lability tended to be more intuitive than sensing, and more perceiving than judging; the fact that the temporal lobe affected cognitive style explained why poets, artists, actors, and women – i.e. those with a more intuitive and creative cognitive style – tended to have more frequent anomalous experiences. Temporal lobe types also tended to associate words with their 'pleasantness', and accordingly tended to use more pleasant-seeming words in conversation (grooooovy, man). Temporal lobe types tended to believe in ESP and telekinesis and other psi phenomena, and tended to report these and other types of paranormal experience. Pseudocyesis, or false pregnancy, in which women developed the symptoms of pregnancy for a time – including morning sickness, abdominal swelling, and breast changes – without actually being pregnant, also seemed to be associated with temporal lobe lability (and with belief in Roman Catholicism) through the amygdala and its effects on hormone production, which probably explained why the sons of God have perennially come in unto the daughters of men, afterwards stealing their foetuses, or in rare cases allowing them to give birth to divinities. 'Sudden remembering', by adults, of childhood sex abuse or satanic abuse or UFO abductions was also associated with temporal lobe lability. Finally, Persinger determined that temporal lobe lability could be reinforced, perhaps harmfully, by techniques such as meditation.

Women with temporal lobe lability tended to believe in the paranormal, witchcraft, and spiritualism, while men with temporal lobe lability tended to believe in extraterrestrial life forms. Temporal lobe types were more often left-handed than non-temporal lobe types, a fact which seemed to support Persinger's view that other-worldly experiences were often related to right-hemisphere processes (which control left-side sensorimotor functions). Overall, temporal lobe types tended to have lower than average self-esteem.

Persinger's general theory, now elaborated a bit more since the late 1980s, was that apparitions and UFO abductions and similar intrusions of 'other' entities represented intrusions of right-hemispheric brain processes, especially those related to the amygdala and hippocampus, into overall consciousness (which normally seems to be dominated by left-hemispheric processes). The fact that men tended to have a greater dominance of their left hemispheres over their right hemispheres than women helped to explain why women were more intuitive than men, and also why women tended more often to report anomalous right-brain intrusion experiences such as UFO abductions and demonic possessions. Moreover, such experiences would have different effects for men and women, based on differences between the male and female temporal lobes:

> The suspected sexual dimorphism of the limbic structures of the human brain should be reflected in the general themes of the imaginings. The insula and adjacent orbital frontal regions are associated with the internal representations of the body. Thus one would expect a predominance of taste and smell themes for both sexes but primarily anal themes for men and both anal and intrusive genital experiences (because representation of the inner vagina and the cervix is within the caudal orbital frontal/anterior insular cortices) for women; this sexual dimorphism would encourage experiences of 'the unexplained disappearing fetus' during real or imagined pregnancies. These themes would be interwoven with more classic temporal lobe phenomenology that would include out-of-body experiences, religious connotations, sensed presences, floating, and 'selection' because there is some special personal characteristic.

In other words, the contents of UFO abductions and related anomalous experiences would contain a certain number of repeating patterns – not because the experiences were endured at the hands of the same otherworldly entities but because they tended to involve the stimulation of the same specific areas of the brain, this stimulation being woven, with idiosyncratic and cultural material, into the fabric of the dream-like 'experience' so that a genital tingle became a forcible artificial insemination – in the same way that, for an ordinary dreamer, an alarm clock's buzz could become a roaring freight train.

On a more hopeful note, Persinger believed that sudden 'healing' or other verifiable physiological changes, such as those reported by Dr X and his Peruvian counterpart, might also occur during anomalous temporal lobe activity, and would presumably have something to do with the brain's deep relationship to the body's immune and endocrine systems.

Persinger's third line of inquiry, related both to his geophysical interests and to his classical neurobehavioural interests, was parapsychology. By 1993 he had performed numerous experiments and analyses of others' experiments in this area. One study suggested that over the past century or so of parapsychological observation and experimentation there had been a significant correlation between, on the one hand, things such as ghost appearances, clairvoyant dreams, and high scores by subjects on ESP tests, and on the other hand periods of low global geomagnetic activity. In other words, the 'noise' caused by magnetic storms might somehow interfere with the processes that give rise to ghosts and ESP and clairvoyance. These processes might somehow be different from the processes involved in, say, poltergeist activity – for poltergeist activity correlated with periods of *high* geomagnetic activity. Persinger wasn't sure what to make of it all, but he seemed to believe that the answer had to be mundane somehow, or at least non-supernatural, probably something to do with magnetic fields. As for his views on religion and supernatural-type experiences, Persinger was more or less the antithesis of someone like John Mack or Ken Ring; he appreciated the connection between temporal lobe lability and such positive attributes as creativity and intuition and self-healing, but he also worried that a lot of strange experiences, especially when encouraged, led to fractured psyches and extreme beliefs and behaviour. In particular, he believed that certain types of religious ideologies not only reinforced temporal lobe lability by their associated rituals, but also, by conflicting with everyday experience, forced the compartmentalization of beliefs – building up right-hemispheric pressures that would eventually burst forth as UFO abductions or voices in the head or ghosts or demonic possessions or ray-firing deros or out-of-body experiences or God experiences or God knew what.

In early 1993, George Hansen, Rich Butler, and Joe Stefula circulated a twenty-five-page white paper criticizing the Linda abduction case. It was published in a few UFO magazines, provoking harsh rebuttals from proponents of the case, and the controversy continued. Responding to Hansen's request for an investigation, the Secret Service visited Linda and Budd Hopkins and interviewed them about the allegations regarding Richard and Dan. Hopkins, enraged by Hansen's interference, alleged to the Secret Service investigators that Hansen was mentally unbalanced. Hansen meanwhile turned his attention to other ufological and paranormal matters. Rich Butler continued research with his own circle of abductees in southern New Jersey, and increasingly began working with the noted artist and psychic Ingo Swann – who believed that by telepathically studying abductees, he could recover information more effectively than a hypnotist could. One day in the spring of 1993, he and Stefula brought a twenty-five-year-old abductee named Cynthia – who belonged to the circle of a major east-coast abduction researcher – to see Swann. Swann scanned her, and reported that she had some mental block which prevented his seeing what had happened. After she left, according to Stefula, Swann told Stefula and Butler that he had made up the story about the mental block to avoid embarrassing Cynthia, whom he had in fact visualized dropping acid with her friends. Stefula was impressed, he told me, because earlier Cynthia had admitted to him that she did take hallucinogenic drugs on occasion.

Stefula renewed his interest in the Roswell crashed-saucer case. All of the other major UFO cases he had looked into, from Linda to Gulf Breeze, had seemed to him to involve hoaxes or delusions. If the Roswell case didn't pan out, he vowed, he would abandon ufology altogether. As of the spring of 1993, though, hopes were high among ufologists that something would come of the Roswell case. Kevin Randle and Don Schmitt, the authors of a 1991 book entitled UFO *Crash at Roswell*, claimed to have tracked down metallic debris from the crash, along with reputable, high-ranking military officers (two colonels and a general) who could testify that the saucer – actually more of a bat-winged vehicle than a disc – had in fact crashed, and had been recovered by the military along with four dead aliens, plus a live one. The *New York Times* was said to be interested, and the cable channel HBO was filming a documentary about Randle's and Schmitt's 1991 book, to be released with their new book around Christmas 1993. Stefula, Hansen, and Butler started work on their own Roswell-related book. They welcomed the possibility that their years of ufological research had not been in vain, but also worried that the success of the Roswell case might have the perverse effect of legitimizing the abduction research of people such as Budd Hopkins.

Tracy Tormé began work on a third UFO epic – his last, he told ufologists – which would deal with the US government's UFO cover-up along with some of the odder parapsychological aspects of the UFO phenomenon.

With the release of *Fire in the Sky*, Phil Klass began another round of talk show battles, appearing for example on CNN's *Larry King Live*, with Travis Walton and Walton's former woodcutting crewchief, Mike Rogers. Klass argued, as ever, that the Walton case was a hoax. He also continued his criticisms of the Linda case, and of the abduction phenomenon in general, and as Kevin Randle's and Don Schmitt's book neared publication, Klass girded his loins to debunk their crashed-saucer claims. Other crashed-saucer witnesses, he argued, had already been exposed as hoaxers – and moreover, in forty years no one at *Aviation Week*, where sensational secrets arrived from government sources all the time, had ever been fed anything to do with crashed saucers or captive aliens. Aside from his ufological work, Klass continued to write two feature articles per month for *Aviation Week* from his crowded, reporterly office in his home in Washington, DC.

John Mack's book about UFO abductions and other anomalous experiences, a book which publishers on both sides of the Atlantic had been talking about since early 1992, was finished in 1993 and was scheduled to be published early in 1994. Mack's view of the phenomenon remained more New Ageish and positive than Hopkins's and Jacobs's, but he continued to support the Linda case and many others of Hopkins's and Jacobs's cases, and all three researchers remained friendly and in touch.

Ken Ring retired and became an emeritus professor at the University of Connecticut, and planned two more books – one discussing the variety of transcendent OBE-type Mind at Large experiences, and the other a collection of essays on NDEs. Whitley Strieber kept a low profile, living in Manhattan and occasionally going out to meetings of an abductee support group on Long Island, where, it was said, he tended to sit at the back of the room, hardly ever speaking.

Eddie Bullard kept up his own steady pace of work at his desk down in the bookstacks at the University of Indiana. He told me that he was working on a revision of his 1987 abduction study, incorporating many new abduction cases. Although he remained confident that something unusual was happening to abductees, he also remained open to the possibility that their experiences were essentially hallucinatory, with a few sensational hoaxes thrown in, and that perhaps his expanded study would support this view.

Dave Jacobs's abductee circle widened, and his book *Secret Life* came out in paperback. The *New York Times* and *People* magazine gave some adverse publicity to his undergraduate history course, 'UFOs in Modern Culture', but despite some consequent censorial pressure from the history department at Temple, he was able to continue teaching the course. His view of UFOs had darkened, however. 'That tremendous, exciting, and sort of amazing and even exhilarating aspect of the phenomenon,' he told me, 'the challenge of discerning what it is and how it works, is to a certain extent over. And we're left with something that I don't like.' That something was abductions, and the havoc they wreaked on people's lives. Jacobs didn't really know what could be done. It didn't seem that the aliens could be stopped. It didn't seem that they would just go away. Their activities could be publicized, through books and movies and talk show discussions and scientific conferences and so on, and humanity could begin to make efforts to defend against them, but even that might not be the wisest thing to do. 'For example,' he told me, 'let us assume that this is a secret, clandestine phenomenon ... There is a reason for that – there are many reasons for that, but let us assume that some people get to learn about it. Well, that doesn't matter. The scope of it is so large, we think ... This is a very large scale phenomenon. Well, supposing lots of people get to learn about it – millions. Well, OK, they could still maintain the secrecy, as long as they're allowed to do their procedures.

'But supposing *everybody* learns about it, and people are actively trying to stop it ... and begin to work out methodologies for interfering with it. At what point does the clandestine element of the programme become simply inoperative, and they don't need to be secret? Let's call this clandestine aspect Plan A. At what point does Plan A simply become non-essential because everybody knows about it already, and they then switch, perhaps, to Plan B? The big question is: is there a Plan B, and if there is a Plan B, *do we want to know what it is?*'

In the spring of 1993, Budd Hopkins hypnotized Calvin Parker, Charles Hickson's companion during the Pascagoula incident. Under hypnosis and reviewing the incident, Parker remembered that as he had entered the spacecraft he had been staring at a patch on the knee of his jeans. In other words, he had been curled up in the same tuck position Linda had been in during her 1989 abduction. Hopkins told Jacobs about it, and suddenly Jacobs began to find that a lot of his abductees were being taken into spacecraft while in the tuck position.

Hopkins also devoted considerable attention to a report from a couple whom he had met on his recent Australian tour. They had shown Hopkins four oddly red-tinted photographs taken at a bayside park on an afternoon in 1978. One of the photos showed two children and the father, but the other three showed empty scenes of the park – although they should have included the couple and their children. When Hopkins hypnotically regressed the couple, it became clear that they and their children had been abducted while the red-tinted photographs were being taken, and that the aliens had planted a screen memory in their minds to make them think that they had actually been standing by the bay photographing each other. Hopkins presented the case at the 1993 MUFON conference, and although his presentation was well received, a number of conference-goers mused on the irony that in this case, nothing was being used as evidence for something.

Hopkins's chief concern remained the Linda case, however, and when he was not attending to abductees or travelling to UFO conferences or being interviewed by journalists, he transformed the case into a book and sought a publisher. He remained confident that the case was genuine, citing undisclosed evidence which apparently supported the testimony of Linda and Richard and Dan. He made plans to fly to Geneva, to attempt to make direct contact with Javier Perez de Cuellar and, hopefully, to persuade him to admit publicly his abduction experiences.

Hopkins's abductees continued to express concern over his heavy workload and his health. He had been diagnosed with renal cancer in the spring of 1992, and had undergone surgery to remove one of his kidneys. Some of his abductees wondered to me whether his frenetic pace of work reflected a belief that he had not much longer to work, or to live. They also expressed regret over his separation and impending divorce from April Kingsley. It was said that Kingsley objected to Hopkins's constant focus upon his abduction work. It looked as if Kingsley would get the house in Cape Cod, the one Hopkins had built after his divorce from his first wife Joan. In the meantime, as part of the separation arrangement, he and Kingsley had split the house on 16th Street into two zones. She lived in the upstairs apartment, and he lived in the studio. The studio area had no kitchen, and when his daughter was home and using her bedroom, Budd was obliged to sleep on the couch in the draughty lower studio, surrounded by *Mahler's Castle* and the Guardians, the dusty Ixions, and the sketch by Léger.

* * *

While researching and writing this book, I was frequently asked for my own opinion on the subject of UFO abductions. My response was usually to profess a wary bewilderment, and, although I was always disinclined to believe that an advanced extraterrestrial civilization would have reason to do, in so many strange guises, the things that they were alleged to be doing, I was at the same time convinced that the phenomenon was anomalous and important and deserved serious scientific attention. There were even times – probably unavoidable, given my immersion in the subject – when I began to entertain the notion that it was all true, that UFO abductions really were happening, just as the abductees and their bruises and their scars suggested.

That notion may prove to have been correct, and in any case I find it difficult to ignore the evidence that, as far as UFOs themselves are concerned, there is something real and strange out there. But I also find it difficult to ignore the phenomenological, sociological, psychological, and apparent parapsychological links between alien abductions and a host of other unusual experiences. I am impressed by the evidence that these experiences have been with us for ages, never far from the levers of history, even though their actual nature has tended to be obscured by religious zealots and scientistic scoffers alike.

These experiences, it would appear to me, can be triggered by any number of things – stress, a desire for attention, a Persinger transient, a dose of peyote, a hypnotic trance – and can be clothed in whatever idiosyncratic or cultural or archetypal material is appropriate, but at their heart, as Persinger has argued, there often seems to be a universal neurological reflex which would explain why those who claim such experiences tend to report fundamentally similar experiences such as bedroom presences, levitation and flight, and sexual sensations* – although some of these may also have sociological origins. In Chapter 7 and elsewhere I have reviewed or mentioned several culturally defined variants of these unusual experiences, including Old Hag visitations, shamanic initiations, and demonic oppressions. Another variant, one of my favourites, was prevalent for a time in early medieval Germany as the witch mania was getting under way: numerous God-fearing women confessed to their husbands that on occasion at night they would levitate from their beds, fly through the walls into the midnight air, and float

---

* Is this why witches ride broomsticks and not magic carpets?

with other such women to distant regions where they would descend upon sleeping men, mutilate them, eat them, and then bring them to life again. The ecclesiastical authorities of the time, foreshadowing the Roper alien abduction survey and other modern measures of dissociative or temporal-lobe-type experiences, devised a questionnaire which read: 'Have you believed ... that in the silence of the night ... when your husband lies in your bosom, you are able, while still in your body, to go through closed doors and travel through the spaces of the world, together with others ...?' Those who answered in the affirmative were diagnosed as demonically deluded and were given heavy penances, including a fifty-day bread-and-water fast, to be repeated every year for seven years – which presumably, by causing further neurological stress, ensured that the experiences continued.

The non-fundamental themes of abduction experiences I also find fascinating, for they tend to highlight the extraordinary mnemonic permeability of the dissociative mind. This permeability, this promiscuous neuronal intercourse, is presumably the basis of cryptomnesia – the production of information one does not remember receiving – as well as of suggestibility and creativity. Practically speaking, it explains why one can find antecedents elsewhere in the lore for so many bizarre and apparently idiosyncratic abduction and close-encounter tales. For example, Nicole's vision of pyjama-clad Javier Perez de Cuellar is remarkably similar to Whitley Strieber's vision of his pyjama-clad father in *Communion* (see p. 84 of this book), while Strieber's own story about triangular rashes on himself and his son is obviously like Dr X's claimed experience.* The reader will also have noted that various ostensibly independent witnesses to Linda's November 1989 abduction with Perez de Cuellar have tended to refer to Linda or to her alienesque twin (the Marlo Thomas woman) using unusual but similar terms such as

* Persinger has suggested, apropos of *Communion*, that triangles and other geometric shapes just bubble up naturally from the right brains of mystics, but of course the fact that Strieber manifested scars or marks, whatever their shape, also belongs to a tradition that extends back through the devil's marks of witches and the stigmata of saints to the self-inflicted wounds of shamanic initiates.

'porcelain doll', 'porcelain mannequin', 'blown glass figurine', and 'angel'.

Finally, I note the remarkable resemblance between the various forms of alien 'mindscanning' and mesmerization and the mundane hypnotherapeutic process within which these alien manipulations are often described by abductees. One could even speculate that the stories of sexual operations performed on prone abductees in space-ships owe something to the fantasies activated while abductees lie prone on hypnotists' couches.

The point, of course, is that even incidental, unconsciously absorbed information can invade consciousness with a vengeance. At the time of writing, I have heard that some female therapists who treat Vietnam veterans with post-traumatic stress syndrome have themselves begun to suffer 'flashbacks' about their own 'combat experiences'. The contagiousness of such experiences, especially among temporal lobe or dissociative types, presumably explains why extraordinary encounter claims so often ripple outwards into mass hysterias – the social analogues (social seizures, if you will) of the putative neurological process which ensures their broad resemblance.

There are still a few aspects of the abduction phenomenon which seem to elude the grasp of the standard psychosocial hypothesis. One is the claim – for which, I admit, I have only her ingenuousness as evidence – that as a child sculptor Nicole could not help but put abnormally large eyes on anything she created. If true, this story cries out for an explanation that includes the concept of archetypes. But what would an archetypal image of large-eyed sculptures *mean*?

I have a wild hypothesis, which leans heavily on a theory put forward by a Princeton psychology professor named Julian Jaynes. In his 1976 book, *The Origin of Consciousness in the Breakdown of the Bicameral Mind*, Jaynes argued that until about the second millennium BC, human consciousness was so different from what we experience today that it should not properly be called conscious-ness. According to Jaynes, human introspection, evaluation, and decision-making in unusual situations were then always performed unconsciously by the right side of the brain, which delivered commands in the form of hallucinated voices – and sometimes visions – to the obedient left side. These voices and apparitions might have originated, tens of millennia in the past, as those of other humans, perhaps parents or tribal leaders, but in the course of time they became the voices and visions of gods – initially, benign and all-knowing gods, to whose authority all religions and sciences attempt to return, while the purest atavistic remnants of that blissful bicameral era languish in mental institutions.

Jaynes's arguments remain controversial and unorthodox, but in having postulated a right-brain-vs.-left-brain basis for such modern phenomena as hypnosis, mediumship, and spirit-possession, and in having envisioned the gradual loss of man's access to the bicameral realm, Jaynes has clearly been thinking along lines similar to those of such researchers as Michael Persinger, and even, to a subtler and perhaps ironic extent, John Mack. In any case, as regards large-eyed artworks Jaynes argued that in the several millennia before Christ, social and cultural pressures began to weaken the neurological hold of the hallucinated gods. These gods increasingly needed to be evoked with external hallucinogens such as effigies and idols. These effigies and idols, Jaynes argued from his reading of the archaeological literature, tended to have abnormally large eyes. Why? Because eye-to-eye contact was and is so overwhelmingly important in the authority relationships of humans and lower animals. Effigies made better hallucinogens when they had larger eyes.

Jaynes, who sought to use his observations that many effigies had large eyes to buttress his theory about ancient hallucinated gods, took this argument no further. However, I cannot help but speculate that the practice of making large-eyed effigies might have left some vestigial mark, not only on the physiognomies of our modern monsters, but perhaps also on the creative impulses of some modern sculptors and painters, who without knowing it might be acting out the hallucinogenic artistry of their distant Sumerian – indeed, Lemurian! – ancestors.

There is another quandary concerning UFO encounters. No one has satisfactorily explained to me why some abductees, contactees, and close-encounter victims, aside from hallucinating and seeming to read people's minds, almost inevitably (and increasingly, once they have attracted the attention of researchers) seem to engage in bizarre and complicated and often ludicrous deceptions involving such things as nasal X-rays, sand-and-seaweed-covered struggles on the beach, mysteriously proffered bottles of wine, disappearing grey-stained sheets, scars and other alien residue on their own and their children's bodies, and evasions of nocturnal surveillance.

John Keel has suggested that such deceptions are practised through unwitting humans by a non-human intelligence – in other words, that the abductee syndrome and its sister syndromes represent forms of spirit-possession. In my opinion, however, Keel is only half right; the abduction syndrome can usefully be considered a modern version of spirit-possession, but both can probably be accounted for by ordinary, goal-directed, conniving human intelligence – acting consciously or unconsciously.

The anthropologist I. M. Lewis, in a book entitled *Ecstatic Religion*, discussed a variety of spirit-possession syndromes found in the Third World. Here is an example from Tanzania:

> The possessing spirit, which manifests its presence by hysterical and other symptoms, demands gifts which reflect its origin. Treatment here is often a lengthy business; and involves not only the usual costly cathartic dances but also the presence for some time of the therapist within the family of the afflicted woman. In this enlightened therapy, the sick wife is made to feel the centre of attention and her husband may even be constrained to modify his behaviour towards his spouse.

Lewis elsewhere quotes a Nigerian anthropologist, M. Onwuejeogwu, on the *bori* spirit-possession syndrome among the Muslim Hausa tribes of West Africa. Onwuejeogwu states simply that possessed wives

> manipulate *bori* episodes in such a way as to reduce their husbands to social and economic straits. Hence *bori* is not only a symbolic but also a real way of defying the male dominance which pervades Hausa society. In *bori* women find an escape from a world dominated by men; and through *bori*

the world of women temporarily subdues and humiliates the world of men.

Lewis makes clear, with numerous examples, that such female possession syndromes are endemic in cultures where women are treated subordinately, and essentially represent the expression of forbidden impulses and desires, including the desire, often expressed with elaborate deceptions, to annoy males and to protest against their domination. Possessees are not always female, but when they are not, according to Lewis, the possessed male can usually be said to occupy a similarly subordinate or peripheral place in society; thus the function of possession as a technique of social subversion and protest would appear to be a general one. However, in practice virtually all possession syndromes are populated mainly by women.

For our comparative purposes, it is also worth noting that spirit-possession, perhaps when it has proved successful as a manipulative or esteem-elevating technique on one occasion, tends to become chronic and to take on a new social dimension. In the following passage by Lewis it is easy to imagine that he is talking about aliens, abductees, support groups, and hypnotherapists:

The primary emphasis is sometimes initially on the casting out, or exorcism, of the intrusive pathogenic spirit. But since such complaints tend to be habit-forming, what is eventually achieved is often more in the nature of an accommodation between the chronically possessed patient and her familiar. The patient learns, in effect, to live with her spirit. The spirit is thus finally 'tamed' and brought under control, but usually only at the cost of recurrent ceremonies in its honour. This process is normally realized by the woman concerned joining a club, or group, of other similarly placed women under the direction of a female shaman.

In the West, where marriage and social customs have meant that women often do not marry, possession has frequently stemmed from female sexual frustration; in these cases, the possessing spirit tends to act out forbidden erotic impulses, at least some of which seem to be aimed at the mediating shaman or exorcist or therapist, who is almost always male.

Third World possession cults, according to Lewis and other anthropologists, are often understood and tolerated by males as necessary outlets for female grievances. In the enlightened West, however, female possession cults have seldom failed to succeed in deceiving their male targets – and when men do finally catch on, the syndromes disappear for a while, and then re-emerge in new and newly impressive forms, especially those which enjoy religious or medical sanction.

For example, in the middle part of this millennium, it became the tradition for aspiring female mystics to undergo a period of oppression by demons – usually nocturnal sexual oppression in the form of erotic dreams or hallucinated intercourse – followed by a visionary 'mystical marriage' in which the young woman would become a 'bride of Christ'. The validity of this mystics' club was never seriously challenged by pious churchmen, although it attracted many obvious frauds. The case of Benedetta Carlini is a good example. Sent to a convent at the age of nine in 1600, probably because her parents had no money for a marriage dowry, Benedetta began her ill-fated career as a mystic by apparently toppling a statue of the Virgin Mary in a convent chapel and claiming, once her cries had attracted an audience, that the statue had bent over to kiss her. Later she began to complain about demonic oppression, and asked that another nun, one Bartolomea Crivelli, be her nocturnal companion. In bed with Bartolomea, Benedetta began to channel a variety of male alter personalities, including Jesus and a young angel named Splenditello. Splenditello, assuring Bartolomea that it was all right to have sex with an angel, forced himself on the young girl, and the two became energetic lovers. In time, Benedetta/Splenditello was observed by other nuns wounding herself to create fake stigmata, and painting a 'ring' on her finger with saffron to symbolize her sacred marriage to Christ – with whom, she claimed (following not only the shamanic and demonological lore but the contemporary lore of female saints), she had rather bloodily exchanged hearts one night while in bed. Bartolomea confirmed that she had witnessed the exchange taking place, although she later retracted her testimony after Benedetta's trickery – which had enabled her to attain the position of abbess – was exposed.

Benedetta was diagnosed with demonic possession, but her possession was probably more related to the multiple personality disorder of today than to the classic convent possession cases of her own day. Of these, the Aix-en-Provence case of 1609–13 was probably the most famous. It centred around the adolescent nun Madeleine de Demandoix de la Palud, the daughter of a well-to-do Marseilles family, who was sent to a small convent at Aix at the age of twelve. She returned home a year or so later after becoming depressed and homesick. There she was befriended by a handsome and popular Marseilles priest, Father Louis Gaufridi, with whom, it was said, eight other women were in love. After Madeleine and Father Gaufridi were rumoured to have spent one and a half hours alone together at her parents' home, Madeleine's parents sent her back to the convent at Aix. There, two years later, in 1609, aged sixteen or seventeen, she began to suffer convulsions, cramps, and tormenting visions of the devil. Just before Christmas of that year, she smashed a crucifix during confession, and it was decided to attempt exorcism. During these attempts, Madeleine's demons accused Father Gaufridi of having seduced her, and of having given her a green devil as a familiar. Madeleine's symptoms spread to five other nuns, one of whom, Louise Capeau, soon rivalled Madeleine by claiming via one of her demonic spokesmen that she, Louise, was inhabited by no less than 6,666 high-ranking officials of Hell. Both girls' demons accused Gaufridi of a variety of offences, including the seduction of Madeleine, grotesque sexual perversions, sorcery, cannibalism, and attendance at the 'synagogue' (i.e. witches' sabbath). During a brief period of confinement after her accusations had proved difficult to confirm, Madeleine exhibited manic-depressive symptoms, and, according to the historian R. H. Robbins, 'had visions, danced and laughed, sang love songs, neighed like a horse, disrupted the services (snatching birettas and tearing a chasuble), told fantastic tales of [witches' sabbaths] (with sodomy and eating of little children)', and so on. Later, when Gaufridi was put on trial, both girls attended and continued their alarming behaviour, Madeleine alternately denouncing Gaufridi, pleading for warm words from him, and simulating (or experiencing) violent orgasms.

She twice seemed to attempt suicide, and also displayed the 'devil's marks' on her body which she said Gaufridi had caused to be put there. The vanishing of these marks, along with the rest of Madeleine's symptoms, coincided with the execution of Gaufridi in the spring of 1613, although Louise continued to be possessed and later that year caused a blind girl to be burned at the stake for witchcraft. Another epidemic at Lille was begun by a Sister Marie de Sains, who had been at the Aix convent during the Gaufridi case, but this ended when a sceptical archbishop intervened and imprisoned her.

In the Loudun case of 1633–4, later novelized by Aldous Huxley, a group of nuns was asked to collaborate in a political scheme against a priest named Urbain Grandier. Their task was to mimic the symptoms of possession, and to accuse Grandier of having bewitched them. Remarkably, however, their symptoms, which included fantastic feats of strength as well as apparent demonstrations of parapsychological skills, did not end with Grandier's torture and execution. In fact, they soon drew crowds of tourists, one of whom, according to R. H. Robbins, beheld a certain Sister Claire while she 'fell on the ground, blaspheming, in convulsions, lifting up her petticoats and chemise, displaying her privy parts without any shame, and uttering filthy words. Her gestures became so indecent that the audience averted its eyes.' All attempts at exorcism failed, but when Cardinal Richelieu, who had sponsored the plot, lost interest and stopped the nuns' payments, their possession fits ceased.

In the Auxonne case of 1660, a group of nuns developed the symptoms of possession and quickly focused their displays upon their convent confessor, a Father Nouvelet. Nouvelet, who seemed to have learned from the mistakes of his predecessors, disarmed any would-be accusers by suggesting that he himself was also bewitched. He also came up with a Monty Pythonesque scheme of exorcism in which he would lie in bed with the possessed nuns or would have them assume erotic, contortionist poses before a chapel altar while he celebrated mass. When the convent's mother superior objected, she became the subject of elaborate accusations by the other nuns of witchcraft and lesbianism – although, after an investigation, it was found that some of the accusing nuns were either mentally disturbed or fraudulent, and charges were dropped.*

The increasing demonological scepticism in such parts of Europe was not immediately reflected in the American colonies. The best-known episode of American possession hysteria, at Salem, began in the early 1690s when the village parson's daughter and her cousin, aged nine and eleven respectively, began to exhibit the usual seizures and invisible woundings that signified demonic possession. Their symptoms soon spread to others, and the possessed began to blame various villagers for having bewitched them. Within a few months some 200 people had been arrested, and twenty hanged, and it was only after important colonial officials – including the President of Harvard and the wife of the Massachusetts governor – were implicated by the bewitched girls that the hysteria collapsed of its own absurdity.† By the eighteenth century, when the accused began to fight back with libel suits, the mass possessions and witch-trials had largely disappeared both in America and in Europe.

In the nineteenth century, one could argue, peripheral possession syndromes in the West took the form of the 'hysterical neuroses', whose mostly female sufferers presented to mostly male doctors any of a variety of mysterious symptoms, including nosebleeds, abdominal cramps, (false) pregnancies, hallucinations, eating disorders, thermoregulatory problems, and amnesic spells – in other words, the usual background symptoms of the dissociative or temporal-lobe-labile personality. One of the psychiatrist Josef Breuer's patients, the pseudonymous 'Anna O', referred to her amnesic lapses in Germanized English as 'time-missing', and when

---

* The *Sacramento Bee* of 12 July 1993 reported that Dr Richard Boylan, a prominent local psychologist, was sued by two women who claimed he lured them into 'naked hot-tub sessions' by convincing them that they were UFO abductees and thus required special therapy.

† In England, the witch hysterias ran a similar course, although on occasion witch-hunters could have the tables turned against them. The self-styled 'Witch Finder General', Matthew Hopkins, who for all I know was an ancestor of the modern Budd, enjoyed a busy three-year career between 1644 and 1646 in which he reportedly obtained the conviction of some 200 individuals – before he was accused by another Puritan minister of being a witch, and was duly hanged.

Breuer, through hypnosis and the exploration of her memories, had finally seemed to cure her myriad symptoms, she suddenly developed abdominal pains and claimed, 'Now comes Dr Breuer's child.'

Breuer and many other eminent psychiatrists of the day took such symptoms to mean that hysteria could be caused by sexual frustration, and could be cured by the alleviation of that frustration, or at least its illumination in therapy. Even Breuer's young colleague, Sigmund Freud, found himself becoming an object of his patients' sexual attention: one threw her arms around his neck after a hypnosis session, and another, 'Fräulein Elisabeth von R', responded unexpectedly when he pinched her leg during a physical examination. 'Her face,' noted Freud, 'assumed a peculiar expression, one of pleasure rather than of pain; she cried out – somewhat, I could not help thinking, as with a voluptuous tickling – her face flushed, she threw back her head, closed her eyes, her trunk bent backwards.'*

Freud's biographer Peter Gay has suggested (somewhat short-sightedly I think, since the concept of talk therapy extends back to primitive medicine) that Anna O's visits to Breuer established the paradigm for modern psychotherapy:

> Breuer visited her daily, at evening, while she was in a condition of self-induced hypnosis. She would tell stories, sad, at times charming, and, as she and Breuer discovered together, this talking-out temporarily relieved her symptoms. Thus began an epoch-making collaboration between a gifted patient and her attentive physician: Anna O described this procedure, felicitously, as her 'talking cure' . . .

The view that problems could be talked out cathartically was echoed in Breuer and Freud's comment that 'The hysteric suffers mainly from reminiscences.' Freud soon realized, however, that his explorations of the reminiscences of hysterics were turning up a common denominator: the memory of a sexual trauma of some kind in childhood, often involving the 'seduction' of the child by an adult or an older child. From this observation – which was heavily

---

* Freud eventually decided that such behaviour represented the 'transference' of the patient's secret loves on to the therapist from some other individual.

influenced by his expectations – Freud developed the radical theory that all hysterical neuroses were simply psychosomatic manifestations of repressed memories of childhood sexual trauma. This 'seduction theory', which Freud hailed as 'a source of the Nile', was widely ridiculed by his colleagues, and he soon abandoned it after deciding that, based on the numbers of hysterics being sent to him by the families of Vienna, it implied an improbably high incidence of child abuse. Freud developed an alternative theory, which corresponded with the general view that hysterics were merely undersexed. Freud's new theory was that repressed impulses or fantasies, *à la* Oedipus and his mother, were the chief cause of neuroses. As this view gained adherents within the fast-growing discipline of psychology, interest in hysteria and dissociation as such began to wane.

Freud's concept of repression had emphasized buried impulses and fantasy, and Freud himself had expressed his doubt that recovered memories were always clean representations of historical fact. Even though psychotherapists in practice made it their business to recover such memories, which might give clues to the drives or fantasies that were expressing themselves obliquely through apparently neurotic symptoms such as eating disorders and amnesias, this did not mean that the memories had to be taken as literally true.

By the 1980s, for a variety of reasons which possibly included the demise of Freudian theory, the rise of feminism, and a rash of horrific child abuse stories, this view had changed, particularly with respect to repressed memories of childhood sexual or other abuse. Recovered memories were taken seriously again. The fact that there had been an explosion of therapists during the 1970s might also have contributed to this change, since many of these therapists had relatively flimsy qualifications – and with so many therapists to choose from, a patient who wanted to discover repressed traumatic memories could easily shop around until she found a therapist who would validate those memories. For therapists, disbelief of patients could be professionally disadvantageous.

Coinciding with this sudden epidemic of recovered memories of child abuse was another epidemic, that of multiple personality disorder, or MPD. Patients with MPD, aside from manifesting various alter personalities, suffered from mysterious amnesic fugues, mysterious allergies and eating disorders, and mysterious scars and bruises. They also, almost unanimously, claimed a history of childhood sexual abuse. And ninety per cent of them were women.

Although memories of childhood abuse were often recovered with hypnosis or after leading questions from the therapist, and were very rarely corroborated, the view that horrendous abuse in childhood had forced the MPD patient to create alter personalities to cope with the distress became scientific orthodoxy. One of the top dissociative disorder specialists, Colin Ross, a former Canadian academic psychiatrist now in private practice in Texas, put it this way: 'What is MPD? MPD is a little girl imagining that the abuse is happening to someone else.' Ross and other dissociative disorder specialists believed that alter personalities, though created to play a defensive role against childhood abuse, would eventually run amok, causing the amnesias, scars, eating disorders, allergies, hallucinations, and various other psychogenic and self-inflicted ailments from which the patient suffered. Only with long, painstaking hypnotherapy, art therapy, dance therapy, play therapy, and talking-out, in which each alter was confronted and convinced to 're-integrate' with the main personality, could MPD be cured. Therapists often complained about how difficult this was, since patients would often take obvious measures to prolong therapy, responding to every apparent therapeutic advance with more scars and bruises, more horrendous stories of the things that had been done to them. George Ganaway, a psychiatrist at Emory University in Georgia, recounted the following anecdote in a 1989 paper which drew attention to the use of fantasy by MPD patients:

Ms A, a 31-year-old female, urgently telephoned her psychiatrist to report that an internal persecutory alter had just emerged and deeply slashed her vagina with a razor blade, leaving her with profuse haemorrhaging. She was instructed immediately to arrange for assessment and treatment at a nearby hospital emergency room, after which she was admitted to the hospital's psychiatric unit. On his arrival the psychiatrist was surprised to learn that a careful gynaecological

examination by the emergency room physician had revealed
virtually no evidence of physical injury.

In his 1989 book, *Multiple Personality Disorder*, which remains a
standard reference work on the subject, Colin Ross argues that
MPD is simply the modern version of spirit-possession. He also
acknowledges that most old cases of spirit-possession – and virtually
all cases of MPD prior to World War II – seem to have been
caused by factors which, compared to modern claims of chronic
physical and sexual abuse, are relatively mild. In fact, he approv-
ingly cites the work of I. M. Lewis and other anthropologists,
concluding that possession was often susceptible to an anthropological or sociological explanation: 'women living in cultures in which
they are politically powerless can acquire power, influence,
autonomy, and partial satisfaction of thwarted needs through possession . . . Demon possession in Western Europe made possible the
ritualized expression of Dionysian impulses and opinions that could
not be stated directly . . .'

This analysis implies an enormous etiological discrepancy
between old, manipulative forms of MPD and modern abuse-caused
forms of MPD. Ross's hypothesis for this discrepancy is not
entirely convincing: 'Since 1944 MPD has evolved into a syndrome
with a post-traumatic etiology, whereas before it tended to have
less severe external precipitants; our society has gotten sicker, and
the abuse of children more bizarre; earlier clinicians missed the
abuse history in many MPD patients, which was not as severe, on
average, as that experienced by contemporary patients. The
incidence of MPD, then, is an indicator of the amount of child
abuse occurring in Western society.'

MPD was rare before 1980. The present epidemic of the disorder
has followed a number of sensational books on the subject, including the bestselling *Sybil*, which appeared in 1973 and was later
made into a film. In 1980 came another sensational book, *Michelle
Remembers*, by an MPD patient named Michelle Smith, who with
the help of her therapist (later her husband) came to understand
that her dissociative symptoms had been caused by physical and
sexual abuse at the hands of satanic ritualists. Aided by the well-

meaning credulity of Christian fundamentalists, claims of satanic ritual abuse, or SRA, began to rise exponentially, and by the early 1990s dissociative disorder specialists were suggesting that 50,000 of America's estimated 200,000 MPD victims were SRA 'survivors'. SRA survivors often told stories of having been abducted to a strange place where they were drugged or hypnotized and were forced to lie prone, and then were subjected to various sexual indignities. Afterwards they might breed babies which would be used in sacrifices by the other ritualists. Such stories have inspired a number of modern witch-hunts, in which many lives have been ruined, although US law enforcement officials have found little or no tangible evidence that such cults exist, at least in the form alleged by SRA claimants. And of course there is no solid evidence that these cults cause people to develop MPD.

In the early 1980s another even more bizarre MPD variant began to confront therapists, after the publication of a number of sensational books on the subject. The symptoms of those who suffered from this syndrome were virtually the same as those manifested by MPD patients: they included amnesic fugues, mysterious scars, eating disorders and mysterious allergies, and claims of post-traumatic anxiety. The sufferers from this syndrome, very much like SRA survivors, claimed to therapists that they endured more or less regular sexual indignities from beings who hypnotized or otherwise incapacitated them, and later harvested their babies for nefarious purposes. However, in this case the trauma-causers and baby-snatchers were not demons or sorcerers or cultists or incestuous parents. They were little grey aliens.

It seems plausible that some or all cases of alleged alien abduction, satanic ritual abuse, multiple personality disorder, spirit-possession, and demonic oppression might be understood not merely as 'unusual experiences' but as self-victimization syndromes – that is, syndromes in which the goal of the symptoms or behaviour is the fulfilment of the role of victim. Other, more ordinary examples of self-victimization would include some claims of prosaic abuse,* as well as some

---

* Not all prosaic abuse is prosaic; in the past few years, psychiatrists have begun to encounter people who believe that they endured child abuse in *a past life*.

of those mysterious maladies, known clinically as somatization disorders, which somehow never yield to a firm diagnosis despite numerous hospital visits by the earnest and voluble patient.

Another example would be 'Münchausen's syndrome', in which patients compulsively and deliberately seek hospital treatment, telling wild stories of traumatic experiences, feigning symptoms of disease, or creating symptoms through self-injury or by tampering with laboratory samples. The classic description of a Münchausenian, by the London physician Richard Asher in the *Lancet* in 1951, certainly brings to mind the alien abduction phenomenon: 'She sometimes comes in with a different name, but always says she's coughed up pints of blood and tells a story about being an ex-opera singer and helping in the French resistance movement.'

In the related syndrome known as Münchausen's by proxy, children are used, usually by their mothers, as vicarious bait for doctors and medical emergencies. The apparently increasing practice by which UFO abductees present their children and their scars or other 'alien-inflicted' traumata to abduction researchers seems frighteningly consistent with this syndrome.

It would seem, from the literature on Münchausen's and MPD, that self-victimizers employ both conscious and unconscious forms of role-playing. Indeed, both imaginary and self-inflicted ailments are common among MPD patients, so much so that mysterious allergies, eating disorders, and scars and bruises are often considered a sign of an underlying dissociative disorder. Münchausen's syndrome itself has been proposed as a distinct dissociative disorder, since the behaviour of Münchausenians resembles so strongly that of MPD patients.*

In most cases, it would seem, the purpose of self-victimization is to grab attention, to act out otherwise forbidden fantasies, and perhaps also to distract attention from the individual's own problems; in other words, it is essentially childish. But as I. M. Lewis has pointed out in his analyses of Third World possession cults, even chronic self-victimization can lead to a shamanic apothe-

---

* This suggestion was made by Wisconsin psychiatrist Jean Goodwin in the journal *Dissociation* in 1988. Ironically, Goodwin suggested that both MPD and Münchausen's might develop, at least in part, out of actual childhood trauma.

osis or transformation in which the victim adopts a new role in society, often that of a healer or a representative of victims' groups. Nowadays, many MPD patients become nurses or therapists (and vice versa). A similar trend is found among people with Münchausen's and Münchausen's by proxy. Breuer's patient Anna O, whose real name was Bertha Pappenheim, became a social worker and a champion of women's and children's causes.

The appearance of such common threads throughout dissociation-related syndromes suggests, with Persinger's work, that more than sociological forces are involved here. Another indication that relatively deep, transcultural processes are present comes from the recurrence of what appear to be archetypal images. For example, in a satanic ritual abuse case in the state of Washington in 1988, a son of the alleged perpetrator was badgered by police to come up with memories of ritual abuse by his father and other cultists. All he could remember were two haunting childhood dreams. In one, 'little people' who reminded him of Snow White's Seven Dwarfs watched him through his upper-floor bedroom window and then floated into the room and walked on his bed. In another, he said, 'Every time a train came by a whistle would blow and a witch would come in my window ... I would wake up, but I couldn't move. It was like the blankets were tucked under and I couldn't move my arms.' The witch, who was obese, hag-like, and wore a black robe, would sit on top of him. Therapists interpreted the dreams as screen memories of sexual abuse by cult members, just as some ufologists would surely interpret them as screen memories of abduction episodes. The ultimate origins of such archetypes are unclear — why little people? why Old Hags? — but presumably they have some relationship to European traditions of fairies and witches, and perhaps also to basic human neurophysiological processes, Old Hags often being associated with sensations of paralysis and suffocation.

Another example comes from one of Freud's more famous male hysterics, a tormented Russian aristocrat whom Freud nicknamed the Wolf Man because of the peculiar dream which he remembered having had as a boy of about four, during a bout of malaria. In the dream, his bedroom window opened and he saw a pack of six or seven wolves — eerily white wolves — staring in at him from the branches of a tree. Freud, who acknowledged that much of this material must have come from children's fairy-tales, nevertheless could not prevent himself from interpreting, with the patient's help, one of the wolves as the boy's father, the opening of the window as a reflection of the boy's sexual fantasies regarding his father, and the dream in its entirety as a symbolic screen for an actual memory of having risen from his cot unexpectedly to watch his mother and father vigorously enjoying each other during an afternoon siesta. The reader will note this dream's similarity to Nicole's dreams of white gorillas, cats, and owls, and to other abductees' dreams of white or grey animals that they have encountered in unusual circumstances – the ufological interpretation of such circumstances being, at least, more straightforward than Freud's.

The Wolf Man's dreams underscore the fact that hysteria and dissociation are not exclusively female complaints. Indeed, some studies have shown that men and women report roughly equal measures of dissociative experiences; and psychiatrists have argued that the relative absence of men from hospital dissociative disorder units is because men who are highly dissociative act out rage and aggression – directing it towards others, rather than inwards as self-injury – and as a result are hidden in prisons. However, it remains the case that severe dissociative syndromes and their associated cults, networks, and groups are often populated almost entirely by women. This may be only a quirk of social and neuropsychological evolution – a reflection, and an understandable system for sub-version, of the male dominance which has prevailed for most of human existence. But we are left with the fact that on occasion, when groups of dissociation-prone or temporal lobe labile women come together, and sexual, cosmological, and other anxieties are set loose among them, strange, obsessing, mind-bending, and life-wrecking things begin to happen – and one begins to glimpse, illicitly, through the modern curtains of feminism and political correctness, the confusion and frustration and even terror that in days past drove some civil and ecclesiastical authorities to seize such women, many of whom were in the flowering springtime of their lives, and lock them safely away.

Of course, the modern UFO phenomenon involves much more

than tricksy abductees. It involves unusual things that fly around in the sky, and groups of people who attempt to study those things. In that sense it should fall squarely and safely within the realm of science. Yet there is something about UFOs and ufology, an obsessing oddness, that attracts like moths to a light not only psychics and hysterics and tricksters and shamans and shaman-esses, but also conspiracy-theorists, schizophrenics, obsessive-compulsives, con-men, cranks, misfits, impostors, and deviants of every description. The ordinary and congenial are there, of course, and I don't wish to offend them, but too often they seem outnumbered, or at least outshouted, and whether the ufological issue at hand is abductions or crashed saucers or government cover-ups, one's sanity is always at risk; I will always remember John Keel's advice to a distraught friend (a UN official, of all things) when the 1967 UFO wave had strained his mind to the breaking point:

> There's only one way out, Dan. This damned thing becomes an obsession ... a fixation. The only way to stop all the nonsense is to stop thinking about UFOs. Get rid of all your files. Take up stamp collecting or chasing women ...

Presumably Keel meant women who had never met a devil or an angel or an alien. In any case, I do not advocate that all ufologists abandon their vocation for less dangerous pursuits. I wish them well, and I hope that some day their phenomenon will become as apprehensible as thunderstorms or shooting stars or Saturn's rings. As UFOs approach this threshold, the brain-curdling system of strangeness that has surrounded them will perhaps fall away, all of the misfits and deviants and hysterics and impostors scurrying off to wherever else Mind at Large or the deros direct them. In the meantime, however, while ufologists wait for silvery saucers on the White House lawn, or for Plan B and planetary destruction, or even for a geo-hydro-atmospheric-electromagnetic explanation, I am not sure that I wish to be among them.

Author's Note

While researching this book I benefited greatly from the cooperation of Joan Baer, Ted Bloecher, Eddie Bullard, Aphrodite Clamar, Jerome Clark, Paul Devereux, George Hansen, David Jacobs, Don Johnson, John Keel, Philip (J.) Klass, John Mack, Robert Naiman, Michael Persinger, David Pritchard, Jenny Randles, Kenneth Ring, Peter Robbins, Ted Rothon, Dennis Stacy, Joe Stefula, 'Lucy', 'Nicole', and, especially, Budd Hopkins.

A number of individuals mentioned in the book have been given pseudonyms: Melissa Bucknell, Jed Burgess, George Fisher, Mina Hobart, Virginia Horton, Gretchen Kelly, Philip Osborne, Howard Rich, Carlotta, Cynthia, Eva, Fumiko, Lucy, Nicole, Ricardo, Sarah, and Steven.

Recommended Reading

Blum, Ralph and Judy, *Beyond Earth: Man's Contact with UFOs*, New York, Bantam, 1974.

Brown, Judith C., *Immodest Acts: The Life of a Lesbian Nun in Renaissance Italy*, Oxford, OUP, 1986.

Campbell, Joseph, *Primitive Mythology*, New York, Penguin Books, 1977.

Cohen, Daniel, *The Great Airship Mystery*, New York, Dodd Mead, 1981.

Evans, Hilary, *Visions, Apparitions, and Alien Visitors*, Wellingborough, Aquarian Press, 1984.

Ganaway, George, 'Historical versus narrative truth: clarifying the role of exogenous trauma in the etiology of MPD and its variants', *Dissociation* (1989), 2, pp. 205–20.

Hopkins, Budd, *Missing Time*, New York, Marek, 1981.

Hopkins, Budd, *Intruders*, New York, Random House, 1987.

Jacobs, David, *Secret Life*, New York, Simon & Schuster, 1992.

Keel, John, *The Mothman Prophecies*, New York, Saturday Review Press, 1975.

Kingsley, April, 'Energy and order: the paintings of Budd Hopkins', *Budd Hopkins: Retrospective Exhibition 1952–72*, Huntington, Huntington Galleries, 1973.

Klass, Philip, *UFO Abductions: A Dangerous Game*, Buffalo, Prometheus, 1988.

Lewis, I. M., *Ecstatic Religion*, 2nd edition, London, Routledge, 1989.

Michel, Aimé, 'The strange case of Dr X', *Flying Saucer Review* (September 1969), pp. 3–16.

Persinger, Michael, 'Predicting the details of visitor experiences and the personality of experients: the temporal lobe factor', *Perceptual and Motor Skills* (1989), 68, pp. 55–65.

Randles, Jenny, *Abduction*, London, Hale, 1989.

Ring, Kenneth, *The Omega Project*, New York, Morrow, 1992.

Robbins, R. H., *The Encyclopedia of Witchcraft and Demonology*, New York, Crown, 1959.

Strieber, Whitley, *Communion*, New York, Morrow, 1987.

Strieber, Whitley, *Transformation*, New York, Morrow, 1988.

Vallée, Jacques, *Passport to Magonia*, London, Henry Regnery, 1975.

Discover more about our forthcoming books through Penguin's FREE newspaper...

Penguin
Quarterly

It's packed with:

- exciting features
- author interviews
- previews & reviews
- books from your favourite films & TV series
- exclusive competitions & much, much more...

Write off for your free copy today to:
Dept JC
Penguin Books Ltd
FREEPOST
West Drayton
Middlesex
UB7 0BR
NO STAMP REQUIRED

READ MORE IN PENGUIN

In every corner of the world, on every subject under the sun, Penguin represents quality and variety – the very best in publishing today.

For complete information about books available from Penguin – including Puffins, Penguin Classics and Arkana – and how to order them, write to us at the appropriate address below Please note that for copyright reasons the selection of books varies from country to country.

In the United Kingdom: Please write to *Dept JC, Penguin Books Ltd, FREEPOST, West Drayton, Middlesex UB7 OBR*

If you have any difficulty in obtaining a title, please send your order with the correct money, plus ten per cent for postage and packaging, to *PO Box No 11, West Drayton, Middlesex UB7 OBR*

In the United States: Please write to *Penguin USA Inc , 375 Hudson Street, New York, NY 10014*

In Canada. Please write to *Penguin Books Canada Ltd, 10 Alcorn Avenue, Suite 300, Toronto, Ontario M4V 3B2*

In Australia: Please write to *Penguin Books Australia Ltd, 487 Maroondah Highway, Ringwood, Victoria 3134*

In New Zealand: Please write to *Penguin Books (NZ) Ltd,182–190 Wairau Road, Private Bag, Takapuna, Auckland 9*

In India Please write to *Penguin Books India Pvt Ltd, 706 Eros Apartments, 56 Nehru Place, New Delhi 110 019*

In the Netherlands: Please write to *Penguin Books Netherlands B V , Keizersgracht 231 NL–1016 DV Amsterdam*

In Germany Please write to *Penguin Books Deutschland GmbH, Friedrichstrasse 10–12, W–6000 Frankfurt/Main 1*

In Spain. Please write to *Penguin Books S A , C San Bernardo 117–6° E–28015 Madrid*

In Italy. Please write to *Penguin Italia s r l , Via Felice Casati 20, 1–20124 Milano*

In France Please write to *Penguin France S A , 17 rue Lejeune, F–31000 Toulouse*

In Japan: Please write to *Penguin Books Japan, Ishikiribashi Building, 2–5–4, Suido, Bunkyo-ku, Tokyo 112*

In Greece Please write to *Penguin Hellas Ltd, Dimocritou 3, GR–106 71 Athens*

In South Africa Please write to *Longman Penguin Southern Africa (Pty) Ltd, Private Bag X08, Bertsham 2013*

READ MORE IN PENGUIN

A CHOICE OF NON-FICTION

The Time Out Film Guide   Edited by Tom Milne

The definitive, up-to-the minute directory of over 9,500 films – world cinema from classics and silent epics to reissues and the latest releases – assessed by two decades of *Time Out* reviewers. 'In my opinion the best and most comprehensive' – Barry Norman

The Remarkable Expedition   Olivia Manning

The events of an extraordinary attempt in 1887 to rescue Emin Pasha, Governor of Equatoria, are recounted here by the author of *The Balkan Trilogy* and *The Levant Trilogy* and vividly reveal unprecedented heights of magnificent folly in the perennial human search for glorious conquest.

Skulduggery   Mark Shand

Mark Shand, his friend and business partner Harry Fane and world-famous but war-weary photographer Don McCullin wanted adventure. So, accompanied by a fat Batak guide, armed only with a first-aid kit and with T-shirts, beads and tobacco for trading, they plunged deep into the heart of Indonesian cannibal country . . .

Lenin's Tomb   David Remnick

'This account by David Remnick, Moscow correspondent for the *Washington Post* from 1988 to 1992, of the last days of the Soviet Empire is one of the most vivid to date' – *Observer*

Roots Schmoots   Howard Jacobson

'This is no exercise in sentimental journeys. Jacobson writes with a rare wit and the book sparkles with his gritty humour . . . he displays a deliciously caustic edge in his analysis of what is wrong, and right, with modern Jewry' – *Mail on Sunday*

READ MORE IN PENGUIN

A CHOICE OF NON-FICTION

Bernard Shaw Michael Holroyd
Volume 3 1918–1950 The Lure of Fantasy

'An achievement of the highest order that no one interested in the dramatic, social and cultural history of the time can afford to neglect' – *Financial Times*

In the Fascist Bathroom Greil Marcus

'More than seventy short pieces on "punk", its fall-out and its falling-outs. They are mostly brilliant . . . much of this book is hate as love, spite as well as delight. But when the professor does fall in love . . . he is a joy to behold' – *Sunday Times*

Visiting Mrs Nabokov Martin Amis

'From the wahooing triumphalism of the 1988 Republican Convention to darting drama in a Bishopsgate pub, from toplessness in Cannes to hopelessness in the snooker-room, Amis is a fantastically fluent decoder of the modern age . . . he is also one of its funniest' – *Independent*

Eating Children Jill Tweedie

'Jill Tweedie re-creates in fascinating detail the scenes and conditions that shaped her, scarred her, broke her up or put her back together . . . a remarkable story' – Glyn Maxwell in *Vogue.* 'A beautiful and courageous book' – Maya Angelou

Journey into Cyprus Colin Thubron

This is the account of a unique journey – a six-hundred-mile trek on foot around Cyprus in the last year of the island's peace. 'Purchased by blistered and bleeding feet, this picture is extraordinarily detailed and vivid . . . An accomplished linguist and historian, his passionate concern for antiquity in all its aspects lends weight and warmth to every chapter' – *Financial Times*

BY THE SAME AUTHOR

Round in Circles

Hauntingly beautiful crop circles started appearing in the English countryside in the early 1980s and were soon seized upon by rival schools of enthusiasts; this definitive insider's account examines 'one of the strangest popular mysteries of our times'.

Were the curious corn 'pictograms' created by currents of air, mystic messengers from the heavens – or hoaxers trying to take gullible New Agers for a ride? To answer that question, journalist Jim Schnabel took to the fields and joined the plasma physicists and eccentric earls, mediums and magicians, ufologists and cerealogists. With sharp but affectionate wit, he vividly chronicles the scandals squabbles and speculations, the lawsuits and love affairs. The result is both a history of a remarkable phenomenon and a journey into the weirdest recesses of human nature.

'Without judging, or being patronizing, he tells the story of each happy nutcase's involvement in the crop-circle saga, mainly through their own words. It's an endearing, absorbing account' – Robin McKie in the *Observer*

'Has all the gentle irony, delicate characterization and warm humanity of the very best Ealing comedy. It also has a rather better plot ... splendidly amusing' – Laurie Taylor in the *New Statesman & Society*